A SCAMMER, A DIAMOND, & RANSOM

A SCAMMER, A DIAMOND, & RANSOM

J MOREWOOD OSBORNE

PRIMIX
PUBLISHING
THE WRITE CHOICE

Primix Publishing
11620 Wilshire Blvd
Suite 900, West Wilshire Center, Los Angeles, CA, 90025
www.primixpublishing.com
Phone: 1-800-538-5788

Published by Primix Publishing: 02/14/2024

ISBN: 979-8-89194-081-9(sc)
ISBN: 979-8-89194-082-6(e)

Library of Congress Control Number: 2024901651

CONTENTS

FOREWORD

This is a true account of a Nigerian scam situation that occurred during late 2010 - 2011 Most of the conversations are actual text from emails of all persons involved some words have been changed and some lines moved to complete the actual sentence during live chats

Some events are totally unexpected and definitely orchestrated by a group of persons. There are many people who may have fallen victim to one of these Scams and there are certainly more that will particularly young girls who are most vulnerable.

While organizations exist around the world to combat this cybercrime little success is achieved as authorities are under manned and unable to offer much assistance.

This scam occurred after the author was widowed suddenly after a long term relationship and although adjusting to the new life let loneliness grab a hold and paid the price.

I hope that this account will help those in a similar situation to realize before it is too late that Internet Relationships rarely work out and if it seems too good to be true it probably is

This book has been four years in the making and even today email messages are still received from the scammer asking for financial assistance. If you find yourself in this situation you should delete your email address without advising the scammer and never give out any address details including mobile phone numbers as these are easy to contact from anywhere as is the case in this scam.

Research has been done by the victim in this story and details are included but even reporting an incident to the police or other appropriate body will not guarantee you any assistance.

Profile 13/11/2010   Beck Hill 31 y.o.

I am a fun loving person I am down to Earth, open minded person with a good sense of humour. caring ,single , genuine romantic ,passionate person love to share time with my lover, love to bring out the best in him and make him feel special, love to resolve issues and make things right. I am here to meet an honest man that is ready to put his miserable past behind him and ready to open a new chapter in his love life with me.

What is more important to us is the love we share, the memories we have or the lover? let give love a chance to swallow us up. Don't just think it will happen in an instant, it will surprise you before you know it, but it will be the most rewarding experience you will ever have.

I want someone that is finally ready to trust I don't want time wasters. I want someone that can decide on his own. I hate people that friends decide for I want someone that can stand by his self, and make his decisions I want someone that is ready to move on with and that really want a soul mate. I want a nice lad to get to know in respect of a relationship life together. I would also love a guy who is caring, loving ambitious and who feel he would be very committed with me. I want a guy from anywhere in the world as far as I am concerned I don't look into handsomeness. I prefer what this person has to offer from his heart I want someone who we will have fun together and travel together to nice islands and countries for visits also someone who would be independent. I hope I get the luck of finding such a fellow in here.

CHAPTER 1

THE INTRODUCTION

It was August 30th and having finally recovered from a relationship with a "bad Czech" I had decided to try my luck at internet dating not, that I particularly believed in the possibility of actually meeting someone on this site but working nights alone gave me not only the opportunity but some entertainment. So by luck I was reading all my face book messages and an offer to join a free dating site appeared, well I thought this will keep me busy tonight. I was expecting to read a local profile or one from an area I had chosen in any case they would have been national only limited to the east coast travel would not have been an issue as fares are cheap. To my amazement I found what I thought a very suitable profile that was international. Immediately that attracted my attention and I reminded myself after the Czech experience that I going tread with caution

The message read

"I am a fun loving person I am down to Earth, open

minded person with a good sense of humour. caring ,single , genuine romantic ,passionate person love to share time with my lover, love to bring out the best in him and make him feel special , love to resolve issues and make things right. I am here to meet an honest man that is ready to put his miserable past behind him and ready to open a new chapter in his love life with me.

What is more important to us is the love we share, the memories we have or the lover? Let's give love a chance to swallow us up. Don't just think it will happen in an instant it will surprise you before you know it, but it will be the most rewarding experience you will ever have."

Well, why is it that you do not read anything on a local site that seems as genuine as this. The interesting issue was that you would expect this message from someone from a third world or former Eastern European nation (that I had just gotten over), but no this was from London why would he be looking for an international date!

I decided that it was not worth any quandary and proceeded to make contact with him. I was not a paying member of the Website in question a website that was advertising on Facebook so naturally I did not give second thought as to the validity of the site., and because I was not a financial member I was unable to read the emails sent to me, but for an unknown reason that was not the case with this email address, something I had experienced only once before hand.

His photo showed him in board shorts, with an athletic build and a darker shade of skin tone. He is Caucasian He has black hair and a clean shaven chest. He stands 173cm tall, a non smoker sexually attracted to men. The profile seemed Devine and I could only think the only thing to adjust here is some height but I'm sure I will manage.

After carefully noting the email address I began writing.

Hello Beck

Thanks for the flirt. I was able to read your message once as I am not a paying member on this site either. I hope this reply is correct with your comments, I am trying to recall as I write. I have not checked this site for a few days so that is why the delay in replying.

My name is John and I live in Sydney in the inner city. Like you I have been widowed for 3 years and although I have friends I miss the relationship and the sharing, there is so much emptiness in my life without a man to love. Like you too I now also share the bed with my dog and often I am living on my own when I am looking for new flatmates. I was lucky to have a relationship earlier this year that lasted 5 months. I thought I was ready now for a new guy in my life and we enjoyed each other. Sadly 29 Year old students from the Czech Republic are not suited for long term commitment and do not want the relationship they thought they did, so it is now again back to sharing the bed with the dog. On this site one month ago I was having an online relationship with a sweet guy in Western Siberia, to my amazement I was enjoying the relationship and the cybersex, and until

I was in this online relationship I was not aware you can actually share so much of yourself with the other person and have feelings. I am sorry that your best friend is getting married It may also mean you have to find another residence and another soul mate. I had this with my Young Russian on line but that ended when he asked me to pay for his airfare to Australia. Like you I have many friends and they are, understanding of my sadness but they are not soul mates, maybe we can chat some more soon if you like.

Regards John

I had broken the Ice the feeling was fantastic and now I hoped he would chat with me again soon.

I had to allow for the 9 hour time difference before any reply might be received, I was amazed when a reply was returned 4 and one half hours later.

From Beck

Am happy you responded back to my email...I really appreciate it...I should tell you

how I really feel. But I'm afraid of what you might say I like you and I really want

good communication, trust and commitment between us...believe me from the very first

time I saw your profile, I have been growing good feelings for you and I hope you have better thoughts about this too. I am an honest, genuine caring, sincere, trustworthy romantic type. I am single 30 years of age... no kids...Am a Graduate...I have my masters

Degree in Hotel Management and Tourism. I am the only child of my family I am a Christian...I do go to church every Sunday. I lost my dad when I was young...I miss him...my mum is still alive, she is 69 years old...she is nice to me and wants the best for me.

I do gym every morning to make my body fit. I have a very simple mind, I hate argument. When I am in a relationship I always want to satisfy my man with everything. I am not the best but want to be for my man...I easily fall in love...I want a partner I can share my life with and someone that is caring and someone that has mind to love me, someone that can love me for who I am someone I can be with till eternity Beck

There is now a good possibility that we will chat regularly and maybe even get to a point of meeting each other. I was hopeful he was feeling the same way. It was no later than the next day that I felt the need to talk with my new found acquaintance.

And while at work the next day I sent the following.

Me: 31/08/2010

Beck I am glad you responded so soon I wrote to you from work I am a Concierge and Night Audit Manager with a five star apartment building in inner Sydney so yes I work in Hospitality, I have more than one job. I am sorry too about your loss so young with your father, I know I am very lucky both my parents are alive and are celebrating their 58th wedding anniversary this coming December. I am guilty of the same qualities as you I have loyalty and honesty to offer my man and a strong commitment I had the first one for fifteen years until he died. I am well respected by my friends and I am a genuine caring guy. I don't want to sound bombastic but if you were to ask them they would agree and this was put to task when my man died, everyone one of them rallied to help me. I admit I am looking for another relationship I will stay away from Eastern Europeans though. I wish I was going to the gym still I used to go 3 times a week for 7 years so my body was tight then. I haven't been to a gym for 3 years. There is so much to do now I am alone and it takes all the time plus two jobs. I don't know why you found my profile attractive but I'm glad you do. I think we have some very similar circumstances in fact my man was a Virgo too. Say hello to your mum for me I bet she is a good cook and a very caring woman I hope she finds new love in her life too I think the more we chat the Stronger, our feelings will grow. I hope you want to share your feelings with me because I feel comfortable being completely honest with you. I will hear from you soon.

I was in luck with a response, again the same day 8 hours later. There were many questions asked this time and these required a truthful answer

Beck:

How are you doing? Thank you for the message I'm really glad to read from you. I'm a very romantic person as well and expect to meet someone who has the same quality. I'm a very decent guy, good looking people say, but I always tell people to wait and get to know me deeply and you will see that my heart is more beautiful. I am an easy going person and a level headed guy, not into games, nor hook-ups. As they say I know you are wondering why I'm still single. I don't like the gay or bar Scene. I'm a very shy type so I'm very much more of an indoors person but I love nature so much. I lost my ex 2 years ago he died to cancer of the lungs so I mourn him for so long as a respect now I feel it's time to carry on with my life. My friends often say to me that I should stop living in the past and focus on the future and what I want for the future is someone who is ready to love and be loved, who I can love and show that I care for someone I will love in and out of bed and someone who will understand me, thru the sun and the rain and that's why I'm here sitting on the computer writing to you. You sound so honest and you seem like that kind of man I have been longing for. I don't want to hang around the site, going from one man to another I just want someone who will take me to the dream land take away the growing pains of loneliness.

I have some questions for you.

Are you single?

What are you seeking for?

What do you like in a guy?

Do you like a girlish type of guy?

What do you do for sex?

As the email continues I realise this will be the email that will hold future reference on Beck's. I must therefore be careful with my answers to these questions. Beck now proceeds to give his own answers

Beck

I am single

I am seeking for permanent relationship with the right man

I like honesty, sincerity and my man to be loving and caring

I'm not a girlish type I like my man to be a man

About what I like in sex...well I love being a top, and I would bottom sometimes for the right man. I enjoy making love to a man and all the things that go along with that even the long hot showers together. Giving and receiving full body massages and seeing my guy in boxers is a turn on but getting him out is so damn hot or just playing with him in his boxers. I love kissing cuddling and licking his toes and I love making doggy style.....

I really have interest in you. There is a lot of distance between us but I don't want you to measure that. All I want you to measure is the good feelings of my heart which I have in writing this to you with good feelings. We can break the barrier to be together I can relocate and I have made up my mind, to go a million miles in search of my man.

Relationship is not a question of how much love you have in the beginning, but it's a question of how much love you are able to build at the end and the memories we share......

I know I don't really know much about you but believe me, I have never felt this good for long...well I guess something good wants to come out of this... I don't cheat and I don't lie, I hate arguing with my partner. I hate seeing my man hurt I love spending my free time with my man. I love the beach so much. I am a graduate that has his Masters Degree in Hotel Management and Tourism. Presently I am not working here in the UK the job is not going well...does it work well where you are? My mum she is the one supporting me for now...I need to move on with my life. I know she will be happy to see me with my partner....am the only child of my family Sometimes I miss the way I don't have brothers and sisters. I am not from a large family...we are not much I don't have a car I don't really keep friends but I have friends. I like keeping things to myself. I love travelling. I love sport like tennis soccer and swimming...I have a positive mind about our communication

It was now up to me to impress this man, he has shown interest and I do not want to miss the opportunity by providing bad credentials.

I began.

Me:

Hi Beck it was nice to receive this message I received it at 2:00pm today and it has really made my day as well as the photo shoot I was participating in today. I understand totally what grief you are going through. It took me 15 months to stop grieving my partner we were together 15 years and had even had a marriage ceremony which wasn't legal then and still isn't in Australia (yet). Everybody grieves differently and in their own time frame, when he died I wanted to move to the Orkney Islands or take a job on a Norwegian Prawn Trawler but my friends got me through and I owe them so much for it. Then, when I thought it was time to carry on with my life. I met Leos. He was a tall man about 192cms. Has light brown hair his skin is very white and his eyes a beautiful pale blue this made them almost hypnotic .He is solid with a hairy complexion on his chest and back. Sadly Czech Boys do not want the relationship with older men they first ask for nor do online Russians. I want for the future the same as you I have so much love and loyalty to give and I want to share my life with a special man again now. I nursed and loved my man until the day he died all 15 years I looked after him he was 44 when he died.

The answer to your questions, are yes I am single

I am seeking another long term relationship to share myself and everything I have with that man.

What do I like in a guy? Well above all honesty but also loyalty a good personality and masculinity. I prefer masculine men it's, fine if they have some hair on their chest and face but equally if not as long as they are masculine.

What do I do for sex? I have tried many things I love being sensual and spontaneous sex with my lover. I am happy to bottom but do like to be on top occasionally. Yes long hot showers in winter, massages I would enjoy wrestling with my man and ripping his jocks off, or washing the car together and hosing each other then, having sex in the courtyard while the suds are still on the car.

I love starting at the toes and working up. I will offer doggy style to the right man.

You mention you would relocate are you thinking of migrating? You mention you love the beach in Sydney you can on some days still go to the beach in winter there is so much sun and plenty of work in fact there are so many pommy's here and kiwi's in hospitality. I know you would be welcome with open arms in my family and in my deceased partner's family for they are still mine too. You say you are from a small family and not much, that is not true, you have a lot of love and honesty to give and everyone is important on this planet (well most people) be proud of yourself you are young and good looking and healthy that is a lot of individual wealth and happiness that no one can have unless you share it with them and there are a lot of sad people that will never amount to anything.

I don't know much about you either but I want to and I'm sure we both have a lot to tell each other. I feel good when I receive mail from you and I will wait for your next letter. I may not be able to reply to you for a couple of days my computer is badly infected with viruses and needs to be cleaned out I will reply to you tomorrow night (Wednesday) from work around midnight Sydney Time EST. Keep your mind positive and I will be in touch soon John

Beck   1/9/2010

Firstly am so happy that we are communicating with each other. You have said everything. I really understand every word in your mail, we seem to think alike and that may make it easier to get along fast.

These are all important sentiments and issues in a relationship. It is about two halves together making a whole. It is about two total beings joining together. Of course with the best intent these are not guaranteed to lead to total and everlasting success but, if the motivation is there to begin with great!

Do you fall in love easily?

Do you easily get attracted to what people do?

Do you smoke or Drink?

Are you a jealous type?

Can you trust again?

Do you believe you can love from distances?

What do you really want in a man?

In your ideal relationship are you the dominant one or not?

Sorry for asking so many questions. The more we know the more the feelings of our heart will rise. I have a very colourful heart and I easily fall for the right one

I don't smoke but drink occasionally. I get jealous when I am in love

I don't really get attracted to people. I follow my heart

and I know it always leads me right, maybe that's why I am writing you.

When I like someone and I think I can trust the person because without trust a relationship will never grow.

I like being with a caring and honest person someone with whom we can be happy together. I need my own man. The man I call mine. You know things fall in place when You fall in love. And when you're in love things come so easy I'm a very caring guy who loves to make his man special, treat my man like an angel I care for him and treat him right in and out of bed.

I have been in a loving relationship with a guy that lasted four years. I lost my ex to cancer of the lungs. It was a bad time for me. Life seems so cold and grey when we lose our loved ones. I felt it was over for me but I had to carry on with my life I miss him greatly, and that's why I have waited this long before wanting to get into another relationship. It's been 2 years since I lost him. All I want is a man with who we will both be happy together a responsible man I must say. Please take care of yourself and will hope to read from you soon.

Kisses and hugs.

Me   2/9/2010

Hi Beck

I think it's quite okay to ask all those questions. I am an open and honest guy I have nothing to hide and don't mind sharing myself with you.

I guess I do fall in love easily It took me two weeks to

tell my man I loved him and we then lasted 15 years. It only took me two days to fall in love with Leon (my 29 yo Czech Student) and I wasn't aware at the time I had fallen so soon, it was not my original intention.

I am interested and Attracted to some things that some people do. I do not intend nor have I followed in their footsteps just because it was or did sound appealing. I know I have strong fantasies I play out in my head for example, I have always wanted to be a famous gay porn star but I have the realities of life to deal with and I concentrate my energy there.

I do not smoke anymore I have not smoked for 7 years, in fact the day I quit I went cold turkey. I know when I was a child both my parents smoked and they have not smoked now for 40 plus years. My partner smoked until the day he died in fact he had an irreversible lung condition and emphysema that was his cause of death. Is that why your boyfriend had lung cancer because he smoked? However I do drink I usually have a glass of wine with dinner and a few beers after work most afternoons. I also enjoy my JD & coke and a G&T at times.

You ask me if I am the jealous type. I would say no but that does not apply when I have been dumped for a younger man and the younger man was my friend before, hand. I am very proud of the fact I have mastered the 7 deadly sins but unfortunately. I would be jealous when my man was with another. In my relationship with my partner we used to have threesomes but this was only when we both agreed and only when both of us were 2 of the 3 guys involved.

Can I trust again/ well I am a trusting person in the first instance and I learned a long time ago to hate or distrust someone makes you bitter To not trust someone permanently they would have to be repeat offenders.

I am hoping you can find love in a long distance relationship! I know I found it easy to love in my short relationship with the 25yo Russian man on line. I am hoping we will not be a short time on line.

You asked me what I am looking for in a man, well really I want honesty, loyalty love commitment and masculinity, and like you someone to have as my lover or boyfriend. I want a relationship where we can .share decisions and where I can be top sometimes. A Relationship, where we are also both comfortable in accepting the decision of the other partner on some occasions, for this is a true relationship.

Next Monday is my partner's birthday he would have been 47. I will be here at work next Monday until 11 pm then I will go home and have a drink or three for him I still miss him but I have moved on and I know he would be annoyed with me if I did not do so.

I am writing to you from the front office in the hotel lobby as my computer has a failed hard drive but fear not I can send and receive on my phone. I hope these answers have helped you to feel better and understand me more. I would like to be able to kiss you good night and I will imagine I will have done so. I will hear from you soon.   John.

Beck

How are you? Thanks for the message it's nice to read we are along the same line. Like many I find it hard to talk about myself. You want to say enough to make it interesting without sounding like a braggart.

But you also don't want to make it boring either. It's a hard thing to do but I'll try my best. Let's start with sports. Not a big fan here but I do enjoy a good game of soccer now and again .I do enjoy going for walks whether it's around the neighbourhood, at the park, hiking or in the woods or on long lonely country lanes (do a lot of thinking there).And to see the sun rising over the water. Or seeing it after the days travel settling into it as into a bed can be a wonder to behold. I also like to walk in the rain when the raindrops come to softly caress your cheeks, but if I would rather stay indoors and do have to go out into it can lose its' magic fairly quickly. Or walking on a street after a winter's storm is over and you're the only one there in the stillness of the night. Finding everything covered in a mantle of white. If you're lucky there might still be big snowflakes coming down to greet you and keep you company while you enjoy that winter's wonderland where tree branches laden with snow make for a fairies playground and even carts buried in the snow become a work of art. Have you ever walked on the Ocean beach with grey skies

a strong wind blowing and where the waves come crashing on the sandy shore to rush up and kiss your feet. It's just fantastic. I also like to sit by a window to see the show in a Lightening storm, or watch rain beating against the window to be let in. They are all natural but imagine doing all this with a partner will be great.

I like going to the movies and also to the park to listen to an open air concert, to stop, and listen to street artists playing. They put all their hearts and souls into what they love and in that fact make their music comparable to a symphony. I don't like the bar scene.

I like to spend some time at home. A nice ride in the country...just spending the day there bringing and having a picnic is great sitting beside the campfire all the wee hours of the morning, feeling good about the world. I like to see new places, try new things taste new foods. If I have to choose between a crowded environment I would prefer the quietness of home nice to snuggle up on a cold winter's day with a good book listening to music on the radio or just to watch TV. Even better to snuggle with someone and do those things together.

I believe in treating others with respect. Family and friends get an extra dose of it... with added benefit of unwavering love. I don't always agree with what they may say or do and there may be some arguments here and there but I will stand by them as I would like them to stand by me in my time of need actually at all times. And yes, we show affection to the one's we love whether it's in the little things, where I think it shows more, up to the big things let me explain. The big things show you care but the little things show you deeply care, and want to make ALL aspects of someone's life more enjoyable. It's nice to walk up to someone you love and give them a hug for no apparent reason other than to show them that you love them, and are glad that they're in your life. To give me a handpicked flower from the yard even if it's a dandelion or a forget-me-not. Or to leave a note on the table or pillow with the three hardest words to hear... the real and not the superficial "I love you"

I don't care if you're tall or not so tall. Slim or of a bigger build. Of course there needs to be an attraction for something deeper than friendship to exist. And when I'm speaking deeper than friendship I mean one on one love between two people .You love your family and your friends with all your heart and might but when it comes to a relationship it goes to the very core of your being. I guess the old people were right when they worded it by saying you become one with each other. It's a love that can't be explained but needs to be felt in order to be known. By the way I don't believe that a relationship is a 50/50 thing but a 100/100 situation. I don't want 50% of you I want 100% of your commitment. You will get all of mine in return. I also believe that a relationship is a living thing (I use the word thing for lack of a better one). A relationship lives grows deepens and sometimes unfortunately can die,,, so as I said it is living. It needs attention nurturing to help it grow. It also needs two people working together to take care of it and not to neglect it.

I am shy at the beginning but as I get to know someone, trust them, open up to them and people seem to like me. I am not pretentious at all. I don't believe that I am better than anyone else. But on the same note I don't believe that anybody is better than me.

We are all equal...well we should, all be. I don't care if

you live in a twelve room mansion up on a hill or in a one room, basement apartment. somewhere..., If you have all that money does it make you better than the man who has none but has a heart that is true?

You may have much and love that plenty. You may have little and lust after the plenty. but in either case if you don't have the love to give to someone you are both very poor and destitute. It's what I think anyways.

The man that I aspire to find should be courteous, affectionate and respectful. He will like home life but also enjoy life as a whole. Going out is a treat to be enjoyed and savoured. Home is where you find the man you love. When there's a disagreement and there will be because we are individuals we will talk about it but never go to bed angry. Our bedroom is the place where we nurture each other..I've written more than I had first planned sorry. I would like to finish with a quote that I heard and liked...."some of the biggest challenges in relationships come from the fact that most people enter a relationship in order to get something. They're trying to find someone who's going to make them feel good. In reality the only way a relationship will last is if you see your relationship as a place that you go to give and not a place that that you go to take.

Take care.

Me   3/9/2010

Hi Beck I actually want to be bold and say Hi babe (hope that's okay with you) I'm always so happy to hear from you, yet again we are thinking alike. I am referring to your reference of walking along the beach with grey clouds and yes. I have done this with my man holding hands with our shirts open and flying backwards like the flag of a victorious army, the waves at your feet it gets so humid here in summer that massive sudden thunderstorms are common place. But what I think romantic is your descriptive walk down the street after the snow has fallen. You see I have never really seen much snow and certainly not ever in any city, Here we all listen to Christmas carols that might start with the words chestnuts roasting on an open fire but to a lot of us (me included) that is very remote. I have been to London and love it but only in the summer months, you have mentioned you have travelled, have you ever been to Australia? or south of the equator? For that matter if not would you want t to?

Something I have not done since I was a child I would long to do with my man is to hire a row boat on the river and row for a day have a picnic lunch and pitch the tent to stay the night in the clearing you found from the boat while you were rowing, then make love at dusk so our silhouettes are pink from the sun's rays and our naked bodies are gleaming in the strange light. You know even sitting on the lounge watching TV with your arm around your man while he is nestled into your bosom would be wonderful too.

You like to go for a ride in the country how about doing it on horseback? I learned to ride when I was young my mother was born on a farm and she believes it is a s necessary as learning to swim, so my brother and I went to riding school every Saturday and then tennis lessons on Sunday. She is so British my mother as the family are all English (except my mother and her brother) they were born here in the country in a place called Ballimore. The property was called Beaconsfield as that is where the family are from and where some still live. I have been there too I have a lot of English and Scottish blood coursing through my veins I was just born in another part of the world that has a very good climate.

You would never have to worry about me treating others with respect I am a nice guy polite and honest. I do not suffer idiots easily and I have no time for selfish people. I do no believe all people are created equal or perhaps they were at conception but something has gone terribly wrong with 50% of the world's population and certainly a reasonable percentage should be sterilized to stop the "bad Seed" .I hope you don't think bad of me for saying this but it's true. I see it here in the Slum areas of Sydney and it is true all over the world. We would not have your British class system if everybody was a clone.

I believe like you we should never go to bed angry and never involve others in your disagreements. If you are looking for a relationship for the sake of what you can get out of it then you may both find it but you will not find love. If you are looking for a relationship where you can share all your love then you will find it but you will also notice the jealousy of others for what you have. You can always find what you are looking for if you seek it. The problem is so many people have no idea what they really seek. I have been very social on the Sydney Scene and met many people and you can form opinions about them, also you would not have to worry with me only offering 50% in a relationship. I will give you 100% and expect it back. This is a mark of binding love and respect.. I never found the words "love you "hard to say to my man, I wish he was still here to say it back.

You mention you are shy at the beginning but I think your letters to me are becoming more open each time. I could have been more open with you from my first letter but then it would not have the romance it now does, well, anyway I think it does, you are easy to talk to and so non judgemental I like that in you, believe you give love from your soul not from your heart, the love that is from the soul is more sincere and is not easy to extinguish .I'm glad you have opened so much of yourself to me with this letter. I have shown my feelings and thoughts to you also. If there is anything you want to know just ask me. If I have said anything to offend you just tell me if I have done neither then respect me and if you want to show emotion then enjoy me. I will wait for you to write (soon I hope). Thanks for your friendship and your honesty.

I kiss you goodnight now.   John

Beck

Good morning babe .and thanks for the mail. I'm an easy going guy I'm a very shy type. I can't stand it for a guy to walk to me and tell me he likes me, Damn that's why I created the add, for a soul mate I know we must have got to know on the internet and there is nothing to be shy about again. Babe the internet is a very difficult place to find true love, there's lots of irregularities on the internet, but these days I'm more hopeful that there is a man out there for me.

I can see we have more than one thing in common. My heart has been broken before, but to death when I lost my ex I almost went suicidal, it took me a year to stand alone, and now I have been so alone for 2 years I don't want to remain this way, I know there is always a man out there for everyone my mom said to me "son don't even think there is no one out there for you, you are loved you have to open your heart so your heart can receive love again"

Right now I want to receive that undying love and treasure it forever I want to be happy again I have a very beautiful heart, and I want to show you in my quest to searching for a new dream. I have made up my mind that even if the man for me out there lives a million miles apart. I will take the step to move to be with him and experience happiness with him... I haven't been to Australia or south before .I will be very glad to be there soon tell me things that bring you joy in life?

Beck

Me   4/9/2010

Hi Babe Joy for me is reading this email from you, how

much my being able to talk to you has relieved pain in my loneliness and hopefully yours since, my partner died in 2007. I have wanted to travel (apart from the Norwegian Prawn Trawler) to put my feelings back together I have thought of a cruise down the Nile and the Czech republic but Leos changed my mind on the latter.

Now that the dust is settling on my sadness I am thinking again of the holiday I still need. One of the destinations on my list is going back to London a city I love so much. I hope you are okay with me saying this and obviously I would like to see you. On the other hand I can wait until you feel comfortable with us knowing each other better and meet you in Amsterdam or Paris if you prefer or maybe you want to travel to the Colony and if you do obviously I would take care of you while you are here. I hope you will say yes to one of the above options I think what I am saying to you as mentioned in your email is that I like you Beck I believe you should not be suffering pain anymore and I want to put my arms around you to help you in your pain I have a lot of love to give and I want to share it – I will now wait for your reply because this email is a commitment and emotional for me. I need your response before I continue.

Kisses John Beck

Hi Babe thanks for all the feelings, wow this is great and thank god for this wonderful gift of the heart, you know I told my friend about you and she is happy for me and my fear now is losing you. I want to be next to you we can make this happen I have waited so long.

My past life is sort of strange. When I was a teenager, like all young guys I was always chasing girls trying to get laid, which worked out pretty well as I had several girlfriends.

My friends discovered masturbation when we were around 12-13. We used to enjoy ourselves as much as possible. A few of them were a little more adventurous and we started doing each other. We sort of kept that up during high school, except when there was a girlfriend around to take care of things. When I got to university I went nuts everywhere you looked there were HOT chicks looking for sex. I thought this was great as you could go to a party and find action. Then I got a place with 2 friends. We were pretty wild, always having a party. Slowly we started making bets on different things.

Somewhere along the way someone decided that the loser had to blow the winner. After much discussion/arguing we all agreed that this was the start of a whole new experience. If we had girlfriends we fooled around with them, but if any of us were single we could always find someone to help us out. Then after I met a guy around my age and we started hanging out together. One night we were at the bar watching the hockey game and getting quite drunk. Afterwards we went back to his place for another drink. We were watching some porno he had and were both getting very horny. At some point we started to make out, and one thing led to another. We woke up the next day in bed together. Over breakfast we talked and I admitted that I had enjoyed it. Eventually he was offered a great job in another part of the country and he accepted it. It was hard to lose him but it was for the best. Then I was single for a very long time. During that time I would say I was Bi but leaning towards gay... Then I met a great guy and we lived together for 4 years. Sadly he was killed by cancer of the lungs. By the time I found out he was gone. Since then I have been so lonely, it's 2 years now never, seeming to find the right guy. Now I'm very hopeful to find my man and be happy again, relationship is not about the

love you feel at the beginning it's a question of what you are able to build till the end of time. I'm ready to plant the seed and see what it turns out to be. I will love to come over to your place at your convenient time I think that's the best for me

What brings me joy in life?

1. Walking along a beach talking with someone I love walking in warm weather cool weather, windy grey weather... love pounding surf and the easy waves as well. Water is always important for me to be near.

2. Certain pieces of opera make me cry for the joy of such beauty

3. Travelling in nature and being away from people with one person I care for is perfection.

4. I love to sleep naked and I can't sleep well in any clothing shorts or anything anymore and

love the feel of my partner against my body. Sadly I still sleep alone on my poor bed.

5. The man I would love is full of joy accepting of my strengths and weaknesses, loving of those I love and one who knows how to give as well as receive in all ways.

6. You give me joy and I want to know that the thought of you alone gives me joy and every time I read your mail, something makes me smile. I want to experience it in the real world maybe to come to your place will be wonderful.

Okay my sexy man, have a great day, and I'm waiting to hear from you. Hugs and kisses

Me

Hi Honey I am so glad that you responded so soon and I am so happy with your reply my heart is actually beating quite fast and I am excited now. You have made me feel so wonderful from the start. I have, like you, been looking around for a partner and like you have been on websites both local and international. I, like you was very sceptical. You have changed that for me and like you also I don't want to let you go either and I promise you I will never intentionally hurt you or upset you.

I have enjoyed hearing all about your earlier years and especially your first gay experience I was going to ask you that anyway. I wanted to reject the whole concept of being gay when I realized that I was. I think I was 19 at the time and I even slept with some women but that did not change the fact that I hated doing it and I still liked men. My first experience was going to a crowded semi straight bar watching the famous drag show and rubbing guys' crotches. I got lucky and drove to a remote area behind a bus depot and did the deed. Some months later I ran into him and realized he worked in the building next to me and I never spoke to him again or even acknowledged him. That was so long ago now I'm glad you want to come to my place. I am so close to the coast and you will have so many beaches to choose from some are even nude.

I live on a very large island so there are plenty of beaches. It must be hard for you in Northampton when you love the beach so much and it is not close by. When you come to my place depending on the time of year we can go there every day, there are small boats that pull in selling food and drinks usually by really hot muscle guys. Even in the city the guys walk around not wearing much for 7 months of the year and there are lots of very good looking men here in summer both straight and gay. I would love to share that experience with you walking around the harbour foreshore which is a large area and holding your hand, jogging along a lonely remote beach with you then resting in the sand and kiss you then a swim together naked.

I could take you to the Opera in that wonderfully unusual building we have here. We can go camping in a remote area swim in a crystal pool and never wear any clothes.

I am actually a member of a local nudist group we do beach visits, bushwalking, warehouse disco parties and harbour cruises all naked.

Like you I sleep naked I have not owned any PJ's for 30 years, I enjoy the naked men behind me cuddling him feeling each others' manhood touching each others' naked bodies as we drift into slumber and waking up to him in the bed beside me is one of the most precious experiences it says so much and with the morning hello kiss you know he's been with you all night but you reaffirm it every morning anyway. Sadly I am alone in my bed too, so you will need to come over and we can warm it together.

I don't want to stop writing to you as you make me feel so good but I want to go to the Diesel sale across the street and buy a new pair of jeans to look really hot for you when you come over and so that you can peel them off my body. Even if I haven't heard from you by the time I have done my chores I will write to you again today my sweet prince You also have a great day From me, lots of hugs and kisses too.

Beck

From the very first moment I saw your profile I knew that we were destined to be together. It has been so long since a man has captured my attention so fully or made my heart beat the way it does for you. Your thoughts lights up my entire spirit. Your letter fills me with joy, and your mere presence will warm any room. I have no doubt you are the man Heaven has made especially for me.

Thank you for the comfortable conversations and for asking me to be yours most importantly thankyou, for sharing your love and wanting to make me your partner to the end of time. No matter how slowly or at what distance our courtship develops, I know standing before god and our future family, vowing to be your partner for life. Was the easiest decision I could have ever made.

Each day that passes makes our love for each other grow stronger. Although I know we live miles apart, but I know we can make it real and nothing can keep us apart forever. Our desires will continue to stretch across any distance, over every mountain and ocean between us. Nothing can stand between us and nothing will stop me from meeting you.

You are my future and nothing can keep us from our destiny. I miss you more every day. Though I have not seen you I am here with open arms hoping to meet you at the airport one day soon really, really, soon.

Love always

Me   5/9/2010

My darling I feel so much the same way, in your last message you finished by saying have a good day, and I did just that, I went to the local shopping village and it was like walking into an Austrian Bier Cafe

There were guys dressed in Austrian costume playing accordions and there were lots of hot guys everywhere wearing only shorts and t shirts. Here it is now the first week of Spring and {I was having such a good day I really thought you were on my arm with me.) You make me feel that good. I do want to meet you at the airport and bring you home and look after you until the end of time. I even have your photo on my cell phone so I can see you all the time. I have spent the whole day smiling and feeling good and that is all due to you my love, our feelings are stretching the oceans and love travels faster than the speed of light so I guess you are feeling it at the same time as me. I am thinking of going back to the gym so that I can firm up a bit for you. I will stand beside you and any vows you want me to and if I have to go to London to do it so be it. I am hoping your partner and my partner are now talking about us up there in heaven and they are both saying to each other "he's the right one" and we both agree they should be together. I know my man would be in agreement and maybe he has something to do with our feelings for each other. If you are coming to my place and need assistance with cash flow let me know. I can help you out. Spring is so lovely here as it is everywhere in the world.

Tomorrow I will go to the beach early I will swim naked after a light breakfast then visit my parents as it is fathers' day here tomorrow. I will then look after my German Frau friend she is hurting after her lover of 18 years has fled to Spain and I will talk to her about you and I and will enjoy the day in the glorious sunshine (that the weather bureau has told us we are having) and I know I will be thinking of you all day. Tomorrow night I will be with my friends I'll be on the dance floor with you my love in a world of my own.

There is a song that is one of my favourites, that is my song to you. You will know the song it is live it up by Mental as Anything but it is the words of the first verse that capture the essence of what I am saying to you and those words are " Hey there you with the sad face come on to my place and live it up" Again now as I write to you my body is tingling with excitement, and maybe anticipation but I really want to hold you in my arms Beck and I want to press my naked body against yours in bed and just let our feelings flow throughout each other. I am already saying to myself that you are mine. Is your mum okay with this? I know she wants the best for you too. What is her name as your partner I think I should know all my best wishes honey, until tomorrow lots of love.

Beck: 5/9/2010

Good evening my sexy man

Hopefully we are going to make something work soon.

I have to make inquire in Australia Embassy what I will need to come over there and I will get back to you as soon as I know all the documents needed, distance is nothing in relationship with good communication and trust we can make things work.

I guess I do tell my mum about you, she said I should send her regards to you that you made me happy, my mum was a retired teacher.

She is also the only child of her parent...am very close to her so sad that I don't have a large family, mum is the one helping me for now I don't like it but what can

I do...am always lonely...believe me I always want to hear from you and I really have a positive

mind that things will work out. I miss u have not seen you before but I know deep inside me we will be happy together. I have been job hunting no luck yet I want you to read this mail carefully and assimilate it in your thoughts because it is food for thought. What do you understand by the word LIFE?

LIFE is like a book of history of what is done in the past, what is going on at present and what is going to happen in the future shall be recorded in the book of LIFE.

You can see that life has lot in stock for us via surprises.

Have you ever wondered why we enter a church, bank, party or any gathering u may find yourself in, you see some dressed in expensive attire and some dressed in tattered clothes with holes begging to be sown.

Come to think of it why are some born with silver spoon then some with (permit me to say) wooden spoon. This and many more is what LIFE is made up of.

You will agree with me then that LIFE is made up of 2 different people.

the rich and the poor, the genius and the dullard, the optimist and pessimist.

The big and the small, the tall and the short, the beautiful ones and the ugly ones, the dark and the fair, the believers and nonbelievers I could go on and on.

Although the road to good life might not seem so smooth, but it's a challenge to us all which makes the saying, survival is the fittest. In other word we have to take LIFE as it comes our way.

Life is 10% of what u make of it and 90% how u take it. I'll say all animals are not equal but some are more equal than others. This also relates to our everyday life activities.

LIFE to different people means different things. To some people it's worth living for a while to others it's worthless.

The difficulties of life are intended to make us better not bitter. Also LIFE doesn't do anything to us but it only reveals our spirit. As I have said earlier LIFE is full of surprises.

If you ask me what LIFE is I'll say LIFE is a never ending story. I hope I have been able to jolt you out of your lifeless routine.

So what is life for you? Think about it. I want you and all these words are from the bottom of my heart....

Take care   kisses and hugs

Me

Today is the day we were told by the weather bureau (bright and sunny), so soon, I will go for my nude morning swim. In your last letter you gave me tears of joy and this letter is no different. Firstly do not worry or get despondent over job searching that has happened to me many times I know what you are going through.

Secondly ,think of life as a deck of cards you must play with the hand you have been dealt until the next game comes around, if your life is the same each game then you are playing with the wrong people. In other words sometimes we have to go to extreme measures and do something radical to change our circumstances for good.

You are now heading down that path, and I am with you all the way. I will include some web links for Australian visa requirements I have already been here before with Leon so I have them on the hard drive.

Thirdly my darling life is eternal but once to die those we love past and future to hold in that eternity (now the tears are flowing again).

I want to ask you for your address this might seem strange but you have a birthday around now and I want to send you a card, something with a stamp and envelope you can open something I have written in that you can put on your mantle for your friends to see something from me to you with love. (I am obviously a sentimentalist) I care for you and that is not going to stop ever.

Remember my song to you "hey there you with the sad face come on to my place and live it up you there on the dance floor what do you cry for let's live it up." I am a very loyal and honest person as I have said already. I will love you till the end of time But as I am reading metaphysics and hope soon to be practicing I cannot lie to myself because this science does not allow it and my Karma will not accept it, so what I am saying honey is this is from my soul to you forever (and the tears are out again).

Say hello to your mum for me I get the feeling I will

get to meet her one day lots of love from me to you my beautiful man. I will hear from you soon

Pic   pic

Beck Hi John

How are you today I am really enjoying our conversation here I just want to get to know more and more about you

These are the things I consider my hobbies...lol

What's your favourite food?

I love chicken soup, that's my favourite, I love Cannelloni, rice and love pastas, don't eat much vegetables and I will 'love to taste more food.

favourite   movie

My favourite movie lots of Will Smith's collections but the favourite of them all is "Seven Pounds" have you seen it?

favourite song?

ANDY WILLIAMS "a time for us" newies a song by James Blunt "you're beautiful"

favourite colour

blue

how do you spend your leisure?

I do enjoy going for walks whether it's around the neighbourhood, at the park, hiking in the woods or on long lonely country lanes (do a lot of thinking there) go to the movies I do this alone, but right now I will love to spend my leisure with a partner soon....

What do you do on weekends?

Cleaning the house and washing, that's pretty boring, but that's what I do my dear...lol... What would you like in your man?

I like my man to be honest sincere, understanding and caring. I'm not a perfect guy so I'm not looking for a perfect guy also, we make mistakes, but the most important is to talk about it, on our bed not to make noise and shout at each other. Would you marry your man if you are sure that you love him?

I'm ready for marriage as long as he loves me and I love him too. I can't wait to put that ring on my man and own him I prey that happens soon, you know to me marriage is not all about the ceremonial thing it's an agreement between us , which can simply be done between me and my partner. What do you like in sex?

In sex I'm mostly top and would love to bottom if my man wants that, like cuddling rimming, kissing and licking my man's toes. It makes me really happy sex is not sweet until you are having it with your lover. Omg that's the greatest feeling I want to have soon. I just don't want sex but with someone who loves me.

How do you like to make love to your partner?

In a dark room will be great, with the doors and windows

closed just a candle on...I have a large cock 8.4" and thick as well so I, love to make love nice and slow.

What is your experience in the net?

The internet has been making it difficult, it's hard to trust people on the internet but I will trust you because without trust we will not grow in feelings

Did you date many guys from the net?

I met my ex on the internet, so that gave me hope that possibly I can still meet another dream on the net so far that was the only guy I dated on the net

Would you like to meet me in person soon?

That will be great, I will so much love to meet you in person anytime as long as you want me I wish I have wings I will fly into your arms tonight. I will love to spend my birthdays with you.

Are you able to host?

no, I cannot host, but I can come if you can host. I cannot host because I don't have a job yet.....take care of yourself I will end with a quote...."From across time and miles I dream of you"

Me: 6/9/2010

Hi Babe it's me John, where are you with this message? I think you have been out drinking, that's okay so have I. There is one thing you share the same thought as me with and that is to put a ring on your finger. I want to do this and so do you.

I hope that satisfies your worries but I want to have a commitment ceremony with you. The choice of cities is yours. It is not recognised in the colony yet but it will happen, but if you are asking me to come to the UK and marry you because it's acceptable the answer is yes and I can come with two rings. In fact I have been thinking about this all day. This is a great commitment for both of us. I'm sorry I don't know the movie you mentioned but I have heard the song. I am happy to spend my leisure with you naked as much as possible and happy for your 8 inches to penetrate me, as I have said I will require some versatility in our relationship myself. I want you to lick on my toes as you said in your first email I want to kiss your feet in fact I want us to have all of our bodies for each other. I am showing concern with this letter that something is wrong. I think I have done everything right, my situation has not changed. I want to be with you if you haven't changed your mind. I hope it is still on offer. I would still like to send you that birthday card but it's okay if you prefer to leave it alone. Please tell me if you still want the relationship because if you do I can book a ticket tomorrow to come and see you.

I know there are no hugs and kisses from you in this last email, please tell me if I have said something I should not have done because from me it's good night babe I still want us to be together let me know tomorrow please

Goodnight   John

Me

Hi Beck I guess yesterday with my email I was anxious to be with you and my friends were telling me to message you with the way I feel about a commitment ceremony so I did that's why it is important to me you are interested. I realize now I did not answer the questions you asked I'm sorry that was rude of me so I will answer all the questions now.

I have been really fine, the more I talk to you the better I am and that led to a great day yesterday.

I do cook and sometimes I explore new recipes, sometimes I make my old favourites but mostly I cook up what you would call "pub grub" (something quick and easy with meat and veg). I eat meat and chicken, fish I enjoy lots of vegetables as this keeps me healthy. I usually cook a chicken schnitzel with veg or pasta. I had a tradition on Friday nights when my man was alive we used to do sausage sandwiches because we would go out drinking and come home hungry so I do this again now I pre prepare the sausages mushrooms and onions and melt the cheese on the sausages, then when I come home I heat them and put them on fresh bread rolls with butter and English mustard. I would love to make this for you. I also make profiteroles and put Frangellico in the custard— Yum…..

As I said in the last letter I am not familiar with the Seven Pounds but I like Will Smith, if this is your favourite movie I will rent it and tell you what I think. I think too that people can show their personality by the movies they watch. Andy Williams well now you show your age we all know that one and James Blunt Your Beautiful I have it on CD,

.it is a song for you "you're beautiful. My favourite colour is purple followed by rich blue or electric blue and in my garden, I have lots of purple flowers.

Like you with my leisure time I will walk to where I am going so I can think along the way although I probably don't do it as often as you because I have the car. I will go to the pub which you don't do and you're absolutely right I too go to the movies alone for now and also wanting that to change soon too. On the weekends I catch up on chores but my new flatmate John is mad on cleaning everything all the time so I can concentrate on the garden or washing the car.

I am very handy with my hands, and I like making things or fixing things (furniture or electrical). I even paint the house when I am bored. When I used to vacuum the house living alone I did it with nothing on but a cock ring, all my friends know this. Monday mornings are ironing day before work and the dog gets walked, twice a day every day she won't let you forget her.

You already have the qualities I am looking for in my man. I am looking for loyalty, honesty, love, looks, health, personality and warmth. I do not argue but if it does ever happen it is in private and we discuss it. It has happened before (not often) and we would talk it through. I am not a violent person and I don't have a mean streak either. that's why all my friends rallied to support me when my partner died, you know how I feel about marriage maybe I was to early last night wanting to come to you with two rings but it is how I feel, I am being possessive of you already. I do believe the commitment between two people and their spiritual being whoever that is, is all that is required to make the bond Holy.

I was originally against having a commitment ceremony when my partner first asked me, but I always wanted to give him everything he wanted so I agreed, and that made me realize, by doing so we were sharing our love with our special friends. All the women we invited cried that night. I am glad you are asking questions about sex, I wanted to ask you too but I was worried you might think I was to forward, and then there is the thought also that when we meet for the first time should it be a surprise but as I now know that you have an 8 inch cock there is no surprise.

I will be really happy for you to fuck me and yes I will scream, you will rim me before you do it and I will already have licked your arse out too, what you will need to do when you have finished fucking me and cum on my face is hold me tight and kiss me passionately because to me I have just given you my inner sanctum and endured the pain for you so I will need your caresses and passion.

By the way I also have a foot fetish so I will be kissing your toes as well. You have answered two questions already for me the first one was, is your cock thick and when you fuck me will it be rough or gentle. I sometimes fuck guys hard and fast but only if they ask, normally slowly with passion. It would be so Hot with only candlelight, you are making me horny already, in fact I have a truth for you I was thinking of your cock in me this morning, I was watching some porn thinking of you and I satisfied myself twice. I have been in a sling before and I have been fisted once but I can't handle receiving that. I have a friend that I shave and fist but this is not reciprocated. Tell me you are a very passionate kisser. I like leather denim uniforms speedos' and suits. I am into rimming wanking bare backing (when agreed) kissing sucking role playing and voyeurism. That is my hidden self.

As, for the internet, I have my profile on many sites, even international ones. I enjoy taking nude pics of myself in the process to post them. I am not currently in contact with any person on any site and I am on these sites before we met . When I am in a relationship I will delete these profiles because they will no longer serve any purpose.

I am very open on the net and I will tell you anything you want to know about me.

I am careful with some web sites not to use email addresses and I never buy online so no one can get my card details. Apart from the short chat with the Russian guy (Arthur) recently for two weeks only, you are the only guy that has gone so far with our internet relationship.

There have only been 3 guys that have replied to my profiles, and only two of those I met for coffee and nothing happened. Beyond that we were all unsuitable to each other, so basically you are my only internet relationship. I did not meet my partner or the Czech on the net Yes I can host, yes I want to have you in my arms tonight as I did last night, and I can't wait either. Have you thought of a working visa here? I so want you now I will await your advice, good night my darling man

xxx

Beck:

John my darling

Good afternoon my love it's so nice to read from you. I have been thinking about you and I know we will be the best partners.

I'm happy I found you, you are my dream man babe, all I need to do now is find my way to your own better place. I have to think about it all and I am ready to submit my life to you. But will you promise me that you will never hurt me. I want to be totally yours and I will never let you down.

Okay babe I just came back from the Australian Embassy I have made inquire what I will need to come over there, and I have all the document needed and I will need your home address and phone number because the embassy may call you to confirm maybe I'm coming to your place and I will need 150 pounds for the visa fee.

Babe I think this is what we need to do, to be together. You mean the world to me now babe, and I just can't wait to be in your arms.

Love you so much

Kisses and hugs

CHAPTER 2

THE VISA

Beck   6/9/2010

John my Darling

Good afternoon my love it's so nice to read from you. I have been thinking about you and I know we will be the best partner.

I am happy I found you, you are my dream man babe, all I need do now is find my way to your own better place U have been thinking about it all and I'm ready to submit my life to you. But will you promise that you will never hurt me. I want to be totally yours and I will never let you down.

Okay babe, I just came back from Australia Embassy I have made inquire what I will need to come over there and I have all the documents needed and I will need your home address and phone number because the embassy may call you to confirm, maybe i am coming to your place and I will need 150 pounds for the visa fee.

Babe I think this is what we need to do to be together. You mean the world to me now babe and i just can't wait to be in your arms

Love you so much

Kisses and hugs

Me

Hello my beautiful man you have just said the magic words I wanted to hear I love you, so do I love you Beck. I wanted to say this to you when I wrote to you the other day and said I like you Beck I actually wanted to say I love you then I love you with all of my body and soul I promise you now I will never hurt you and my promise is until the end of time. I will be unconditionally faithful to you I will share everything I have with you what is mine is yours. I hope we can figure this out soon I so want to put that ring on your finger my darling, if you want to give me your bank details I will get the money transferred to your account this might take a few days because I have to request a transfer of funds into a nominated bank first then I will get them to do the conversion I will let you know when it is done just tell me when you want it and allow say 3 working days.

The information for the Australian Embassy is below. Name: J Morewood Osborne

Address: xxxxx   xxxxxx   Nsw   Australia

Home phone (612) xxxx xxxx Mobile (cell) +614 xxx xxx Email: xxxx@xxxx.com

I work late shifts on Mondays, night shift on Wednesdays and Thursdays I am on the road driving between 9-4 Tuesdays and Wednesdays and 12-4 pm Thursdays. There is an answering machine so they can leave a message and I will get back to them when I wake up I sleep some of the day obviously.

This is your future new address it is a Victorian Terrace 2 bedrooms built in 1886 with a large courtyard I can give you further details if you want as soon as you want them.

I love you babe take care

Your man John   hugs and kisses

Beck: 7/9/2010

Dear Love

Thanks for the information provided I am very glad and really appreciate I just wanted you to know how truly I deeply care for you. We've been together for a while now and nothing could change the way I feel about you and us as a couple. You are my one and only. I don't think there could ever be enough words in this world that could really capture how I truly feel about you   I love you so much. I just don't know how I could ever explain it but I do know that the one person I can count on always is you. I hope you knew this and if you didn't hopefully you'll know this now and forever I love you very much.

Sweetie the easier way to send the money is Western Union money transfer I think that will be better 150 pounds is equivalent to 200 Australian dollars.

To send the money via Western Union money transfer using the information below NAME ...Beck Hill

ADDRESS....112 Levita House (Chalton St/ Ossulston St) NW I 1 State CAMDEN LONDON

Country ...England

Babe, after making the payment make sure you get back to me with the information you will receive at the western union ie:

SENDERS NAME....?

MTCN # NUMBER....?

TEXT QUESTION &

ANSWER AMOUNT SENT.

.............................?

My life with you love you from the bottom of my heart Beck Osborne

Me

Hi Babe

I've printed off the information I was actually thinking maybe I should try Western Union so that's fine. I will request a transfer today and it maybe in my account tomorrow. I'll be looking at sending this Thursday or

Friday I'm off to work now all day and tomorrow too. But when I have it transferred I can find a Western Union in an area I am In. and send it there. Have you got any ideas when you might be coming I would like to get some Gym in to look good. Also as it is Spring here the airfares are higher and will get higher again into summer

Have a great day darling I love you

John

Beck:

My love you have this power over me this indescribable undeniable unmistakable power. You consume my mind. You invade my thoughts...my love you are the ruler of my dream world. You bring a smile to my face, a sparkle to my eyes, and a tear to my cheek.

Everything you do for me re -assures me that I am appreciated baby hearing from you always makes me happy. I want you to know that you mean so much to me. From the first day we met here you were determined to get to know me baby you tell me how beautiful I am you tell me how you love every curve of my body. You just make me feel extra special, make me feel a sense of warmth inside. I want you to know that I love you for this I love you for being so caring and genuine. I love you for the happiness and joy you bring to my life. I love you for you. I want you to know that I want the best for you as well. I want you to succeed and i want all your dreams and fantasies to come true. I know that in me you see a young man full of kindness, understanding and compassion, a young man with an open heart a young man who puts a smile on your face everyday.

I will be that man who's there for you just as you're there for me the one who encourages you through life's ups and downs but ultimately I want to be the man who is your everything.. Not an hour goes by that I don't think about you. You have brought so much joy to my life and you give me so much to look forward to when I wake up every morning. I want you to know that I sincerely appreciate you and I can never tell you enough that "I LOVE YOU" Sweet heart I will keep on expressing my love to you until the day we meet in person. I want you to know that I don't have a job I would not have asked you for the visa fee but remember that I don't have a job.

I was told by the embassy that the visa will take 3 working days before it will be intact. I will be waiting for fee, love you

Sincerely yours

Me   8/9/2010

Hi My Love

I am off to work now so I will send you a good long message at my other work. I have transferred the cash but I have missed the 7:00pm cut off time last night so it should be available tomorrow or Friday. I am not happy about using Western Union a bank account is better. Is Western Union Faster? Don't think it's safer, what visa have you asked for?

I think you are too old for a student visa but you do have a university degree so that will help. What are you doing for the airfare? I will message you late tonight must be off now Bye my love.

Beck

Good morning my darling, thanks for being there for me I swear I do think about you much and I always want to read from you...My love the easier way to get the money to me is Western Union it's safer and very faster...Meeting you was fate becoming your friend was a choice but falling in love with you I had no control over. "believe me sweetheart if dreaming is the only way to be with you then I'll never open my eyes...when I was a young man my mum used to tell me that you will find only what you think you deserve.so am so happy I found you and am happy we are getting along well....I've been alone with you inside my mind and in my dreams I've kissed your lips a thousand times. I sometimes see you pass outside my door. Hello, it's me you're looking for I can see it in your eyes; I can see it in your smile. You're all I ever wanted and my arms are open wide, because you know just what to say, and you know just what to do, and I want to tell you so much. I care for you and I love you

Kisses

Me: 9/9/2010

Good morning my sweet man

I am here at work alone writing to you I have transferred

the money and that should be available tomorrow. But there is only 1 western Union in Sydney in the city centre and I will not be able to get there tomorrow as I will be in a different area and on Friday I'm going away for the weekend back Sunday evening. You may not be aware but I can pay for your, off shore visa application here in Sydney and that will save me exchange rate. All I need is the details and that I can do tomorrow at the government office in the area I will be at. You must be requesting visa 417 working holiday visa 18-45 yo. This will give you up to one year, Have you applied for the visa yet? How long have you requested or have you only been granted 3 months? I really want to see you soon, I am planning what to do when you arrive but I'm not going to tell you what that is.

I did not know you live near Camden markets in North West London I think the local station is Euston I went there once. You know honey I am so happy I found you I do feel like I never want to let you go.

At all times I think you are with me and when I get home from work it seems like you are there waiting. Let's have the waiting over soon. I will keep checking my email via the phone. If you supply me the information I will pay the visa tomorrow if you have applied already. I will be thinking of you all night. Babe

Kisses forever   yours   john

Beck

I feel so much falling for you. I really want this to work out between us. It's 2 years working visa I requested for

I haven't applied for the visa yet I have to submit my application with the visa fee to the embassy here, so you was the one delaying now babe you should look for another western union store or go to any bank they will have Western Union branches there, because that's the way it is here. Guess what I told my mum about you so fast she said I should send her regards to you and that you make me smile and she said I should ask may be you won't hurt my feelings or maybe I trust you....I told here truly we have not seen in person but I trust you and I know you trust me as well....I really will love to be in your arms one day, did I ever tell you I noticed I was gay at the age of 22 and I had my first man then. Am happy I have a new life now and am moving ahead with it...hey have you charm me? I can't stop thinking about you here...

Kisses

Me: 10/9/2010

Hi Babe

I think I must have been dumb I have just keyed in westerunion.com.au and there are lots of places newsagents and post offices that are agents it even gives me the amount with fee. This is great news as there's one now close to home. I'll send you a message tomorrow with the details. Love you

Me:

Hi Babe

The money is available now

Details are

NAME   Beck Hill

ADDRESS   112 Levita

House STATE.   Camden

London

COUNTRY   England

Babe after making the payment make sure you get back to me with the information you will receive at the Western Union i.e.

SENDERS NAME...........?   xxx   xxxxxx

MTCN # NUMBER...........? 1029789818

TEXT QUESTION AND ANSWER ....?   And name of your first Pet   Xxxx

AMOUNT SENT ......? 150 British pounds

This cost me A$300 with transfer fee and exchange rate I was going to send a little extra but I ran out of money that I had on me so that's why you got 150 GBP

This must make you happy and excited. Hopefully next week you will have it I am off to snooze for a while now my love. I will hear from you later Babe Hugs and kisses

Your address is not required as you collect this from the Post Office you will need to show ID I was advised that the text question and answer are not required when sending from Australia to the UK so this information may not have been put into the database.

I have the original receipt.

Beck:

Sweetie thank you so much I am very glad and really appreciate I got the Western Union information now am on my way to the bank because I have to submit the requirement to the embassy today I will write more as soon as I come back from the embassy....I love you from the bottom of my heart

Kisses

Me:

Hi honey I guess you were asleep when I sent you the message I stayed awake to go to the post office early and get this out of the way for you. I have an early train to catch to the river so I will pick up your message if I get reception. The area I am going to is world heritage listed so no mobile phone towers are allowed on the headlands. One day I will take you there.

Enjoy your day my love somehow I think you will
Love you kisses

Beck:

Good afternoon my darling. I just came back from the embassy I have submitted my application to the Embassy and I was told to check back on Wednesday. I have always believed nothing happens just by chance.

Everything in the universe is pre planned and I believe we were destined to become lovers. All of our previous encounters were a preamble to what was about to happen with us. You are all I now want from life and I thank god every day for your presence in my life. I dream about you and often they are of a sexual nature but then neither of us are getting any male contacts. My life is sworn to you and only you. You have won my heart 100%   have fun over there hope to see you

soon

Me: 11/9/2010

Hi Babe

That is great news I bet you are happy. I have just arrived back from my river cruise with a bit of red skin as well I will send you a couple of photos of today later. This morning I was thinking of you I even made you a cup of tea you seemed so real. We will be able to move on I agree even with our emails. I have no doubt I want you to be with me and when you arrive we will have other things to discuss about us. You believe we were destined to become lovers. What is strange I am not a paying member of this site, this is where you first contacted me on August 30th I cannot open or read emails on this site

But yours opened for me once only and I copied your email address. I was only browsing this site in Australia and you were browsing International. I replied to you with a wink because I saw your profile and even though I knew you were in the UK I didn't care.

Your email said contact me with your email address so

I did. This email was not even supposed to be opened in my browser. Maybe this is something special time will tell.

I showed a lot of people on the boat your photo today. I hope to be able to introduce you to them soon.

I love you my darling I wait for your next message

Lots of kisses

Beck:

John my Darling

You brought love and laughter to my empty sad and boring life. My heart had known only emptiness until the day you came and filled my heart to overflowing with your jovial ways. Your sense of Humour has turned my frown into a smile.

You taught me how to love again you taught me to give and receive love by trusting in you and believing. You taught me to go the extra mile. And though there are miles between us, I never stop thinking of you. You have bought a change into my life and my heart is forever yours.

I can never forget you or keep thought of you out of my mind.

Thoughts of you warm my heart. You complete me. You are everything my heart desires I love you I will be waiting for the pic

Kisses

Me: 12/9/2010

Good morning babe (well its' morning here)

I am going to have a very busy day with a long lunch and visiting, then Sunday night out as always don't worry you will have lots to see and do. I just want to say thanks for all the nice words you say about me and I'm glad you like my sense of humour. It can be "Wicked" sometimes. I had a pretty amazing day on the river yesterday and have included some pics of me and some of my best friends that I have known forever. I wanted to ask you do you want to tell me about your dad and your partner. If it hurts and you don't want that's okay. I just want to know all about my beautiful man. Your story to me of the first time you got off with a friend after watching a hockey game is such a horny story maybe you have more to share. I will hear from you later babe take care lots of hugs and kisses John

] river pics]

Beck: 13/9/2010

My love how are you doing? (Lol))

Are you there?

I will be right back 15 mins hope to chat with you soon

Me:

Yes

I am here waiting for you my love

Beck:

Babe why did you go without informing me? Did I get you angry? I am not happy with this please get back to me

I love you from the bottom of my heart\ kisses Byeee

Me:

Hi babe

I am very sorry for logging off without saying goodbye I thought you had logged off. I finish saying I love you Honey I am so sorry if I got you upset I was being inconsiderate you have a lot of things to finalize and you need a certain date to go I will request the transfer today if you get back to me in time. I have to have the request in by 7:00 pm What I need form you urgently is the exact price because the post office will have a different conversion rate to me and there are transfer charges. Last week the GBP was 60p to $1 Aus that is a good rate maybe I can still benefit from this I need an exact Amount from you ASAP so I can ask the post office for a price and request the withdraw. Hopefully then a flight next Thursday or Friday should be fine. See if you can get an arrival time in local time here to fit in with my roster. I love you babe I am sorry Hugs and kisses john

Beck: 13/9/2010

Sweetie are you there/? Are you there my love?

Me:

Hi babe I'm here sorry I am at work and was away are you alright?

Beck:

Yes I'm alright now

Me:

Have you got yourself into moving mode yet? I wanted to ask you when is the last day you have in your place? As I said before I can get a total price tomorrow and move the funds about Thursday

Beck:

I will love to move this week or next week

Me:

That's not a problem I was only thinking that if you can't get a ticket this week because there is no room do you have more time so let's aim for this weekend but if you can't then next weekend.

Beck:

That will be fine with me this weekend or next week during you off day at the office

Me:

Either way you're here soon and before October

Beck:

Yes babe

Me:

Yes, if you can confirm local arrival time when you book that will help otherwise any flight Friday, Saturday or Sunday should be fine. I found the post office too busy today I was on my way to work, so I'll sort the price tomorrow and arrange a transfer I don't want you to worry my love. I think I will be up for around $1750 inclusive.

Beck:

Yes I will confirm that, and thankyou very much my king because you have been here for me in anything and I promise I will not let you down. Yes $1750 Australian

Me:

I want you to be happy and it wouldn't hurt me either. How long is your flight 24 hours?

Beck:

Yes babe 24 hours

Me:

Okay that gives me an arrival time to workout I have not had a call yet from the immigration office but I guess maybe they don't call everyone

Beck:

Really!

Me:

Yes not yet

Beck:

Yeah you right I hope you stay close to your phone

Me:

There is an answering machine at home and I have just missed a withheld call number on my phone. I have one friend who calls me withheld but she would not call. Are you going to have a garage sale and sell all your things?

Beck:

No oh okay, I will leave everything for my friend and my mum

Me:

...........Phone rings..............

I have the Embassy now

Beck:

Really?

Me:

Yes I am speaking with them

Beck:

am happy am very happy what did they say?

Me:

They will call me again tomorrow visa available Wednesday No shit man that was the Australian Embassy in the UK. They are very hard to understand.

Beck:

How? I don't understand what did they say?

Me:

I think they said they are going to grant you a two year visa but you have an appointment with them on Wednesday and they will grant this on Wednesday or Thursday, they will call me again in a couple of days, I think the missed withheld call was them they called on my mobile and he was obviously Black and hard to understand.

Beck:

I was told that very day I went to submit my application to check back on Wednesday

Me:

I'm so excited I told them I was online with you and expecting you to stay for 2 years with me

Beck:
Really!

Me:

Yes

Beck:

I am very happy now my love hopefully we will see each other soon I think they may call you on Wednesday or not I told them already

Me:

He was saying something I couldn't understand the voice kept wavering, anyway you will find out and let me know.

Beck:

Okay my love

Me:

Maybe you should get them to call my landline number +612 xxxx xxxx

Beck:

That will be on Wednesday if they want to call again

Me:

It maybe that you can go this weekend but they want to talk to you. I think they wanted to make sure I exist if you are coming to stay and that I can support you

Beck:

I think they may call you on Wednesday or not, yes! I told them already

Me:

Yes I think so too, now the time is 7:45pm I think you are 10 hours behind me so, if they call at the same time on Wednesday, I will be at home. It might be that you need to tell them, because, if I am driving, it will be hours before I can answer. See if they can give it to you on Wednesday but they did say Wednesday or Thursday

Beck:

Ok

Me:

Hey honey this is fantastic news, you must be so excited

Beck

I think it should be Wednesday because they told me to come for collection on Wednesday. I am very, very excited.

Me

Fantastic, then they will call me Wednesday, hopefully I can understand them better

Beck:

Yeah

Me:

I have just looked at the phone number, it is withheld, so I did miss the first call and they called back 10 mins later

Beck:

Uh okay, and we are just talking about them what a life

Me:

Just start packing babe

Beck:

Yeah my love you got it

Me:

He even said "I am calling from the Australian Embassy in the UK on behalf of Mr Beck Hill"

Beck:

Really!

Me:

Then he said "Do you know him? Is he coming to stay with you? I said yes to all

Beck:

That's nice

Me:

That is amazing, we were just talking about it and it

happened, that's spooky. I don't know of any situation where that has happened before

Beck:

(lol)

Me:

I feel a bit strange now, I feel like we have connected

Beck:

When you told me you was talking to them I am so surprise

Me:

I know, I was typing to you to let you know they were on the phone. I thought you're not going to believe this but it is true for us my love

Beck:

Believe me you got it you was talking to them and still typing to me

Me

Yeah, that is true I was short of breath and excited myself

Beck

Wow, I am so happy now my love I swear

Me:

Can you please message me as soon as you've got it, I

will probably get the call first, but they might confirm with me after they have spoken with you. This also puts us in their system

Beck:

Yes babe, I will get back to you as soon as I got it

Me:

To be able to claim residency later, we have to be together two years, before they will consider us, so now it is in the database

Beck:

Wow, that's very nice my love

Me:

I have to go

Beck:

Okay my love, I know you at work right now just take good care of yourself, I love you so much hope to see you soon, Kisses byeeeeee

Me:

All okay I had someone wanting mail, they are sorted now. Bye honey sleep well now kisses

Beck:

Byyyyyy

Me:

By you beautiful man I love you

Beck:

I love you to   byeeeee

Me:

Bye

Me: 14/9/2010

I don't want to log out without saying goodnight my love so I will say goodnight for now, just keep packing and it's okay if you have more than 2 suitcases we will find a place for everything

Beck:

Okay babe

Me:

Goodnight babe

Beck:

I love you good Night, Kisses

Me:

Love you too

Beck:

Byeeeeee

Me:

And hugs I love you bye honey

Beck: 15/9/2010

You there now.

Me:

Yes

Beck:

How are you my love?

Me:

I am fine I have been out all night I have a friend coming over early to play how are you what time is it there?

Beck:

It is 7:30 pm here babe

Me:

That gives me an idea of time it's 4:30 am here

Beck:

Really?

Me:

Yes I don't work until 3:pm on Mondays I had a great night out got hit on a few times wasn't interested. Is your mum pleased with your decision?

Beck:

Yes babe she's very happy

Me:

I hope she doesn't get lonely

Beck:

She will not my love

She said I should send her warm regards to you that you make me happy she wants the best for me love. I really love the pic you sent to me it's very nice

Me:

The pic was taken yesterday those guys are old friends I wanted to give you an idea of the countryside. It is different here even with a river everything is dry

Beck:

You would let me understand everything when I get there

Me:

Yes it is that time now with this application we have the waiting game

Beck:

Yes babe

Me:

I hope yesterday had the right answers with the visa

application we are so ready for each other I hope the news will be good

Beck;

Yes babe I will get the visa for sure because I have all the requirements needed I just can't wait to be with you there.

Me:

Me neither I want to have you here ASAP I am cleaning the house and making it spotless

Beck:

LOL thankyou my love

Me:

Are you going to have a farewell?

Beck;

Babe I have to check the flight ticket is very expensive

Me:

What price have you got? I have been speaking about that today with a friend of mine who is a travel agent.

Beck:

I got 995 pounds which is $1650 Australian dollars

Me:

I will see if my friend can do any better she is English

and owns her own travel agency. She has just returned from the UK and she knows the cheapest fares. I want to have some cash left over for us as I need to support you until you get a job that's why I want to be as sensible as possible if I can get a cheap fare that will be okay with you..Can your mum help at all?

Beck:

I don't know how to talk to her about that because I told her already that you are capable enough that you are there for me anytime and she's very happy:

Me

today the Aussie $ is 60p that is a good rate I have the cash to do that. I have some bills to pay but I want to replace that money ASAP that's why if I can get it cheaper all the better that will leave me a little

Beck:

Okay I got you my love I understand that.

Me:

I don't have as much as I want

Beck:

I will also check some cheapest as well but KLM is nice airline because I don't want to have any problem when I am coming there

Me:

If the Immigration Department rings me they may want to know that I can support you

The answer is yes but I will then rely on wages helping us and not spending much

I will be okay especially when you get a job we just need to get to that stage. Can we wait until you have your visa, then see what I can do your visa will have a start date that should be when we make the flight you don't want to waste any of the allocated time

Beck:

I don't want to waste it my love. You would have known how much I want to be there with you

Me:

I am so looking forward to our time together .I will be happy later this week when we can plan our lives together. Did you request a start time on your visa application?

Beck:

Yes If I get the Visa on Wednesday I can fly anytime. I want to even if I want to fly on Thursday I can

Me:

Okay that s good to know as I mentioned in a previous message

I have some bills to pay including Visa which is full, limit, otherwise I would pay with that .I might pay that off and use and use that or I may do it over two pays, but I don't want to delay either. Can you leave this with me and I will do my sums. I still want you here as soon as possible. Will you have any spending money of your own? I may have to consider that in the equation, we will need to go out I don't want us to sit at home and wait for payday. I will have some cash left over but I like to have that for emergency. I want your help on this when you get a job.

Beck:

Babe I will understand you that you have spent a lot on me don't think I will bother you for anything when I get to your home.

Me:

I will look after you I told you that

Beck:

Don't worry my love when I get a job I would pay you back

Me:

No I don't need you to do that

Beck:

And I will not like it if only you is taking the expense we need to do it together I have to contribute as well my love because that's the only way we can enjoy our relationship we both have to contribute to it.

Me:

That is what I was going to say, it is not the paying back so much as saving together. I want to see you with your own cash and we can share if I need some from you I will ask.

Beck:

Yes Babe

Me:

It is more important to get you on your feet n that is my promise we will get the finances sorted anyway

Me:

Yes I agree with you we are now in this together, as a couple

Beck:

So I need to be there and get a job so you would not be doing all the expenses

Me:

You are a honey and I thank you for that, it will be fine thankyou you are a wonderful guy you are fair and I appreciate it so much

Beck:

You don't need to thank me my love is for the sake of each others

Me:

Remember this is your place as well we are a couple yes and I will look after you I promise.

Beck:

I am happy to hear that that's why I will always be proud of you

Me:

I will buy new linen for us and we will have to spend an hour sorting the hanging spaces for your gear.

Beck:

I promise I will not let you down

Me:

Do you have many cases to bring? Will they all fit in my Hyundai Getz? I feel good about you Beck and I don't think you will let me down either I had that happen with the Czech. I feel good vibes with you babe. I so want you to have a new great life with me

Beck:

I don't have much luggage just 2 bags

Me:

Cool we will find room easily I may have to work for friends this first weekend in October and it involves travel , they will pay me for this so I need to allow that time plus when you arrive to bring you from the airport.

Beck:

Babe I want to be there before first week of October

Me:

okay that can be done . I do have some bill to pay about $880 , I get paid this Tuesday to cover that the next full payday is 28th which is a Tuesday if that is too late then we will be looking at the 21st.

Beck:

I think 21st will be fine with me

Me: but as that is a Tuesday it means the flight needs to land after 4:00pm I work Tuesdays and Wednesdays 9-4

Beck:

Okay babe

Me:

I also work 3-11pm on Mondays so a Monday morning arrival is fine or a weekend would be better, also I have Fridays free from 7:00 am but I will need to sleep for several hours

Beck:

Okay I will let you know the time

Me:

Yes please see what you can get from them I will see if my friend can get me a good price maybe I can arrange it so you can collect the boarding pass at Heathrow. I think all flights to Australia leave from Heathrow

Beck:

I will love to by my ticket here because I don't want any problem or embarrassment during my departure

Me:

okay I understand that I do have residents where I work that do get me to print their boarding passes that they have emailed to me from overseas and they all fly okay that is the only reason I suggested it I don't want to upset you

Beck:

Okay, but I don't want that my love

Me:

I will ask my friend if she can guarantee ticket collection it might be possible with no problems. I like you would not want any problems. If it were me either, I won't buy the ticket from her I will see what she says first.

Beck:

I would love to buy my ticket here that's the best thing to do

Me: you are so headstrong okay don't worry honey I will get the ticket after you have got the visa I will check Webjet for the best price .I am a member of Webjet. Is the weekend of Sept 22nd okay with you?

Beck:

Babe try to get me better I am not headstrong I am telling you my mind

Me:

I am sorry if I have offended you it was not my intention that's cool, no problem

Beck:

Okay no problem let me get the visa before we continue about this

Me:

Sure   I love you   bye

Beck: 15/9/2010

I love you so very much sweetheart. Congratulations John I just came back from the embassy I was issued 2 years visa, I am very happy now babe, you are the love of my life.

I have a hard time explaining how I feel I have never felt anything like this before. You are always there for me no matter what. I do not know what I would've done this week without your love and support. You are the most loving, caring, compassionate and absolutely I want to marry you now believe me. I want to be your man forever I want a baby with you (LOL). That is the most awesome experience nothing compares to that. You are a wonderful man to me, but you deserve more Thank You for always being there for the flowers they are beautiful, for your kind words hugs, kisses, and the unconditional love. You are a dream come true and I want to spend the rest of my life with you as your

Man, lover and best friend I have never in my life been so very happy. I feel much loved, beautiful and very happy.

I am so very proud of you .You are a strong person. It is really cool that we are strong for each other in different ways. We totally understand each other and feel for each other.

When you hurt I hurt When you are happy I'm happy, I'm happy I just love you so much sweetheart and I never want to lose you. I give you my heart my love and my life for now and forever babe I will be expecting the flight fee tomorrow Thursday I can't wait to meet you soon. I love you

Kisses

Beck Osborne

CHAPTER 3

THE PTA FEE

Me: 16/9/2010

Hi babe

I'm sorry I missed you on line I was busy. You will have the fare tomorrow, I had to change my bank limit and have half of it at home in the drawer. As soon as I have finished this email to you I will collect the other half as it will be after midnight and I can drawer it out I will be leaving work at 7:00am and am going home to sleep so around midday Sydney time I will send the money, The Western Union Form is already filled out I will be driving after that and may not be able to give you the number until later that afternoon. However I have an ace up my sleeve .I will try to go home and send you the number as soon as I have it. You will probably still be in bed so tomorrow will be a great day for you when you wake up.

I am so looking forward to you coming and being with

me always, thankyou for all the beautiful words and feelings towards me. I love you Beck with all my soul.

I am so happy you are happy and so looking forward to kissing you and I want to meet you at the airport if you can get the right flight. I am starting to make plans for us to be together, (on paper) for immigration purposes. We have to wait 6 months from your arrival date to apply for residency as a couple I will be glad if you can get a job real soon as my Flatmate Josh was very unhappy about this and I didn't want to tell him until we had confirmation from the embassy I don't see him until the next day, he was worried, you might not look after his dog and other things but I have had a talk with him and come to an agreement, I will pay two thirds of everything when you arrive until you are working he is happy with that he really is a nice guy and I don't want him to move out. I promised him we will not push him out and keep the karma happy. He is about 40 and has a 6 year old kelpie named Bella. The other Kelpie// Shepherd in the house is mine her name is Cindy. I want to look after you Beck I want to cuddle you in my arms. I want to protect you, and I want to wake up beside you. We have already shown our honesty to each other and tomorrow morning when you wake up we will have shown trust. You will have the fare and I will have flight details from you.

I know the embassy would have done a history check on me as well. The fact that you got a two year visa proves you are of good character, I believed this from the start, what I have not done is tell many people that I have paid for this I could not stand their criticism, besides it is our business. We are a couple now honey, that sounds really good to me it's what I want to this is a big step for you and takes a lot of guts I am proud of you and pleased you have taken that step. I won't let you down and I know you won't let me down.

Here's to a new life together for both of us and sharing everything. I have made room for your things in the bedroom cupboards and your house keys are cut. The time is now 12:20 am I am going to go out the driveway door to the bank behind this building and get the rest of the airfare. Good night my beautiful man, we will talk tomorrow.

Kisses

love your partner   John

Me

Hi my darling

I have some good news, go and buy your ticket here is the number you need. 8328059197 995GBP in the name Beck Hill from John Osborne sent 11:41 EST I love see you here soon.

Bye babe have to go to work I will chat with you tonight at my other job. Kisses

Beck

My dear lover

I appreciate what your values are and I do hold dear

to them and I admire you have them. However my principle in life is availability honesty and genuine love which conquers all. Your last email almost makes me cry. I know how Josh feels please tell him that I will be good to him and his dog it's a promise. Yes my John I too long to hold you in my arms, have my hands run through your chest, arms and down to your groin and my mouth sucking on your family jewels and god's gift. To hear your voice groaning and begging me for more is all I need now. Okay "cum" on and give me your juice. I long for your dick to penetrate up my ass as I beg and scream for more.

I feel deep down that you are for me and that I would do anything to see you, I will be tied up and spread on the bed with you, licking you all over. Come on lover! So have no doubts about me I'm all yours. I got the information you sent to me, I have to take a shower and leave for the bank from there I will go and buy my ticket, I will let you have the ticket details as soon as I am back, love you from the bottom of my heart.

Kisses

Me

My beautiful darling man

I am so sorry this email upset you. Josh was very concerned and I had told him about you beforehand I will show the first part of this email to him to satisfy his worries thank you for providing that to show to him. My darling I cannot express how much I want to hear your voice, smell your odour know every part of you and be as dominant with you as you will with me if you want that. I'm feeling as much the same way as you and I know you were going to wake up early and check your email that is why I wanted it there before you woke. I will be at work all night and I will wait for your email on flight details. I have been under a lot of scrutiny and questions about this and I have not mentioned it to many people at all but I have mentioned it to one person that was the wrong person and now I have to convince them which will be no problem soon. I have not told my parents I have mentioned to my best friend you are paying for yourself (with him it needs to stay that way even when you arrive) and I hold my neck out like a horny cock after a brood of hens through all of this because to me from the start this was going to work with us. I am so much looking forward to us meeting I am not even sleeping much you have already changed my life and I am making plans for us now.

I thank you for telling me everything about what you want tonight .I want to please you I want to love you I want to fuck you and I want to taste all of you and wake up beside you, and if the end of time runs out then I will find you. I want you to be mine and I don't intend letting you go either. I will hear from you later today, for you it will be maybe 5 hours but I have 9 more to add to the wait and I will wait all night

I love you

Kisses and hugs babe.

The next email subject line read "Confirmation London-Sydney (YYXBZQ) "17/9/2010 I was feeling at last we were actually getting close to meeting each other I was feeling quite excited. There were booking details AF1181 (Air France) depart Sat Sept 25th via Paris and Singapore arrive Sydney Mon 27th 05:10am. There was now much to do as I had to make room for my guest in the bedroom

Beck

Sweetie I am just back home and very tired, there is no available seat again so I chose for next week Saturday, and I will arrive in Sydney on Sunday this is the flight details below and I will be going to immigration office tomorrow. I have to confirm all the documents I will use to travel so as for me not to have any problem the day of my departure. I have to take a shower now and have a little sleep I will check you online soon hope to see you soon -Kisses

Beck:

My love how are you doing?

Me:

I'm here did you have enough sleep? Have you finished packing?

Me:

Hi babe are you excited yet?

Beck:

Yes my love

Me:

Did you have enough sleep?

Beck:

Yes my love

Me:

When you pack your things you should allow for a long sleeve shirt or sweater when you arrive

Beck:

yes babe I will

Me

It's still early spring and cool at that hour, how is your mother taking this?

Beck:

She's very happy because she really wants the best for me

Me:

That's good I don't want here to be upset. I guess when you get settled and have a job and are financial we'd better bring her here for a holiday

Beck:

Yes my love you got it that's a very nice idea

Me:

Besides, I guess I need to meet my new mother in law

Beck:

Lol

Me:

I think there are a lot of things we will think of honey we are going to have some wonderful experiences

Beck:

Yes babe we will have a chance to think better when we are together

Me:

I know I am slowly breaking the news to those that need to know, what about your friends? Are they giving you a send off?

Beck:

Lol, yes babe I only told one of my friends

Me:

Okay if that's what you want, I have a number of friends I guess you will meet them that is if you want to I know you said you are not into the scene and I respect that but if we go out occasionally I would like to introduce you to them

Beck:

Yes babe no problem I would love to meet your good friends that will be nice

Me:

Is there anything you need me to have here for you that you aren't bringing with you but will require?

Beck:

Nothing babe I will be fine I will see what I will need when I get there

Me:

I have to have a couple of hours sleep

I have my mother-in –law (the old one) coming for lunch. Yes I guess so now next Sunday seems such a long way off, but as I said I have to finish making room for you

Beck:

Yes you told me, Sweetie about John, I did not get upset it's just that the message made me cry

Me:

I am so sorry about that I really do apologize and I would not send anything like that normally but I had told Josh I would mention it, unfortunately I did not word it correctly. I promise you darling I will not write anything like that again. Also honey I will check the flight details online before I go to meet you just to make sure what time the plane lands.

Beck:

it's okay babe

Me:

Thankyou I am a nice person I do not do those things (unless there is an idiot on the other end of the phone). Honey I am going to let you do what you have to it is now my turn for bed. I will chat with you again later bye kisses

Beck:

Ok my love I will go to the immigration office tomorrow

Me:

What do they have to do?

Beck:

To confirm all my travel documents

Me:

Okay is everything else covered?

Beck:

Yes, if they confirm it I will not have any delay or problem during my departure

Me: that is a very sensible idea

Beck:

Yes my love

Me:

Do you still have only 2 bags?

Beck:

Yes babe

Me:

I am making one side of the wardrobe available for you

Beck:

Thankyou my love don't let me delay you, you can go to bed now I love you and my regards to John

Me:

Thanks Honey I love you too and I will pass that message on babe bye I love you

Beck;

Kisses, Byeeeee

Beck   18/9/2010

John my darling

Sorry for not getting back to you as earlier of the result I was too tired when I came back from the immigration office, then very pissed off, am not that happy as I found out what I will need .I was informed that I will need to hold PTA fee. It's a certain amount of money that all new travellers need to present before they will be allowed to get on board.

They said I will need A$5000 which will serve as PTA

fee. The PTA fee is a refundable fee, all you need to know about the PTA fee is it is a regulation which is formulated by Britain states in conjunction with the Australian government, as a result from the fact that most people travel from England and end up living on the streets of Aus, roaming about the streets, due to this reason they stipulate the regulations. Sweetie the PTA fee is refundable, it will not be taken from me, it is just to show that I meet the requirements of the immigration.

Babe I just can't wait to be with you. I have been thinking about you. I just wish I can hold you now and make love to you I feel so tired tonight I wish I will be sleeping in your arms tonight while you massage me. Love you so much

Kisses   Beck Osborne

Pic   Pic

Beck:

My love how are you doing?

Me:

Hi babe what is the situation with the PTA fee I don't have that kind of money to splash around

Beck:

Babe I was not really happy about the PTA stuff but I was told by immigration that the money will not be taken from me

Me:

Well whether it is or whether it isn't I am not able to transfer it to you

Beck:

How do you mean my love?

Me:

If they are so interested (as was the Embassy) they can ring me as did the Embassy. If this is like a sponsorship then I will be the sponsor but I would check again with them because I'm sorry that is a ridiculous amount that you have to have

Beck:

Babe, just try to understand this situation

Me:

Am I supposed to transfer this amount of money to you so you can show them you have it?

Beck:

The money will not be taken from me I will give it to you back as soon as you pick me at airport

Me:

I still don't have that available. I put my money in all sorts of things some where the cash is not available. The thing is, I don't have that amount of cash to give you anyway. That is why I am saying recheck the PTA I can't provide it anyway

Beck:

Babe are you mad at me? You sound like someone mad at me. It's not my fault I am not happy with it

Me:

No I'm not mad to you honey I am honest I do not have that money available I really don't

Beck:

It has been giving me a headache since morning

Me:

There is nothing much I can do even if I had the money I would lose so much in the transfer and the fee for sending anyway. This is upsetting for me as well please believe me I am more than happy for them to check with me surely there is another way around this, refugees come into both countries without this kind of cash maybe you will have to explain this to your mum.

Beck:

I have done that and she told me to inform you about this

Me:

My flatmate tells me you need that amount of money to leave the UK but I don't have it to give you. I have some cash available but not A\$5000. I have the funds tied up in shares and term deposits. Well I don't know what to say now.

Beck:

Babe so what are we going to do now because you are the only hope I have

Me:

I don't know what to do I don't want this to stop you from coming my immediate suggestion is can we get someone from immigration or the embassy to check with me I mean you have the visa, you have the ticket this is a government red tape there has to be a way around it. Why would they give you a 2 year work visa in the first place if they weren't going to let you go. The ticket is probably set travel time not adjustable so surely they are aware of that

Beck:

You know babe Embassy is different from Immigration Officer

Me:

is there an office I have to ring from here to talk to someone? Yes I know they are different and from different countries

Beck:

Babe I don't think so

Me:

They are obviously not talking to each other

Beck:

I don't think that immigration have anything to do with you. I am very tired now not happy at all because of the PTA stuff

Me:

But that doesn't help we know as the famous line goes (Houston we have a problem)

Beck:

I have been thinking that you may not be able to get it for me

Me

I don't know what else to say or do Beck I really don't I'm a bit shattered at the news myself you know. Can you take out an international loan at an affiliate bank and start paying it back when you get here that is what my last boyfriend did.

Beck:

Seriously babe this makes me so down now

Me:

Me too

Beck;

And I am going crazy about it

Me:

Me too. I do not have A$5000 available I did before I sent you the fare

Beck

yes I understand you my love because you have done all you can to make me get there but I don't want this PTA thing to stop me coming over there I can't do without you now you have taught me how to love I have fall in love for you already

Me:

I have no answer for you at the moment and I don't think I can get a loan for A$5000 we are Talking dollars not pounds I hope because if it is pounds it makes it unrealistic….. I am thinking

Beck:

It's about 3000 pounds babe 5000 Australian dollars

Me;

That doesn't help I can't raise that kind of cash and the reason for that is I am already committed to bank loans and credit cards that are full limit and I will not be given a loan on that basis. I have tried recently about 2 months ago and was told no. And yes I want to see you too honey.

Beck:

O my God

Me:

Yes exactly that is what I have been saying I wish we both knew about this earlier

Beck:

Babe I have suggestion can you borrow from Josh? Yes babe the earlier may be better

Me:

Can you ask them to waiver the PTA and call me I will confirm I am sponsoring you can we at least try that?

Beck:

Baba all because I am new traveller

Me:

No sadly I can't ask Josh, his boyfriend ripped him off so he is very wary

Beck:

The Embassy will not do that they just want to see me with the money during my departure

Me:

Then it is back to the same question I don't know what to do at the moment

Beck:

Babe I guess I should talk to my mummy about this I told her already she asked me to tell you

Me:

Honey I have to go and sort something out on a time frame I will chat later I just have some urgent things to do we need a clear head to think at the moment

Beck:

Okay babe am not just happy about this stuff I will chat with you later Kisses

Me:

I do love you it would have been easier for me to come to you but that would not have helped your situation anyway

Kisses

Beck:

Yes you got it don't let me delay you, you can go for now . Please email me whatever you think about this stuff. Hope to chat with you soon

Me:

This is something we need to resolve, I would ask my parents but they are broke from a bad business bye love.

CHAPTER 4

THE LOAN

Beck: 19/9/2010

John... King of my life.

I know you have been doing a lot for me and you want the best for me, you told me you will get me a job I am very happy and I really appreciate everything you have done for me., that's why I am ready to give you my life don't have any doubting thought on me because you will make me feel so stupid, all because I can't do anything in my life without you. You are the one who built the trust in my heart please don't take it away. John the PTA FEE IS REFUNDABLE IT WILL NOT BE TAKEN FROM ME IS JUST TO SHOW THAT I MEET THE REQUIREMENTS OF THE IMMIGRATION.

Sweetie, as soon as you pick me up at the airport in (SYD) I will hand over the money to you back. I look so terrible with the stress I am going through now, hope to chat with you soon

Kisses.

After, reading this I had a sinking feeling in my stomach as to knowing I had spent the night making room for his belongings and the only resolve would be to pay the PTA fee, But, I was reluctant to part with any more money as I felt my original obligation was fulfilled I replied

Me: September 19th 2010

As I said Beck no PTA fee, if you can't find it then returning my money will be great thanks bye. I had felt it necessary to write Beck a formal letter advising him that my status in life is not ask for money, that it was not proper or acceptable. It was also necessary to remind him he too was also responsible for some of the expenses.

My letter to Beck My Dear Beck

I am a bit concerned that you do not understand what I wrote in my email to you last Friday.

I do not have this money available in cash to offer you. A man in my position does not ask for a loan unless from a financial institution, and I am asking myself now, if my judgement with you was correct. Yesterday I had lunch with a friend, and his friend both of whom you sent the same email to as you did me on the same day. A valid point was made to me by both of them and that is, that there is no guarantee that you will come as you have not put any finance of your own into this relationship, and there is no guarantee if you do arrive that you intend to share your life with me because there is no way of knowing how many men you have contacted off shore. It is obvious that you intend to apply for Residency I do not have a problem with that and will support you but please realize you have not made any commitment to me yet. I have shown you my trust and honesty and forwarded to you all you required I am guilt free and have proven myself to you. Now it is your turn if this is to be a relationship. As I have also suggested to you get a credit card loan which you can pay off when you arrive, my ex boyfriend did just that he didn't speak English when he applied and got accepted.

I have got something for you I was going to wrap .it up as a surprise but I guess I will be wearing it myself if you don't arrive.

You have got a golden opportunity with a nice Guy to be your friend, your lover, your soul mate till the end of time. I guess you are not really ready for this, it must be frustrating and upsetting for you, your bags are packed your ticket and visa paid for, accommodation overseas organised, but you can't do one thing for yourself in this life changing experience not even for the man that wants to love you.

Yes I am strong and I want a strong man too, I can help make you strong if that's what you want but I need to see some commitment from you honey.

Earlier today my ex boyfriend contacted me wanting to see me as soon as possible. His last possible Visa is due to expire and he will have to go home to the Czech Republic for good, I think I know what he wants and I'm not sure if I will take him back to keep him in the country. This is a decision for you to make now as I can show my love and loyalty to only one man. I will not go to the airport on Sunday unless I hear from you, I would still like to go and meet you. It is now up to you my love.

Beck   the poem is for you

"When a man takes his partner he takes that man for life
They share their love a holy love as if were man and wife
Together they will bind their wounds and rub the ill away
Together they will always be forever and a day
There is love this is love there is love.

For no matter how far the distance
Our souls can be as one. To wake beside the man
I love another day begun.
This is love there is love this is love

Your sweet lips touching mine while bodies are entwined
Will always make the day ahead to never be a grind
And thoughts of coming home again to be with you each night
Makes the loving and our life, our souls our union all our life
This is love there is love this is love

I do love you bye Babe

Beck:

Sweetie I know how you feel about it but you make me feel so sad on your email don't think I love you because of money or I am coming to Sydney because of residency, I will never do that in my life, you should be thinking that for the fact that I want to come over there all the way from 6000 miles without being there before in my life, I would have you know I have already submitted my life to you and full trust I have in you so why would you have been doubting me, I know it's not your fault I guess this is all because your friends try to convince you, and don't forget that they can never how the feeling we have for each other, don't let anyone play with our feelings, well I have talk to my Mummy

already before I got sad email from you and she's willing to take a loan for me so definitely I will get the money this week and I will keep you up dated.

Kisses.

Me: September 20 2010

My darling Beck I'm glad you were sad because that was my intention to make you sad, yes it was deliberate and as I speak I ran into a friend tonight who has been living in England for the past 10 years, he is now snoring beside me but wants to fuck my arse and tie me up, he also wants a relationship with me I said I will let him know in a week Please believe me I do not have that amount of available cash to give you I have come under a lot of pressure over our situation with my friends and I promise you now we can pay your mum back before we think of my bills. I am naked typing this so is the hot man on the bed with the PA.

I meant what I said Beck I do not have $5000 to give to you I do have some but not that much that is what I have been trying to tell you. I welcome you to all I have and that will never change. I have to go I have a man waiting (maybe for the last time if you arrive)

I have a lot to say but as I have a man in my bed I have to please him so I will chat tomorrow

Thankyou I love you Goodnight babe Kisses

Me:

Hi Babe

I want you to know nothing happened between me and the guy I brought home last night. He threw up 3 times on the carpet beside the bed and on the linen so I cleaned it up and slept on the lounge. I have just finished cleaning up now and he has gone home. I want you to know that I intend to be completely loyal and faithful to you and I expect you to be the same. I am sorry if telling you that last night upset you I had been out to my nightclub and it was their birthday party so all my friends and I were in a good mood Chat later

Kisses bye Beck;

Hi

Me:

Hi Babe

Beck;

I don't understand the email you sent to me, what is the meaning?

Me:

I do love you I have been avoiding chatting live because I cannot and would not give you the PTA fare, what do you mean about the email, is that the one I just sent you?

Beck:

Yes

Me:

okay my love this is what happened two hours ago I went out tonight to my favourite club.

Beck; okay

Me:

It was their 29th Birthday party, the staff do drag, guys turn up from all over the continent because it has that reputation anyway.

Beck;

Okay

Me;

I ran into an old friend that did not know my partner had died so he is hot and horny and asleep and snoring in my bed after throwing up on the carpet and I'm not happy about that what I wanted from this guy tonight was a good fuck, he was going to tie me up and make me scream, the same thing I want to do to you, that is what I meant by tonight and the previous message. I have had a lot of flak from my friends about what I have done and most do not know the truth. I was hoping to prove them wrong about us. I hope I still can what do you think?

I have read your message and my message to your mum is we will pay you back immediately, but I am just not able to get him here by providing the PTA.

Do you think she will be happy with that I have already proven myself to you I never had any intention of hurting you Beck but you were not listening to what I was saying $5000 is a lot of money and I don't have that amount available. I did until I gave it to you so I had to try and make you understand. I must go now I have to sleep

Beck:

I have a question to ask you

Me:

Yes

Beck:

Do you really love me/

Me:

Yes

Beck:

I don't think so because you prove me wrong just now, if I told you I was with a man right now and he wanted to have sex with me how do you feel? You just shared sad news with me right now and I don't think I will be in good mood for a while. Is that how you will be cheating on me when I arrive to your place? Or don't you know cheating is what they call what you are doing right now

Me

you don't think you have upset me at all?

Beck:

How?

Me:

because my love I gave you my unconditional love to love one only until the end of time during our conversation over the past few days you were never going to come to me so I decided that I must cut my loses and what I had done for you and move on: I do not expect to have anyone but you and I expect the same

Beck:

Did I mention I will never come to you? Babe if I upset does that mean you should make me cry? You know I have been doing my best to make this work that's why I talk to my mummy and she has agreed to go for the loan tomorrow

Me:

I apologize if this has upset you but I promise it's the last one now that I know what you are doing I will never cheat on you and I would not have gone to this much trouble if I did not care for you in the first place, I apologize now if I have upset you but when I give you the key to the front door we are one, and only you

Beck:

I know you have been telling your friends about me and they try to confuse you regarding this matter. Do you think listening to your friends is the solution to the problem?

Me:

What do you mean?

Beck:

do you think listening to your friend criticise is the solution to this issue?

Me:

What s my friend criticising? I do not know what you are trying to say

Beck:

I know they would have been talking shit about me

Me:

Uhm no I have been trying to justify my actions about

the fact that I spent that much money on a visa and airfare for someone I don't know a lot of them have done it and been burnt I want to prove them wrong that it does work and I know in my ex boyfriend's house it does. I have not berated you, I have had to defend myself, you must realise I have told everyone you are coming and we must meet .Then you couldn't get yourself here so I had to apologize because I looked like an idiot. I meant every word I said Beck, I do love you and you know what I want us to do, and that is to walk into that venue as a couple and say "yes it can and has happened meet my boyfriend Beck, ".and I don't care if it doesn't happen to you but it has happened with us. Are you happy with that Beck?

Beck

Yes I am, Babe my mummy agree to help us with the loan but the problem is the bankers told her that they can only give loan of 1500 pounds to her, we need 3000 pounds

Me

Okay we need to find 1500 pounds, is that correct?

Beck Yes babe

Me

I am only able to offer $1000 because that is all I have to give you

Beck;

Okay it's fine. Babe if you offer $1000 where do you

want me to get the rest, because $1000 is 600 pounds here. Sweetie, the total money we need is 3000 pounds and my mummy will get a loan of 1500 pounds

Me:

I can't offer you more than $1000 because it is all I have to give. If I gave you more it would have to come from my pay which means you need to change your ticket to a later time

Beck

Babe I can't wait to be with you soon, you know I am willing to be with you soon so I can have rest of mind

Me

Me too, I am glad you are happy with what I am telling you about the man in my bed, because so far while I have been chatting to you he has thrown up on the carpet, woken my flatmate up, and now he's moaning. It was a bad idea but he's a good kisser and that sucks anyone in. He is snoring and I am going to sleep on the lounge I won't do this again as I said to you, and you to me. I can only love one man and I want that to be you.

Beck:

Sweetie the total money we need is 3000 pounds and my mummy will get a loan of 1500 pounds

Me:

I can't offer you more than $1000 because it is all I have to give .if I give you more it will have to be from my pay which means you need to change your ticket to a later time.

Beck:

Babe I can't wait to be with you soon you I know I am willing to be with you very soon so I can have rest of mind.

Me:

Me too

Beck:

If I am still here I will be having doubting of mind that you are cheating am not just happy with this situation

Me:

Why do you say that when I have given you the visa and airfare?

Beck:

The remaining money is 2500

Me:

And I can't get it either

Beck:

Babe I am not there now so what you are doing with the other guy I do not want you to do that again that's why I want to be with you soon

Me:

Can we chat tomorrow about this I need to sleep I have been partying all night I also need to figure out this problem with the shortfall of cash. I don't know how I can do anything but I need to think tonight

Beck:

Okay babe no problem

Me;

Now if I didn't love you would I actually bother telling you this?

Beck

I will be going to the bank with my mummy tomorrow morning

Me;

If you can get more fine if you can't I have $1000 when we need more we must act fast you and I the flight is a week away, I don't know if I can get any more money as I said I have tried recently I need to think

Beck:

Okay I will see what I can do babe we will chat tomorrow.

Me:

Thanks babe, by the way I am not getting any sex out of the man in my bed tonight he is too far gone and I want you to know as you are here next week, this is my

last chance anyway and I have now missed out. I love
you beck I will chat tomorrow

Kisses

Beck;

Love you too Bye

Me

Bye babe

Beck

Babe, how are you? Are you there? Me and my mummy
just came back from the bank right now

Me:

Hi sweetie you must have been there very early

Beck:

We fill a loan of 3000 pounds it's 11:45 now but we was
told at the bank we can only give 1500 pounds or more
than that but it would not be up to 3000 pounds.

Me;

Is your mother with you now?

Beck;

Yes babe, is with me now Hello Mrs Hill babe let me
stand up for her she says hello my in-law how are you?

Me:

Tell her I'm fine I hope she has a nice day and you too my love. You said to me yesterday you thought only 1500 pounds, well then the usual question to ask is we are still short all I have on cash reserve is the $1000

Beck;

babe we can only know tomorrow because we haven't know how much the bank will give out. I guess the bank will give a loan of 2000 pounds because my mummy talk to them that 1500 pounds is not going to be enough for what she needed it for and they told her to be expecting 1500 or 2000 pounds.

Me:

Is that definite that you have been approved for something? I can give you the $1000 but that money is to be used to look after you when you get here until you get a job that's why I don't want to use it

Beck:

Have you forgotten that the money will not be taken from me? As soon as you pick me up at the airport I will give it to you.

Me:

If she gets the 2000 pounds I can use the $1000 that will give you 2600 pounds. If you want 400 pounds I won't be able to do anything before next week I don't think this will be until Tuesday afternoon.

Beck;

Babe I think you can get it, borrow from Josh

Me

No way, he has it quite clear he has no intention of being out of pocket when you arrive Anyway, he is Jewish they don't do that sort of thing. If they only give you 1500pounds we are screwed I will have to contemplate it will take possibly a week to get that money from a dodgy Finance lender, I will have to search the net. As I said before I cannot get an increase on my credit card or from the bank as I am already committed to both and they work it out on your salary. Can you change the departure date? Do you intend to pay that money back to the bank as soon as you arrive?

Beck;

Yes babe

Me:

Because then I will need what I have got in hand for us to use until you get a job. I won't touch what I have here this is our safety net so we may be looking at 1500 pounds it is not a lot of money really

Beck;

It's a lot here babe

Me:

A nasty thought comes to mind Beck, Have you thought of prostitution this week to get the cash? (lol)

Beck:

Ahahah trust me I will never do that

Me:

Okay let me know what they offer tomorrow

Beck:

Yes babe I will get back to you

Me:

Can we go to the authorities and see if they will let you go on 2000 as you have a place to stay and a sponsor when you get here. Will that work?

Beck:

That will not work babe everything just make me weak because I have packed my luggage already

Me:

I thought you would have packed already. This is very awkward I want you here too. Okay I will look on the net and see if there is anything I can do but if there is we will have to pay this back straight away, can you change the flight date?

Beck;

to when?

Me:

In case it takes a while to find something in case we need to make it next week around Wednesday? Because if you can that makes it a lot easier. I can do the (borrow from Peter to pay Paul routine.)

Beck;

You mean I should change the flight to next week, Wednesday?

Me:

If need be can you?

Beck;

Yes babe I will I have no option because I know you have been trying for me

Me;

Or the weekend after if you want I was just saying Wednesday because that may be the time I need, you see I get paid fortnightly, from this my main job. I will still have the bills to pay but if I send the money to you and you give it back to me as soon as you arrive we can use it twice, do you understand what I am saying?

Beck:

Okay I will give it back

Me:

That's fine I will have around $1500 available next week and if I use the $1000 I am saving it might just be enough but it has to come back. We won't have much to spend for a week or two.

Beck;

Okay babe so I should change the date to Wednesday or when?

Me;

If they only give you 1500 tomorrow then I need you to change your flight date. .Do you still want to fly on a Saturday? You can move it back to the next week if you want that is up to you honey. But if you want to come as soon as possible then book for Wednesday that will put you here on Thursday I will be at work but we will cross that bridge when we need to.

Beck:

Okay I will come on Saturday

Me:

Thanks babe I appreciate it I will see what I can do I don't want to send the money in small groups because it costs so much to send it so I will do it all at once.

Beck:

Okay babe

Me:

I won't spend much this week myself okay?

Beck:

Babe please can you do me a favour I just don't want you to tell your friends about me anymore I want it a surprise when they see me arrive

Me:

Ah yes so do I and when they do meet you, you paid your own way okay? They will kill me if they know I have paid for the fare and some of the PTA, you will also get more respect from them if they think you paid your own way

Beck:

Okay babe thankyou my love that's lovely thank you so much

Me:

That's necessary

Beck:

Don't let me obstruct your work you can go now, kisses

Me

Bye honey Kisses

Beck

I will chat with you soon I love you from the bottom of my heart byeeeee

Me

And I do you my love

Me   21/9/2010

Are you there babe?

Beck:

I am doing great my love I just got home about 10 mins ago babe the loan has been approved but it is 1500 pounds

Me:

That's what I thought you'd say I would have preferred 2000 pounds

Beck:

Yes babe I would have preferred too

Me:

Okay this is probably what is going to happen and I need you to read what I am about to say and take in every word okay? I am able next week

Beck:

I will email you with the loan approved now

Me:

To provide $2500 now that leaves me a shortfall of $750 that I need including the fee I have spent today and last night at work looking for loans and unless I take out a long term loan at 35% no one will give me one, basically I told them all to get fucked. So apart from the fact I have one avenue to go tomorrow if it doesn't happen this what you will do no questions asked because I am playing with my bills and credit rating to do this for you You will book a flight any day from next Thursday on (I would say Wednesday but sometimes my boss pays me a day later so Thursday covers that Saturday is fine if you want, you will change the pounds you have into A$ at Heathrow because you should get more for your money there than if you do it here. I will meet you the morning you arrive unless I am at work

Beck Okay babe

Me

And I will take half of the money you then have in A$ to pay my bills, this is not negotiable. That also means you still have to find about 150 pounds and I don't care if you rob a bank or turn to prostitution for the night to do it. I am not angry I am frustrated and stressed you have managed to upset my account balance and I have not even held you in my arms yet. Yes I want you here and I am sorry for saying this please do not get upset, I want you to know as I said earlier I will look after you and I need finance to do so

Beck:

it's fine babe

Me:

I do love you and I can't wait to see you

Beck:

I don't get upset I know you have try for me a lot

Me:

That is why babe it has to be the next week because I am providing my own money to do this and I might not have enough left over to pay for the parking at the airport

Beck:

Babe I know everything will be fine when I get there

Me:

I am doing this because I love you and I trust you and because I believe you can learn a lot from a relationship with me that will be beneficial to you. I am sorry babe I just realized I am interrupting your conversation to me did the bank give you the money today?

Beck:

Yes babe I have the money with me now

Me:

Thanks for understanding but this request or demand is necessary for me to stay on track. Do you remember last night when I said I can borrow from Peter to pay Paul? (an old saying), well this is how I can do it. Now remember I still have one more try tomorrow night with some friends I am meeting and that is for 750 pounds shortfall but I can't guarantee it yet. Are you able to book the ticket for Thursday or later after I speak with you tomorrow night?

Beck:

Yes babe after you speak to me tomorrow

Me:

Or do you need to do it now and we just make it that date next week, anyway we are talking about September 29th

Beck:

I will wait for your response tomorrow

Me:

Thankyou honey because if I can get all the finance together next week you can come earlier

Babe

How much you want to get from me now?

Me

Babe, if my boss pays me on Tuesday I will need to wait until Wednesday anyway because I need to use the rent money Josh gives me which is automatic every

Wednesday I can send this while you are still asleep Do you understand all of that it is very important.

Beck:

Okay babe

Me:

Thankyou I have to meet my friend tomorrow around 5 pm EST as I am working tomorrow night I will be able to chat with you then in case I do not do so earlier

Beck:

Okay babe thankyou so much

Me:

Cool that is great what I want to think about in case it is needed is where you might get the shortfall of $750 I think that means about 325 pounds. I don't know that will be the amount at the moment I am using today's exchange rate from the post office that western union are selling for, so it might change slightly up or down

Beck:

How, what do you mean by $750? You mean you will not get the money complete for me?

Me:

In any case you are going to be with me shortly and I can't wait but I don't want to be stressed out when you arrive so that's another reason I need you to do it the way I have said. Do you think you will fly on the weekend/,

Beck:

Babe, when do you really want me to fly?

Me:

If you do a Thursday flight it will put you here on Friday but it depends on what time any flight that lands at 6:30am should be fine for me to get you

Beck: Okay babe

Me:

If you want to come as soon as possible and I know we both want that so I will leave that up to you

Beck:

I don't understand what you are telling me about $750 you mean you will not get $2500 completed to me

Me:

What I am saying is for me to send you 1500 pounds it is going to cost me $2750 I am able to come up with $2500 perhaps that will mean a minimum of $250 I haven't got but it may be as much as $750. That means you will still be short on your 3000 pounds by as much as 350 pounds. I just don't have any more available cash or reserve that is if my meeting tomorrow is unsuccessful.

Beck:

Okay I got you

Me:

I have used everything I have in my own cash for you and I'm sorry but there isn't any more, that also means that the money I had put aside for expenditure for you is now also gone. We will need to get you working asap.

Beck:

Okay babe

Me:

There will be time for travel and lots of fun but I have to sort finance first that way you will be looked after as promised.

Beck:

Okay babe thankyou my love

Me:

I want to start setting up some job possibilities for you

Beck:

Don't let me take your time since you are at the work

Me:

Babe, I am not at work tonight I am at home in our bedroom typing to you. What do you want to do for work? I want to start spreading your availability now

Beck:

Okay sweetie I haven't know how that place is, but I know we will talk about it when I get home over there

Me:

Okay but you will need to be employed asap. The holiday comes after that I run a tight ship but it is not known as the Titanic.

Beck:

Yes babe I want that so we can have a lot of money

Me:

You will if you do as I ask

Beck:

Wow that's nice yes I will, you know your wish is my command

Me:

And maybe we will be a comfortably well off couple for the rest of our lives if you decide to stay with me so honey I will shop around a bit more for rates and loans and if something appeals that is not a rip off (which I doubt) I will make an online application tonight.

Beck:

Okay babe I am ready to spend the rest of my life with you

Me:

Good, so am I with you

Beck:

Babe do you mind me do some rest? Because I am so tired now and I need to find something to eat

Me:

Honey please yes do that I am going to have another G&T I love you, good night honey kisses   bye

Beck:

Okay love you kisses

Me:

Thanks for sending me the loan form it wasn't necessary but thanks and thanks to my mother in law for this as well

Me: 23/10/2010

Hi honey I'm here now how are things for you today?

Beck:

How are you doing? Have been waiting for you here for the past hours am about to go now I have to go to the market for my mum how are you doing?

Me:

I'm sorry I checked earlier and you were offline then I had to get ready and come to work where I am now

Beck:

Oh okay how is it now?

Me:

Do you want to chat later then? I am here for 8 hours

Beck:

Yes I will be back very soon I will come online when I am back

Me:

Okay I will wait for you to get back

Beck:

How is it now, do I have to change the date?

Me:

Things are okay, we have to stay with our original plan. I've spent all yesterday trying to secure a loan, but because I have casual jobs and not permanent no one will give me a loan, so I think we should stay with next week's pay okay? Much the same as what I said last night about Wednesday I can get it all together

Beck:

Okay babe that's okay

Me:

So you should be able to fly after that

Beck:

I will check you back soon okay?

Me:

Yeah sure see you later

Beck:

I will check you back soon okay byeeeee

Me:

Hi Babe I'm here

Beck:

My love how are you doing?

Me:

I have been checking regularly to see if you were on line I'm fine, how are things proceeding? It's probably too early in your day yet for much to be done I will be going to work in 3 hours though

Beck:

Oh okay babe I will go and change the flight date soon

Me:

No worries

Beck:

I just took my shower

Me:

I wish I was there to soap you up and down

Beck:

Lol don't worry I will be with you soon

Me:

I have a question or two the first is, what is your favourite colour? (I think you have told me that) and the second is I know you don't have a car do you have a drivers licence? I also know you will be with me soon

Beck:

My favourite colour is Blue and, yes I have a drivers licence

Me:

That is what I thought, blue is Mine too. Good boy I'm glad you have a licence because I don't want to do all the driving anyway, these are just little things I wanted to know.

Beck:

Okay babe

Me:

What I want to do now if it's alright with you is to go and lie down for 2 hours before work and catch you online later I am tired, I worked last night with 2 hours sleep and I worked all afternoon no sleep

Beck:

Okay babe no problem

Me:

Thanks honey love you speak with you soon ...kisses

Beck:

I love you from the bottom of my heart kisses byeeeeee

Me:

Okay I will wait for you to get back

Beck:

How is it now, do I have to change the date?

Me:

Things are okay, we have to stay with our original plan. I've spent all yesterday trying to secure a loan, but because I have casual jobs and not permanent no one will give me a loan, so I think we should stay with next week's pay okay? Much the same as what I said last night about Wednesday I can get it all together

Beck:

Okay babe that's okay

Me:

So you should be able to fly after that

Beck:

I will check you back soon okay?

Me:

Yeah sure see you later

Beck:

I will check you back soon okay byeeeee

Me:

Hi babe

Beck:

Are you there hello my love

Me:

Yes I'm here

Beck:

Okay my love

Me:

I have not been successful in securing any cash so I will have to use my own next week okay? I have already taken the other $1000 for transfer and will get that on Friday as I can still only do $1000 per day. On Tuesday then hopefully there will be another $1000 and on Wednesday next the rest $800 will be available. The only hold up will be if my job here at Hyde Park pays me a day late that does not often happen but sometimes does. So I would say the same as before, confirm your flight for Thursday or later at your Convenience, over the weekend if you wish I want you to confirm with me when you have received the funds and what flight you will be on. Are you bringing a laptop?

Beck:

I am using old model PC I will leave with my mummy.

Me:

I was hoping you would be able to email me from Singapore if you are travelling via that direction, but that doesn't matter I only have a desk top pc anyway. What you might need to do is sort out you cell phone though I asked my service provider here today about someone in your position bringing a cell phone from another country

Beck:

Okay

Me:

I was told it will be locked and not work here unless you contact your service provider in the UK prior to leaving and get them to unlock it

Beck:

Okay babe

Me:

Have you decided which day you want to fly?

Beck:

I haven't since I am waiting to hear from you I will have to change the flight tomorrow

Me:

Yes so that you can get a seat because I'm desperately going to need some money from you to pay the rent when you arrive it is the rent money I am using and Josh's rent money to me as well

Beck:

Okay my love you told me that before

Me:

Sorry I'm not stressed I have had drinks tonight with my friends they did not want to help financially and really it is up to us anyway. I have had some comments made from the local pub where I drink about the situation I mentioned some time ago so they are now all very annoying.

Beck:

I understand babe

Me:

I want us together as soon as possible now there is also the possibility of getting you a job as Concierge with the new Apartments that have just been built. That is if you have the qualifications to do that, one of the Concierges there used to work with me here, it is only across the street from here anyway. Do you want me to ask him for you? It might involve shift work.

Beck:

Babe I think I will have to arrive before you ask him so he can see who want to work I am willing to start work the following week I arrive there

Me:

Okay have you got your resumes etc.? Otherwise you can email them to me and I will print them later, that's fine too. Will you let me have the new flight details as soon as you get them I am looking at having everything transferred next Wednesday afternoon

Beck

Yes babe I will let you know everything

Me:

thanks

Beck:

I will have to change tomorrow .I have pack all my luggage I just can't wait to be with you.

Me:

Good idea I'm sorry it can't be this week I know we were

both looking forward to it but that is the only way I will have the cash and I'm pleased that we can probably plan more when you have the flight details.

Beck:

Babe it's okay really I understand you

Me:

Thanks honey

Beck:

I know you have been trying your best

Me:

I just want us to get on with our life together now and all the critics can go to hell

Beck:

Yes babe I am happy now

Me:

I will be online earlier tomorrow evening if you like otherwise I will be here at work again from 11:00pm EST (Eastern Standard Time)

Beck:

Okay I will check you online my love

Me:

Will you thank your mum for obtaining the loan it

makes life so much easier that way I love you honey take care see you soon bye

Beck:

Bye my love kisses I will check you back soon byeeeee

Me: Kisses

CHAPTER 5

THE JOURNEY

Me: 25/9/2010

So what's going on with you? Hey babe, are you really intending to come here and be with me I get the feeling there is something you're not telling me. I am going out all day and again tonight I will check online when I can. Originally you were going to be in the air by now flying to be with me. I'm a bit sad that didn't happen and maybe isn't going to for a while. I am trying to sort it all out 12000 kms away.

If you were here today we would be going to a new Polish Restaurant in the gay quarter with friends for lunch with drinks first at the Irish Pub across the street. Then tonight, with my German friends to a Thai Restaurant in the same area, then to a gay night club and watch the show. I am sharing this with you to make you feel good. Wish you were here.

Kisses....love you babe.

Beck   25/9/2010

Sweetie I am very sorry for not being online, is just that
I was sick with Flu but now I am getting better babe.
No available flight on Wednesday but I have changed
it to Thursday, hope to meet you soon

Thu 30 Sep 10   1710 London/(Heathrow Airport UK)
Thu 30 Sep 10   1930 Amsterdam (Schiphol Netherlands)

Thu 30 Sep 10   2121 Amsterdam (Schiphol Netherlands)
Fri 1 Oct 10   1430 Hong Kong (Hong Kong Int'l Hong Kong)

Fri 1 Oct 10   2100 Hong Kong (Hong Kong Int'l Hong Kong)
Sat 2 Oct 10   0755 Sydney (Kingsford Smith Int'l Airport Australia)

I love you from the bottom of my heart   Kisses

*With flight details now confirmed I had to set aside time to
make room for Beck in the house. The next morning I was
rather excited it was actually happening I told myself as I
emptied some drawers and wardrobe shelves to make space
available. How much space do I give him? "Let's start with
two shelves and drawers each. I will worry about hanging
space when I know what he has the requirements for.*

*I vacuumed the room and proceed to concentrate on the rest
of the house .I then decided to go and purchase new bedding
and remembering that he had made mention of making
love in a dark room with only a naked flame I proceed to
the local gift shop for a candle, this had to be of the sort that
would give a fragrance and burn in on itself. I wanted him*

to notice. The only thing left to do was buy flowers Blue flowers Dutch Iris and Corn flowers would suit the look and the mood but as it was still 3 days until arrival I decided to leave them until the last minute, I wanted them to be fresh.

It seemed now that all conversation between us was heightened, we had attained another level in our relationship and that something that had begun one month earlier was now a Reality, we would meet face to face and I would be at the airport to meet Beck and bring him to his new home. I was eager now to speak with him.

Beck:

Are you there? I am waiting here babe. Where are you John? I have waited for you here almost 3 hours maybe I will check you back soon

Me:

Hello babe I'm home I told you my schedule for today but unfortunately it went longer, Okay babe we have to talk urgently and it is serious. Beck I will be online to talk to you 12:30pm GMT London time that is 1 hour from now.

Me:

Honey, it is 9:30pm here I am tired so going to bed, will be up early and keep checking for you on line, otherwise I will send you message I really do need to talk to you it is important... Kisses

Beck:

Babe I'm just coming online I will check you soon   Kisses

Me:

Hi babe I am sorry I never meant to upset you and I don't doubt you just hurry up and come to me love and kisses

Beck:

How are you doing? I'm just back from church now I will check you later kisses hope to meet you soon

Beck: 26/9/2010

Love, are you there! are you there? Babe its' 12 am here now suppose to be sleeping but I waited because of you I will be going to bed soon where are you? Are you there?

Me:

Hi

Beck:

Hello

Me:

I am here I have just had my shower

Beck:

Ok I am feeling sleepy but I just have to wait for you to come its' 12am now babe

Me:

I have got your new flight info

Beck:

Ok babe how is everything with you?

Me:

Okay, we can chat later if you are tired

Beck:

Let's chat now babe

Me:

I was very tired yesterday and went to bed at 9:30

Beck:

You told me it's very urgent that's why I am here by this time

Me:

Okay if you are happy to chat now that's fine. Ok this is the situation when I hadn't heard from you for two days I thought you were scamming me. The result of that is that I have already now spent about $200 so you will be short on $1500. I also then realized how easily I can lose this money next week and have no trace of it so what I will require from you are 2 things, firstly a bank account to deposit the funds into and secondly proof from the airline you are on the passenger list. I am sorry to request this but it also proves something to you that should make you comfortable and that is that I too have some intelligence and that you can be comfortable knowing that is something good in the man you are going to be with. You see at the moment you only exist as an email address you are untraceable and I am not prepared to send money I might not get back next week.

Beck:

John, wait its' okay you just give me ache in the heart right now

Me:

You can also prove to me you are coming with a copy of your visa stamp in your passport maybe a copy of your driver's licence which has a traceable number on it I don't care which. I will leave it up to you

Beck:

So you mean you have been doubting me ?????? doubting

Me:

Not until I hadn't heard from you for 2 days and remember I did not know you had the flu. If I had been doubting you, why would I have paid for your visa and ticket?

Beck:

I have had flu and I was thinking of you and you don't even send me email and I got angry with that because if you don't hear from me you suppose email me but you don't do so

Me:

I, am not doubting you and I have been feeling good vibes all the way with us what would you do if you were in my shoes? This house is still here for you. I was afraid you might be upset with this request but I have already spent $2100 on you and I want you to be with me that is true. I don't want to upset you but it's true you do not exist other than an email address and your name I know that is correct

Beck:

Okay babe but you know I really want you in my life, because you have tried for me a lot I will let you decide what you want to do

Me:

I have got the first $1000 instalment with me now and the rest on Tuesday and Wednesday as mentioned earlier

Beck:

I really want to be with you over there if not this PTA stuff I would be with you by now, so you don't need to have any doubting mind with me babe

Me:

Okay then convince me. Also I am so looking forward to us being together I don't want to be upset if it doesn't happen

Beck:

Even my mummy she's missing me already because she knows I will be leaving for your place soon.

Me:

I am sending a text to my Ex asking for half the money he owes me I doubt I will get it but I do need it

Beck: Okay

That was the realization I came to as well. It was strange to me that you are an only child and your mum is a retired teacher and she didn't have 1500 pounds to give you? Also you are 31 and had no savings all this seemed very strange to me that is all I'm saying .on the matter. I am only asking for my peace of mind here, in any case there will not need to be any doubt between us ever when you are here I have already proven that to you.

Beck:

Babe, just try to understand mummy is retired for a long time. My love, just flush all the doubting away out of your mind.

Me:

Yes I understand that and it's none of my business to know her finances all I am saying is that it seems strange to me, what do you want to do? Remember I don't know how much I'm going to be short on $2750 on Thursday morning, .but you may need to come up with some and

I guess your mum will have to help you, it may be as much as $250 that is the amount I am asking my ex for

Beck:

Okay babe

Me:

The flight details look good and the arrival time is better than before

Beck:

You have been trying your best to get me over there don't worry my mummy will help me with that because she's very happy you are caring for me a lot oh! Okay babe

Me:

Please believe me babe I love you, I don't want to be hurt by you either you know. Do you want me to check with you later?

Beck:

My love I am ready to spend the rest of my life with you since you have promise you will never disappoint me and I will never disappoint you either, hope you get me babe

Me:

I won't disappoint you I mean what I say!

Beck:

So put your mind at rest I will arrive by next week my love and we will be living as couples.

Then send me the details for the bank account it will also be cheaper than Western Union, and send me the passenger list these items are also good to show immigration in Australia how long we have been together.

Beck;

I will not have any problem with immigration in Australia,

Me:

I know that, what I am talking about is, that if you want residency, there are documents they require to prove how long we have been together, these emails are a good start.

Beck:

Love, bank account is not good idea and it will also take some weeks before the money will reflect to my account. Western Union is the best way to send the money.

Me:

If I do Western Union I still need something from you re passenger list or licence etc.

Beck:

Babe why??????? Yes I said it

Me:

This is my money we are talking about

Beck:

I know you are still doubting me meaning you don't trust me, If I don't trust you I would never planning of coming over there, even if I told my mummy about this she would never be happy with it

Me:

What is the problem with you not wanting to help me out here?

Beck:

Love is trust, if you don't trust me, how come you love me? I guess you have been telling your friends about me

Me:

I thought that as a couple we help each other, we are still trying to know each other at the moment, I am only being fair, I have told some of my friends about US and they think it is great what we are trying to do. Why don't you show this conversation to your mother and get her opinion on what I am saying or she can call me here at the house even if that will make you feel more comfortable.

Beck:

Babe I have to go to bed now I will chat with you tomorrow

Me:

I guess you want to think about this so I will go and have breakfast now love you, kisses, bye

Beck:

Love you too   Kisses   Byeeeeee

Me: 27/9/2010

Hi babe, you gave me an internet virus, it is actually a head cold due to change of season. I am allergic to pollen it affects my sinuses badly so I am here at work with a very red nose, no one yet has called me Rudolph. I have a problem with my internet connection at home and cannot access the internet. I have spent this morning on the phone with the help desk and they were unable as usual to find the problem. I have had a call from their technical support department giving me all sorts of codes and reset my passwords to correct the problem. I need to be online and call them from home and they are only open until 10pm and I finish here at 11pm. Tomorrow I am driving from 9am until 4pm and won't be able to sort it out until after that time , if it does not reset tonight when I get home. I have no access to a computer tomorrow as we only have one in the house and I do not work here tomorrow to access the PC, so if you do not hear from me this will be Why, however I can read your emails on my phone. I don't know about replying, it does have the facility attached but I do not have a keyboard with my phone, I am letting you know this as to why you might not hear from me.

However now on to more important matters, I am going to try and send you the complete 1500 pounds but as I have told you I have spent some money. As of tomorrow morning I will have A$2210 available, I believe I need $2740 including fees to complete the transaction and that was based on last Thursday's exchange rate so there will be a variance. I am telling you this because you might need to find up to 200 pounds by Thursday it will depend on what I can send in pounds with the dollar amount, .I have on me on Wednesday afternoon when I go to the post office .and of course I still need you here on Saturday to recycle the cash. I am telling you this because obviously it is now too late to do anything else. Anyway honey I am here until 11pm EST tonight, and I can chat with you later today lots of love. Kisses

Beck:

My love

Me:

Hi babe

Beck:

I have been waiting for you for the past 1 hour how are you doing? how is the flu now?

Me:

I'm sorry for the long message I just wanted to let you know what was going on

Beck:

Yes babe its' okay don't worry about that

Me:

I have been on the checking if you were there but I have been busy and had to leave my post

Beck:

Oh okay babe

Me:

It's still busy here

Beck:

How is the flu now? Hope you are getting better ok babe don't let's disturb you if you are busy my love

Me:

Much better

Beck:

Okay babe

Me:

Sorry I have had to talk to a resident, back now are you okay with my message?

Beck:

Yes I am okay with your message babe

Me:

I will withdraw some more cash tonight

Beck:

Everything will be fine

Me:

My pay from here will be in tomorrow with the other pay but I have to take that out over 2 days it looks like Wednesday afternoon at this stage.

Beck:

Oh okay babe its' fine pls take good care of the flu my love because it will not make you feel comfortable

Me:

I'm sorry about the short amount if it happens

Beck:

Its' fine babe I understand you

Me:

Thanks

Beck:

You have been trying a lot my love. Don't worry everything will be fine. Are you still busy at work? If so don't let me disturb you babe

Me:

I know honey I had had a couple of fellow Concierges want to help and give me money but they are paid less than me and don't have any, no I'm okay now just heating dinner

Beck:

Okay babe you will be driving tomorrow?

Me:

Yes tomorrow and Wed all day 9am til 4pm, so I will do the transfer after 4pm. If I don't get my PC fixed I can email you the details from here on Wednesday late shift

Beck:

Okay babe I got you now

Me:

will you let me know when you have it I can read it here then

Beck:

Yes babe I will let you know as soon as I have it I will email you

Me:

What time on Thursday are you leaving the house? When is the last time I can contact you?

Beck:

I will be leaving the house in the afternoon so we can still chat in the morning

Me:

You have a 5 hour stopover in Hong Kong you may be able to send me a message there

Beck:

Yes babe I will

Me:

Okay I will be driving Thursday afternoon and sleeping in the morning I won't be home on Thursday until 4:30pm so I might miss you but that's one of those things that may be unavoidable

Beck:

Okay babe I will email you if you are not online

Me:

Thanks, I will be at the airport one hour after the plane lands. I will check landing website first, it will take you about one hour to clear customs and immigration

Beck:

Babe, brb back 5 mins going to toilet, okay babe that will be nice

Me:

At this stage I'm not sure what the weather is going to be for Sat. but it is the long weekend in Sydney with the Gay Sleaze Ball and the football grand finals in two states including NSW so there will be a lot of people around the airport

Beck:

When is that babe?

Me:

That is the day you arrive with the exception of the NSW grand final which is on Sunday but that is also the Sleaze Ball recovery party as the Monday is a public holiday

Beck:

Oh okay

Me:

However, I still have to work my normal shift but paid double time

Beck:

Okay babe, my mummy is missing me already

Me:

Do you have any spare money for duty Free shopping?

Beck:

I gave testimony in church yesterday shopping? Yes babe I will sort that with me

Me:

I think when you arrive allowing for the time difference you have to ring your mum from the house, tell her you are okay.

Beck:

Okay babe I will

Me:

If you want that is anyway I guess you want to get on with your day now

Beck:

Okay

Me:

I am still busy

Beck:

Okay babe I will chat with you later, that's if I catch you online. Hope to see you at the airport soon

Me:

Me too If they fix my PC when I get home I will send you a message to let you know

Beck:

Okay my love... kisses I love you from the bottom of my heart

Me:

Take care honey

Beck:

Kisses Byeeeee

Me:

I am so looking forward to kissing you in person bye kisses

Beck:

Wow I can't wait for the day to come yes I want the first kiss at the airport Bye babe

Me

Sorry I missed you babe I am here now. Babe, its' midnight and I have caught the flu from you so I am going to bed goodnight Kisses

Me: 28/9/2010

Hi babe I am sending this from my phone can you send me the flight number and Airline please, so I can check with arrivals on Saturday.

Apparently I need a new modem. This will take several days to fix as the service provider is an idiot. I will send a

message tomorrow from somewhere and chat tomorrow
night at work Kisses

Beck: 29/9/2010

How are you my love I have been busy since morning
since I have 2 days left I got my police clearance in case
I will need it for there, am so tired now I will email you
tomorrow Kisses my love

Me:

Hi babe I don't know about a police clearance requirement
here. I should have my PC fixed by Saturday. I think
I can only send 1300 pounds will chat at work tonight
kisses

Beck:

Sweetie have been waiting for the information I have to
go to the bank very early today hope to hear from you
soon. I have talk to my mummy and she agree to help
me with the remaining 200 pounds, my love get back
to me with the information I will be waiting for you I
will check you online soon.

Me:

Hi babe, number is 9062906613 1300 pounds I will chat
later this has been sent via cell phone   kisses

Beck: 30/9/2010

Sweetie I got the number I have to rush down to the
bank before the closing hour and I will have to go to

the store to change the money to dollars because I will receive here in pounds so I will get back to you as soon as I come back kisses love you so much

Me:

Hi honey that's cool I will chat later kisses

Me:

Hi babe I might miss you on line so I will send this now. The weather here on Saturday is between 11 & 21 degrees with showers so you might need a light jacket. Also can you let me have the flight number from Hong Kong to Sydney? The government has installed new software at all airports and the program is faulty causing some flights to be processed manually taking several hours, so I want to ring and check if this is the case. I don't want to have to wait and pay all the extra parking rates. I can retrieve the info from my phone. Hopefully I will hear from you before tomorrow afternoon Kisses.

CHAPTER 6

THE ROBBERY

Beck: 30/9/2010

Hi babe are you there I am just coming back from the hospital. I was rob on the way to the store to change the money to dollars....pls we have chat asap. I have call the KLM

Airline for the cancellation of my ticket, but I haven't pick any date yet, my mummy was so frustrated right now babe I will be waiting for you online

It is very hard to explain how I felt after reading this message, there were several thoughts had come to mind, but mainly an overwhelming feeling of despair had engulfed me, not only was our meeting delayed and that all expectant first kiss for both of us not going to happen soon but I had the feeling of being robbed too as this was my money.

Naturally this meant a delay as the PTA fee now had to be replaced and I was quite sure Becks' mummy would not have

available funds. My immediate concern lay with Beck we needed to chat asap. I had received this message at 5:30am while still on shift I would not hear from Beck until 2:00am the following morning.

Beck: 1/10/2010

Thank god you are here babe

Me:

Yes I'm here I have been waiting and then the screen dropped out just now as it does on this PC.

Beck:

John you got my email? I am just coming from the hospital/ the doctor asked me to stay till tomorrow, but I told her no I have to inform you of this

Me:

There is not much I can do

Beck:

I am just going crazy now my love I am dying now

Me:

I guess you will have to wait to come and see me now

Beck:

John, I was beaten like hell, I am having bad headache now

Me:

So am I

Beck:

They are 4 peoples I was rushed to the hospital by emergency my mummy is so frustrated right now

Me:

I am concerned for you of course but I now have problems of my own .with you not coming

Beck:

Yes babe I understand you because you will need the money when I arrive you want to use it for house rent. I hate myself right now babe

Me:

The best thing you can do is cancel the airfare and return it to me

Beck:

Good idea because I don't want you to face any problem I will do that babe I am so fucking bad right now having a bad headache but I just have to be here and chat with you

Me:

I am sorry this happened to you, where are you hurt?

Beck:

In my hand and head

Me:

Is there any likely hood of the police catching them?

Beck:

"They was escape babe, police late before they come"

Me:

Well I guess that's the end of us then

Beck:

How do you mean?

Me:

I would be grateful if you could get the airfare back to me ASAP

Beck:

What do you mean by "that's the end of us'?

Me:

Well, you can't come and see me now I do not have any more cash and I'm not going to go through it all again, so that's what I mean

Beck:

Babe, you don't have to make me sad again

Me:

Nothing else I can say Beck

Beck:

I will kill myself if I will never meet with you in this life

Me:

Well, there is nothing I can do now

Beck:

I understand you have try a lot

Me:

Yes indeed

Beck:

Babe, I don't expect you to do anything again

Me:

I can't

Beck:

I will find every way to get the money and come over there my love

Me:

Good luck with that idea

Beck:

Remember I have promise to never disappoint you in life

Me:

I will apply for a small loan with some friends to pay

my rent then I will sit in my shell and never contact anybody else. I guess it was a bad idea in the first place

Beck:

You have done a lot to bring me over there and I don't want your friend to see you as a stupid person, babe I will make you proud.

Me:

Too late, I don't think there is any need to promise something you can't keep

Beck:

Babe I can, don't say that

Me:

How?

Beck:

You know both of us are not good mood now, pls babe, don't make me crazy

Me:

What makes you think I believe you anyway?

Beck:

You have been making me happy since all this days

Me:

It is actually 1 month today

Beck:

I trust you for real and I know you trust me because you love me with all of your heart

Me:

Well! I'm still trying to. So now you are stuck with a visa you can't use, and no job and no way of being able to do anything about it

Beck:

Babe, you know I have all my hope in your place because I know I will get a job when I get there so I have no option than to come there

Me:

I think I will just accept my life as it was

Beck:

I can see you really want the best for me and I want for myself as well babe please don't say that am on shame now "because I have did thanksgiving in church on Sunday"

Me:

It just seems very unusual that's all

Beck:

"Everybody in my church has known that I am coming to you this week"

Me:

Then why don't you ask them all to find the money for you?

Beck:

So what I want to say again babe I am not feeling comfortable right now

Me:

I'm sure you're not I don't know what else to say Beck I can't do anymore

Beck:

I don't know if that can work. Babe I'm just concerned about you now for the house rent. I don't ask you to do anymore. I said I will make everything work myself

Me:
Thanks

Beck:
I will see you I will get the money

Me:
I would like that

Beck:
I know how you feel now babe

Me:

very sad actually

Beck:

Just give me 2 weeks everything will be alright my love I will do everything myself babe

Me:

That would be nice I will have a loan by then to right my finances but if you can do it yourself that would be good. If I were you I would see if anybody in the church can pool in for the 3000 pounds

Beck:

Thank you my love

Me:

Good luck I guess you will let me know one day when you are ready to come

Beck:

Babe, just give me 2 weeks. I can't wait to be with you

Me:

I don't need to chat with everyday about it from now I will wait for you to tell me

Beck:

Babe I want to start a new life with you my love just give me two weeks

Me:

I have to sort myself out now as you can well imagine and you probably want to go to I will see you around one day, bye

Beck:

My love pls always know in your mind that someone is here and care for you babe.

Me:

That's nice. I do hope you are not to hurt

Beck:

Babe I told you just 2 weeks, don't make me feel uncomfortable, you know I am not feeling comfortable already, why are you doing this to me?

Me:

I thought you were doing this to me! I will wait for you to tell me when you are coming I will let you contact me, when there is something to say

Beck:

Babe, when your PC will be ready? I think you at home now

Me:

I hope tomorrow, or maybe later today, when I had finished driving, and after a heated discussion with

████ (my Service Provider) last night they advised a new modem should be delivered today or tomorrow

Beck:

Okay babe. How I wish you were here, you would know how I am feeling

Me:

I think I can say the same thing

Beck:

I know how you feel already, both of us not feeling happy, but I will make things work my love

Me:

I am sorry, but I am feeling this way, I need to go and rob a bank now. I do hope you can sort this mess out in 2 weeks

Beck:

Babe, you don't need to feel that way my love, yes babe I promise to do that

Me:

I don't want to feel this way but it's a natural feeling, I would call it human nature

Beck:

I understand my love even my mummy is so frustrated right now she has been calling me to go to bed now.

Me:

How did they know you had all that cash on you anyway/

Beck:

I don't really know my love. I think they have been watching me when I was in the bank.

Me:

Maybe under the circumstances the PTA fee can be waived if you tell them you are to stay with me. If there is a record of the theft, tell them you had a job to start here see how that works out

Beck:

Good idea my love. The police already know about this I think I will have police report to the immigration.

Me:

Then get the fare sorted out and see if they will let you come without the PTA, they can call me to confirm this anytime, that's a good idea show the police report to immigration I don't think you should fly today though, but you don't have much time to change the fare.

Beck:

I have called the airline when I was at the hospital to cancel my ticket. I told them to put a hold on it

Me:

That's good will they do that?

Beck:

Yes they will

Me:

Anyway, you can sort it out. Well, there are your two options 1) get the parishioners to chip in together, or 2) see if you can leave without the PTA with me as your sponsor. I will let you go now.

Beck:

Okay babe

Me:

Bye

Beck:

I will do my best to make things work out. I can't wait to be with you there and start a new life

Me:

I would like that I was so hoping for that for us but I'm a bit shattered now, nothing we can do I hope they apprehend the robbers and find the cash (or what's left of it)

Beck:

Babe, just give me the 2 weeks the police have been investigating

Me:

That makes me feel better, besides you will have proof you had the money, you would have got a receipt from Western Union., and that might help with the authorities about waiving the PTA.

Beck:

Yes babe I think so I will work on everything and I will let you know how is going on. I love you from the bottom of my heart.

Me:

All you can do is to try I would like you to be able to send me a message soon and say I am coming. We don't know yet but I hope to hear that from you soon.

Beck:

Okay babe I will my love I know you will not be happy now, but I want to make you happy you will get good news from me soon.

Me:

I hope you are right with that babe, I soooo much want that good news. I will keep myself busy for 2 weeks doing other things, to make me not remember this morning

Beck:

I hope I will be chatting with you my love I hate missing you I don't want to miss you at all

Me:

So that is why it took you so long to get back to me last night, I thought that was strange .

Beck:

Yes babe

Me:

I want to hear your voice. I want to kiss your lips, I want to hold you so I will go home and wank myself to sleep. Good night babe

Beck:

I want to suck your cock as well my love, I want to make love to you babe, I know that will happen soon

Me:

Well I can practice my knot tying for when you arrive, that will at least give me something to do. Then I might just have to punish you for losing the cash you might even like it.

Beck:

Yes babe (lol) hum...

Me:

I will chat with you when you have some news for me

Beck:

Okay babe, I think you should get your PC early tomorrow

Me:

Hopefully I will check tonight if the modem has arrived, I should be online then. I think you should go to bed.

Beck:

Bye for now kisses

Me:

I love you and I want us to start a new life together, and really soon, I have plans for us.

Me:

Good morning babe, are you there? My PC will not be fixed before next Tuesday. How are your injuries, I think your hand will take a long time to heal Josh told me he has had his broken too. Hopefully we will meet soon love you   kisses

Beck:

My love, are you there?

Me:

I am fine I am surprised to hear from you, are you recovered or are you still bruised?

Beck:

I am not yet recovered I just come here to check you I even need to rest.

Me:

What damage have you got or should I say sustained? Yesterday we were both quite upset

Beck:

My shoulder and my head with bad headache

Me:

Do you have any broken bones?

Beck:

Yes I have in my hand babe

Me:

I am really sorry I have spent all day wondering if you had really set me up and I realized yesterday I didn't ask you how much damage you sustained. I suppose now how did you let that happen to you?

Beck:

Babe you would have know I can't lie to you because coming to your place is the greatest thing in my life

Me:

I guess your typing will be slower too now with broken bones

Beck:

I want to start a new life with you and have better life

Me:

That's what I was telling myself

Beck:

I have put all my hope to your place my love

Me:

That is what I thought you wanted, then, I was telling myself that is what I want to believe

Beck:

You taught me how to love, I have fall in love for you 100% in this life

Me:

You know that now you would be on the plane to me

Beck:

I may commit suicide if I will not meet you in life, yes babe this is a very bad experience in my life

Me:

Do you think you can organise yourself in 2 weeks?

Beck:

Babe I will get better by next week and I will find a way how to get the money because I cannot ask you to send me anymore again you have try a lot for me so I need to try myself

Me:

I guess it is a very bad experience in anyone's life, and what makes it worse is the situation and circumstances on which it has occurred. You see they have stolen from me Have you had any news from the police? Maybe the money had marked serial numbers this might be a regular gang under surveillance

Beck:

I haven't hear any news from the police

Me:

what about the loan your mother took out is this insured to be replaced? So many times with a loan that can be a prerequisite!

Beck:

She has to pay back the loan

Me:

You know I can't help you financially now it will take me several pay periods to recover myself.

Beck:

Yes babe I understand your side

Me:

That's bad I hope they find them but then all will be spent I know London is the most surveilled city in the world maybe they will find something on camera

Beck:

You have try a lot for me

Me:

I really did babe

Beck:

Yes I know babe

Me:

But I have no cash now and I had to request an extension of time to pay my Visa, otherwise I get fined. There are not many friends know exactly how much I have spent and there are a few I have to tell, there won't be drinks on Sunday to meet you. The only one that knows you are not coming is Josh

Beck:

Okay babe

Me:

I am still offline at home I have received my new modem but the service provider cannot get it to work and will send a technician so this will probably be Monday.

Beck:

Okay babe

Me:

I am not here at work now until Monday so I can read and reply by cell phone only. I won't tell anyone you will be coming in 2 weeks I will just say at a later time

Beck:

Okay babe

Me:

Do you have to wait 6 weeks for the bones to knit and the plaster to be removed?

If you can fly with the weight on your arm they will charge you as extra baggage (lol)

Beck:

Okay hahaha

Me:

I know you are not sounding very happy and I probably not helped matters with telling you my thoughts, but I have been hurt by this too honey and I feel frustrated.

Beck:

Yes I understand you my love that's why I cannot ask you any money

Me:

I think I will keep myself busy all weekend I am not going to spend much as I don't have much to spend but I will go to the beach, the nude harbour beach and get a tan. I will have some drinks in a cheap bar and maybe shout myself a Thai meal

Beck:

Okay babe

Me:

Then it will be Monday and back to work with at least one payday next Tuesday

Beck:

I will be nursing myself then

Me:

Things will get back to normal

Beck:

Okay babe when you will come online again?

Me:

I think you need to do two things, the first is to heal fast and the second is to focus on your original dream with more determination than before to make sure you come here as you wish. By the way today is our 1 month anniversary from the day we first spoke, so happy anniversary

Beck:

Okay yes babe wow

Me:

Just imagine I have bought you some Iris's (the Dutch blue ones)

Beck:

Wow babe I can't just wait to be with you

Me:

Get yourself better have faith in yourself, focus on the need which is to be together and somehow things will happen. Talk to me over the weekend I can reply by cell phone or maybe my PC will be fixed by then. Let's tell each other how each day has been for us (over the next few days,) this should help you in your sadness and stem the distance between us, do not feel suicidal. Remember you have someone else in your life to think of now I'm still here babe. Would it help you if I actually called your house that is if you have a fixed phone .I would like to hear your voice I don't know what I would say but it would be nice to hear your voice maybe we can chat a bit later honey, bye for now I will come back in a couple of hours

Beck:

Babe, do you mind if I go now I need to rest.

Me:

That's okay bye we can chat later

Beck:

Thankyou my love okay I will check you online later

Me:

Be strong Beck

Beck:

I love you so much kisses   Byeeee

Me:

Hi babe, how is your hand and head today? I still don't have my PC fixed

Beck: 2/10/2010

My love how are you doing? Have miss you so much my hand is still paining. I just have to check you here I will chat with you soon   kisses

Me:

Hi babe sorry to hear you are still in pain it is cloudy here today the time is when we should have now had our first kiss. Josh is cleaning the house and I am planting spring flowers. My PC still no internet until Tuesday and from tomorrow our time difference is 11 hours apart, hope to hear from you soon kisses.

Me:

Hi babe, my PC is now fixed it was the service providers problem as I said all along. I will be on line 9:00pm London time for a live chat (that is if you read this in time)

Beck: 3/10/2010

How are you my love, sorry I was not here then I went to the hospital for treatment. I know you will be sleeping by now ...hope to chat with you tomorrow I miss you so much my love Kisses

Me:

I miss you too honey recover quickly and we will chat soon, love you kisses

Me:

Hi babe, here is something to cheer you up. It is real London weather here today, lots of rain so I thought I would send you this to cheer you because I have been playing it as well to forget the rain today.

(I have sent to Beck photos of me and an MP3 file "live it up" Mental as Anything)

Beck:

My love, are you there? It's 8:30am here I miss you my love

Me:

Hi babe I'm here I am getting ready to go out and catch the next bus to Oxford Street. It will be a busy night after last night's Sleaze Ball Party. There is plenty of arse out there tonight, that wants to be satisfied and I can help out.

Beck:

Hum

Me:

Honey I am going to get in the shower now, back in 10 mins......Hi babe

I am missing you and needed to talk to you. I love you .... kisses.

Beck:

Okay babe, have miss you so much

Me:

What did the hospital say about your hand? Gosh I wish you were here too

Beck:

I was told it will get better soon...., yes babe

Me:

Will you be able to push weights with it again?

Beck:

Nop babe I can't for now

Me:

Will it repair enough to do so in the future?

Beck:

Yes babe I think so

Me:

There are so many bones in a hand and it can take so long to repair if there is one broken one missed.

Beck:

Yes the doctor said so babe. How is Josh?

Me:

That's good honey I have to have a shower and catch the bus. I will be online about midnight here. I will see if you are online then. I love you.....kisses

Beck:

Okay my love, make sure you take good care of yourself. I love you....kisses.....byeeee

Me:

The time is now 6:45 pm I will chat at midnight Kisses

Me: 4/10/2010

Hi babe

It is Monday afternoon 4:15pm I am at work even though it is a public holiday. I will be home at 11:30pm and available to chat. I am sorry I was not on line as previously stated I went to my club in Oxford Street and caught up with friends, my best friend abused me when he found out I paid your visa I cannot tell him about the rest he will never speak to me again if he knew. After most of them went home I stayed around until 4;00am. I met a really nice guy and we danced and got very sexy on the dance floor, so I took him home for the night and dropped him at the station on my way here to work His name is Greg.

He is 35 and he has an 8 and a half inch thick cock. I was practising for you my love he fucked me twice with it once doggy style so I am a bit sore. I will meet him again next weekend, as I said before I will not sleep around in a relationship this is only until you arrive.

How are your injuries progressing with healing are you seeing results yet? It has been raining all weekend but this cleared up today, even with the wet weather there are lots of cute men in Sydney for the Sleaze Ball and they aren't wearing much clothing either (lots to look at) will chat tonight love you kisses

Beck:

My love, are you there? It's 11:30pm here now I have to go to bed I will chat with you tomorrow, love you kisses.

Beck: 5/10/2010

My love, I am waiting for you

Me:

Hi babe I am here, time here is 7:10pm you must have got up early and just be about to do breakfast. I am about to cook dinner and have just come back from the local, sweetheart, I will be up and down to cook dinner and reply to you don't go away.

Beck:

I am here babe okay babe

Me:

Hi so am I

Beck:

How are you doing?

Me:

I might have to go downstairs and turn the rissoles in a minute but I will be back, they're black on the bottom already anyway, .how are you honey? I am fine but you are the one with the injuries not me

Beck:

Am doing good babe okay no problem go and turn your rissoles Okay babe I will be back in 1 hour kisses

Me:

Hello I'm back, or should I say I'm Beck

Beck:

Okay I am here babe

Me:

It has been a busy night, I am supposed to be socialising on Friday and Saturday with different people and I as do you have a cash flow problem for a week. Anyway what are you having for breakfast?

Beck:

Just coffee babe

Me:

I've run out of coffee so I think I'll stay on alcohol tonight. So what are you wearing?

Beck:

I wear a top and jeans

Me:

I guess it's too early for a cup of tea yet, I can make a plunger up but that would be a waste and anyway Josh is drinking wine and he is about to pour me a big Drag Queen size glass. What colour is your top?

Beck:

Blue wow, how I wish I was there with you guys

Me:

I have the feeling you look really sexy at the moment
so fucking hot

Beck:

Lol, thank you my love

Me:

You know, with my day job driving in this city in this
climate (which will continue until next April now) I am
always so grateful to have been born here

Beck:

I am happy for you my love

Me:

Today, as normal I have to drive to supermarket chains
and beaches, there are 100 of each almost and the guys
are not wearing much at all usually a singlet & cargos.
It's a shame you are not here now this city is going off
as it always does at this time until the end of January.

Beck:

Every time I do think of your place

Me:

It is still here for you, you know that

Beck:

yes babe

Me:

What is the situation with your hand today?

Beck:

Babe I am still feeling pain but better than before thank you my love

Me:

I care honey

Beck:

Yes I know that because you have showed me a lot that you care that's why I always proud of you

Me:

Me too of you my love, one day we will tell each other face to face that is the same for me

Beck:

Yes babe I just can't wait for the day to come

Me:

That I will leave up to you I do have spring and summer ahead of me and I will be fine, I wish you could be part of it now. Every year it is like that in Sydney

Beck:

Yes babe I wish

Me:

I think you are more positive with yourself at the moment. I am glad for that there is a song by Miquel Brown (1981) you may not know it but the lines do go "So Many Men So Little Time". I am trying to make you sorry for yourself that your aren't here

Beck:

I haven't heard of the song babe

Me:

I personally would rely on charity for your airfare, and cry poor

Beck:

I feel sorry for myself babe because I always think of your place every minute

Me:

Well I do feel sorry for you too. I will need you to decide what you are going to do soon and then talk about the finance situation. In the mean time I will spend another couple of hundred. The ball is in your court Beck and only you can make the decision

Beck:

Okay babe I will let you know if I have any plan, have been thinking a lot here how I can get myself over there

Me:

I won't wait all summer by the way. I have just had my father admitted to hospital again, he has had 2 heart attacks in the past 11 years and all the money I have now is for his funeral. I need to have a cash reserve for this purpose. My father is a wonderful man and has come from the old school when the eldest son has the responsibility and takes control, that is me babe and I won't let him down he is nearly 82 and the second last of 5 brothers and the only one that has reached this age, they all died younger, he has one younger brother now in a wheelchair.

Beck:

Okay babe

Me:

We respect him and admire him

Beck:

I am happy for him he is a great man.

Me:

I think your mother would be happy if you settled and made a life here then we could pay for her to come and visit, remember what I said "If you keep losing don't play with the same set of cards everything is now up to you, BTW I do still love you.

Beck:

I understand you babe I know you want the best for me and I will make you proud babe

Me:

I hope so I want you to be with me and I do not make idle promises, even on the net, but you already know that if you are willing to be with me. I will never hurt you that is from my soul Beck .I guess I just need you to be happy and think about what you are going to do.

Beck:

Okay babe, thank you very much

Me:

At the moment I am living 2 lives with one being 25000kms and 11 hours without a chat window.

Beck:

God will bless you I am very happy to hear that from you

Me:

It is not me he needs to bless it is you. I have my spiritual goodness and it looks after me. I know you go to church on Sundays and that is good I just have it in a different way

Beck:

Okay babe

Me:

I think with what has happened to you, if that is the case then he needs to shine on you and help you out but you see, to me he doesn't help you out I do hope it works for you

Beck:

Okay babe

Me:

Christianity was good to give the masses some education and to control them in the early years, but I have a problem with a religious sect that tortured more people than the Nazi's and if you mention it to them no one wants to know. I am not criticizing you for your beliefs. I am just expressing my view and experience.

Beck:

Okay babe

Me:

There is hatred and bigotry in that group. Sorry I have said my piece now, I feel better. I apologise, to you if that was strong but I am a fire sign and things need to be said sometimes. Are you okay? I have not given you much chance to chat sorry

Beck:

Yes I am okay babe

Me:

Good I did not mean to be rude to you, sometimes I have a bee in my bonnet so to speak and I have to say what is on my mind, but then if you don't speak out you can lose the battle.

Beck:

Yes I understand you. Babe who is that your friend you told about me?

Me:

My friend Rupert is my best friend and I need you to meet him if you come, he is my mentor. He is a teacher and he went to school with my partner for many years. When Lynton died, Rupert was there for me and we are great friends I would never go against his wishes

Beck:

Oh okay but I am not happy with it

Me:

Why?

Beck:

Why! He was blaming you for paying my Visa

Me:

Rupert is a very logical guy, I love him dearly but he lives alone and does not have a boyfriend, and he sees you as someone who is going to rip me off so to speak that is why I want you to meet him. He is only thinking of me and, this is his way of being proactive but from me he demands that I am not a fool, now you know why I cannot tell him the whole story. I will not lose him as a friend but I will no longer get the same respect from him that I do

Beck:

Okay babe I understand him but I know I will prove him wrong if he sees me arrive at your home.

Me:

He keeps asking me when you are coming and when I keep saying you are delayed with problems he believes you are bullshitting to me. I want to prove him wrong. Rupert sometimes says to me this is only in John's world but in saying that he likes to be part of it, and he only came out when he read the eulogy at my partners' funeral. They were the same age so I much want you to prove him wrong Beck, for both of us

Beck:

Yes babe I will soon

Me:

Rupert is hard, he owns his own apartment outright he travels overseas every year, he is extremely intelligent and a very practical man something I aspire to, and for you to prove to him that my judgement and trust was correct, and that love can bloom on the internet through trust. Rupert is a school teacher so he has to be careful of what he does with his life or he can lose his job.

Beck:

I have been asking my friend to borrow money from her daddy and she's willing to do that but she hasn't told her daddy yet. I told her I would send the money back to here by Western Union immediately I arrive to Sydney.

Me:

You do know that if you do arrive we can sit down you and I and work out a payment plan, it is still possible to pay money back to London from Sydney, we get you a good job and we work it all out. I am prepared to help you do that, if we are to be a couple that is normal. I think maximum 3 months for money to start going back we will live off my wages until you get a job. then we have to sort your mum out

Beck:

Okay babe yes babe

Me:

That is quite viable Do you want to chat in 1 hour you seem busy too

Me: 6/10/2010

Hi I just got to work I have a few things to do and can come back

Beck:

How are you my love, okay I will be waiting!

Me:

This is concierge change over time so I will be about 40 Minutes; I will be back as soon as I can   kisses

Beck:

Okay babe

Me:

Okay babe I am back now. I am here for the next 8 hours and I am not feeling well I have the runs and I am throwing up but I will sit in the bosses' office, and hopefully be able to not do much. I still have to drive at 12:00 tomorrow but I will eventually go home and sleep until 11:00 am and not even the dogs will get walked, hopefully this is only a 24 hour virus. But as you know I need the money to pay the back rent so here

Beck:

Yes babe I know that

Me:

Sorry I didn't mean anything by brining that up. What are you doing today?

Beck:

I feel weak I will have to check with the doctor in the evening time

Me:

That's okay then it might mean I have to chat to you at the same time tomorrow then

Beck:

Yes babe

Me:

I feel horny !!

Beck:

Yes babe

Me:

I guess if you can't do much you will feel tired anyway we will wait until after this weekend maybe you will have some good news. I have the house to myself this weekend, Josh is going away and he takes his dog as well

Beck:

Okay babe

Me:

I guess you aren't feeling in a chatty mood tonight, do you want to chat tomorrow instead?

Beck:

Yes babe. Where is Josh going?

Me

John goes to his family, one weekend each month. He does their cleaning and cooking and visits more than one home in opposite ends of the city so he has some travelling.

Beck: Okay babe

Me

Cheers   kisses

Beck

Kisses my love byeeeee

CHAPTER 7

THE ACCUSATION

In this chapter the first two pages are letters I wrote to Beck after my disagreement with sending any further cash to him most of the statements in these letters are lies and I am not expecting to meet Beck now but I am wanting whatever I can for the money.

Me   8/10/2010

Hi babe

What I wanted from the start was a ring on your finger if you remember.

I also have excitement reading your emails and wondering what you are going to say, and yes I have also made love here thinking about you, but I am hurt. I have given you everything I have to come here and something went wrong. I ask myself how many people do I know in the world who have ever been robbed, other than $50 here and there and you are the only one that comes to mind not only that, but it was my money to be RECYCLED. I think you have forgotten that even if this was not your fault. Yes I want you here but I have nothing more to give other than my love life and protection forever as promised. I do not tell lies I never have done (other than as a child to avoid a spanking). Why don't you take the other option and believe me this has been checked out today and it is available to you now. You take the 1500 pounds from Katie's father (maybe even less required) and buy a return ticket to Sydney with a 3 month tourist visa granted to everyone in the UK by the Australian Government, and you do not need 3000 pounds with this visa. At the end of 3 months you can maybe even go home with the 3000 pounds but remember it will need to be paid back to me as I will be supporting you all this time. That should still put you on a flight to me this week. I suggest you show this to Kate and Sarah and get here asap and for your information don't think I am not hurting because I am. I would like to try and start a relationship with you for the rest of my life as promised, I hope you mean to as well. Enjoy the rest of your day I am going out to meet Greg tonight so as far as hot young men with big dicks are concerned there is no problem but just remember Beck I chose you, that choice is now yours to make it work for us, wanting to love you

Kisses

Beck   8/10/2010

Honey I have been sad and depress all day since I read

the mail you wrote to me, you know I got my account deleted in that site because I don't want anybody to write to me again since I have found you in my life. Is you I want not your money. I know you have tried a lot for me that's why I can't ask you anymore again but is Kate told me to ask you since we don't have any alternative again, I don't mean to hurt you in any way hope you understand my love . I have the strong feeling that you are my dream man I have been searching for, I feel you are the one I want to live forever with.

You are a real gem a precious stone of brilliant beauty. We have kissed and hugged and made love so many times in my mind. I want and need that so much. I believe your mind is one of the most miraculous wonders of this life and very powerful you have won my heart, it is us torturing to me as it is to you for us to be in each other's arms kissing, loving each other making love together. I desire to be loved by you so much. I think we're beyond attraction. As for me, I have a burning desire to be together with you.

When I see your letters in my email, my heart is pounding with excitement. Just like a child at Christmas, eagerly waiting, to see what Santa has brought him. You give me hope of a reason to smile, the desire to carry on. I can't explain it better than that. It is crazy but it comes from my heart and I love it.

kisses

Me: 8/10/2010

Hi babe I am here now. How is your hand today?

Beck:

Am good my love, have been waiting for you since your letter

Me:

Sorry, I am only available now I had a few things to do like filling the spa and clearing the compactor. I am free to chat now I am feeling much better today I think I had food poisoning judging by the symptoms. By about 6:00 am this morning I was feeling much better now I am great.

Beck:

You have to be careful my love

Me:

Last night, when I came to work I was very sick, vomiting and had the runs so I worked (slept lol) all night here now all is fine, and you? Are you still feeling tired?

Beck:

Yes babe, but is getting better now

Me:

All I had to eat that day was a bacon & egg roll from the same shop I always buy from but then at Manly for lunch I had Hungry Jacks it must have been that.

Beck:

Okay babe

Me:

I have a boozy day on Saturday with my German Friends to celebrate 39 years in Australia so we are going to all their special venues. As I have the house to myself this weekend I think I will enjoy being alone, although it would be more fun if it were 2 of us

Beck:

Yes babe. Kate will tell her daddy tomorrow have been praying that her daddy will borrow us money.

Me:

I hope so too, do you think the idea of giving it straight back to him will persuade him to lend it? Would it help if he had some credentials from me? I have a blank Western Union at home waiting for you, maybe it will take him a few days to decide. Does he know why you are coming to Sydney? Or just that you have a work visa and a sponsor.

Beck:

His daughter just told me she will follow her daddy and talk, but she don't tell me what she will tell her daddy.

Me:

I guess that's not a problem. Does she know about us?

Beck:

Yes babe she is my best friend. I know by the grace of god her daddy will borrow us the money because her daddy love her so much, and he gives anything that she wants to her.

Me:

I hope so I am praying too. That sounds good to start with. I hope he does it this time maybe he thinks you and I are a couple. Is she an only child?

Beck:

Yes babe she's my best friend

Me:

That is why she gets what she wants, and maybe why you and she are friends you have similar circumstances. Is there anything I can do to help? Like maybe write him an email?

Beck:

(lol)

Me:

Does her father know what happened to you?

Beck:

It's fine because she reads some of our emails

Okay that's cool,

Beck:

She knows that you really care for me a lot but no, her father doesn't know

Me:

Thankyou, I was just thinking that if he did, he might want to help out of sympathy for you but as you say this is none of my business. You can tell Kate, or even show her this that I love you.

Beck:

Yes, she knows everything about us my love.

Me:

I am just wondering, has she seen ALL of our emails? You know what we have said in some of them OMG. Oh well it doesn't matter I am not worried. I would like to tell the world about you. How long have you two been friends?

Beck:

For the past 5 years now

Me:

That's a good friendship with that period of time. If her father says yes to you, when are you planning to fly?

Beck:

I will be coming by next week

Me:

That's cool, do you think Kate will want to have holiday here too and come and see you?

Beck:

Yes for sure she has been telling me that

Me:

That's what I figured that's fine. Then you could give her back the money in person When does she want to do this, at the same time as you or a bit later? You know we won't have any accommodation available for Kate but I'm sure we can arrange cheap accommodation close by, if that's what you want. How old is she?

Beck:

Babe, yes I know that we will get accommodation for her if she's ready to come. She is 27 years old babe.

That's cool there are a lot of serviced apartments for lease close by and some hotels too. I would love to meet her. We can show her around the city, by then you will know some of the places to take her. I guess I have to wait for your all, important email over the weekend. Do you have to go to the hospital today? Does your mother know Kate wants to come too?

Beck:

She told her daddy already

Me:

I was going to ask you if she was there with you now

Beck:

Yes, she's here now we are together now, she can see what you are writing

Me:

Hello Kate, I'm John, nice to chat with you so now I can't talk dirty (lol). I presume she has left the house to give him time to think about the request. Is your mum there too?

Beck:

(lol) she was laughing when she read that you can't talk shit. My mummy is in the room she said hi how are you doing?

Me:

Then I will only say nice things, Hi, I am fine sitting here at work, nothing else to do but chat to my boyfriend who I haven't met yet

Beck:

She said thankyou for taking good care of me and make me happy, and she said you will meet me soon.

Me:

I only have four and one half hours to go the no more work this week. I usually get a long weekend, every weekend. I planned it that way. I look forward to meeting with you too Kate and I promise you I will always look after Beck. I long for that first kiss.

Beck:

She was laughing,.. she said she liked you already

Me: Thankyou

Beck:

My love she already talked to her father

Me:

Has he agreed? Or do we have to wait, sometimes these decisions are not made easily and not straight away, I understand.

Beck:

Babe is sad that her daddy doesn't want to help fully

Me:

That is what I thought you were going to say, so now we are back to the starting block.

Beck:

Am not really happy now

Me:

I don't imagine you are

Beck:

Her daddy promised to help with 1500 pounds. Half of the money and that cannot help us at all, because no where to get the other half of the money from

Me:

Well, that is a start, what about your church friends?

Beck:

I don't have friends in church

Me:

Oh !

Beck:

I only have church member, and I can't ask them for money

Me:

This is for Kate, tell Beck to turn to Prostitution for a couple of weeks, that will get the rest (lol). Well I guess you have to wait a while longer but at least you are only looking for half now

Beck:

She was laughing she said hahahaha. She said she will never support that because I am made for you alone.

Me:

She doesn't know I might be serious but, that is nice, thankyou. I also can only be with one man. I don't have any ideas now for you

Beck:

Okay babe. Babe I know I can't ask you for any more

money and my friends know everything that happened to us. If I may ask when do you want to pay the debt?

Me:

I don't understand what you mean, can you explain/? Do you mean when you arrive?

Beck:

I mean the money you want to pay to the debtor, the money you are late in owing

Me:

I will be paying 2 weeks back rent next Tuesday and one later the same week, when Josh pays me. I also have one other bill I requested an extension on to be paid next week. I have paid the rest. That then does not leave me with any reserve .I still need to look after you as well,

Beck:

Kate says she have an idea

Me:

I don't have anything else available I gave it all to you. That is good I don't mind helping you as I said. You will need to pay me back but I have no more at the moment and I also need some in reserve, what is Kate's' idea?

Beck:

She said why, don't you use the money for me now then you will pay it immediately when I arrive there

Me:

I need to pay this rent this week it is 3 weeks behind. I cannot let it go any further. I also have another bill to pay that I extended, that will give me a bad credit rating, and then there is money for food and spending also required out of the same pay week. I am not able to gamble with the rent anymore.

Beck:

Babe, she said today is Thursday, so I can arrive on Tuesday if that's okay with you

Me:

That doesn't help you find the 1500 pounds. I will only have about $200 for the week next week. and then I have to wait again for another week for the fortnightly pay period from this job.

Beck:

I don't understand what you are saying babe. Please make me understand

Me:

I am not able to leave myself in a vulnerable situation owing so much back rent I have a responsibility to Josh, 2 dogs, and myself. You have 1500 pounds from Kate's father correct? You coming here next week is great, but I don't understand where you are getting the other 1500 pounds from, that is what I am trying to say. Yes we can pay back your debt but obviously, it will not be all of it immediately, as I am already behind.

Remember I have already tried to get a loan last week remember,....and no one will finance because I only have casual employment. I don't know what to suggest to you.

Beck:

What Kate mean, is you send the money you want to pay for rent, then I will arrive on Tuesday so you can pay the rent, that what she's trying to say.

Me:

Cannot be done

Beck:

Okay I told her already because I did not expect any more from you

Me:

I am paying rent on Saturday for the pay to go through on Tuesday. This will clear out that account.

Beck:

Yes, I understand you my love.

Me:

I am sorry honey I am not able to help. I am desperate for this pay to sort it out and it has taken 2 weeks. I guess this needs some more planning

Beck:

So what are we going to do now, because I don't have any option than Kate and her daddy, only give us half of the money.

Me:

I really don't know Beck I am not in a position to have spare cash for a while anyway.

Beck:

Yes I understand.

Me:

See, honey 1500 pounds is a lot of money for anybody, for me it works out at $1800. I don't even get paid that amount in a fortnight between the 2 jobs, so you are asking the wrong person. Is Kate still with you?

Beck:

Yes she's still here she's seeing everything.

Me:

That's okay I don't mind that I'm just unable to help out that's all I'm saying. Remember I even tried getting a loan for you. I have come to a brick wall. I am sad for this and I know you are.

Beck:

Babe, can you get a loan from a bank?

Me:

I have tried that too, I told you I have the car loan I wanted to extend on that, but because I have $10,000 Visa they will not lend me the money. The Visa card has no credit either. I have run out of options

Beck:

Hum ok babe am just tired a lot now

Me:

Okay babe I have to go next door, we can chat tomorrow

I just wanted to make sure you are going to be okay and not do anything stupid to yourself   Kisses.

Reading all of these previous chats should make me realize that, there is something wrong, but I find myself compelled to continue with funding as there is intrigue in this mystery. I find it necessary to remind him I have a responsibility to myself and others, and still, after the deliberation he requests for further funding. I am aware now that my concern is to not lose the money I have committed to the project already, and this means maybe to spend more to make the project work. My original idea was to outlay cold cash to a cause, that should work and it would need to recycle money twice, so to have discussions with each other for further funding is necessary for me. I had sold myself on the idea it would make me money and give me a lover. I wonder if I would have been more successful in the slave trade! I knew I was not able at this point to provide any further cash and, now it had to come from Beck. He needed to be more committed to his cause, something I wanted to see happen, this of course meant a delay, being concerned

I was upsetting Beck or shattering his dream (if it was genuine) the conversations continued.

Me: 10/10/2010

Hello I'm home

Beck:

Have been waiting for you my love where have you been?

Me:

I have been to my local nightclub as I do on Sundays. I met up with Greg who should be here with me now, .but asked me if he could go home with Steve what can I say "If that is where you feel you want to go". My day darling is not good for you.

Beck:

Ok

Me:

I was intending to try one more option to get you here then something occurred to me

Beck:

What option is that my love?

Me:

that is, that you are not upset, that you will not be coming here because you do not have the money. I have now withdrawn the one possible option I had that I admit was dodgy but something has occurred to me tonight

Beck:

What occurred to you?

Me:

I am not prepared to give you anything at all anymore. I don't know who you are

Beck:

What happened to you my love tell me!

Me:

You have given me nothing but woe. It's summer in this city for the next 5 months, and I am not prepared to be broke over you, someone that should have been here a week ago tomorrow I am ringing the Immigration Department and, making sure that my name and address are, no longer associated with your Visa. I believed in you and you are obviously not the person in your profile

Beck:

My love I feel sad sometime, if I remember that you allow a 3rd party in our relationship.

Me:

Your choice with me is this "You will arrive here on your own finances ASAP. If you do not my offer is permanently withdrawn. There are a lot of Hot, Hung Cute Guys in this town

Beck:

I know you have been given wrong advice in your local club again. John, you are talking like you want to break my heart. Why would you allow anyone to play with our feelings? I know you truly love me as I do because you have proven it to me in many ways

Me:

I should have known better, you have let me down I am looking for a partner that can make half of the decisions regarding us. Clearly you are not capable therefore please do not send me sorry messages. I am not interested. Tomorrow your name will be mentioned in Canberra. by me I will get to the bottom of your crap.

Beck:

Why do you want to let me down at this time? You know I have submitted my life to you already

Me:

You have been spinning me

Beck:

What are you talking about!

Me:

I am not going to talk anymore

Beck:

I will commit suicide if you break my heart. Because I was beaten and a broken hand because of you, why do you want to rule my life? You spoil my day already.

Me:

I will expect something from you to tell me what is going on. Maybe you and Kate are in a consortium. I do not know, but I do know I now have no intention of helping you goodnight!!!.

Beck:

Remember this is not what you promised me. You promise to be there for me.

Beck: 11/10/2010

John I am highly disappointed in you, with what you told me now. You have broken my heart already. Kate will be really mad at you if I show her these messages.

Me:

Hello Beck, Yes I promised to be there for you and I still want to. I want this relationship to work. I am sorry for being abrupt but the situation is that you are not able to get the rest of the money from anywhere, so are not able to come here. That situation is not going to change so you are still not going to be coming. I told myself this after it was pointed out to me by some friends, all of whom now think I am stupid because I believed in you and said he would come. I am pretty shattered at the moment that I am not going

to hold you, but you don't seem upset that you weren't going to get the 1500 pounds to come, so that tells me you never intended to. I hope I am wrong. Above all I still want this to work. Please answer me this, how do you intend to get here? You know I have no more to give you and I don't have you here with me now so I have nothing to show for all I have done. I am hurting Beck, I hope you have an answer for me, please tell me something good. I will be online tonight at work if you want to talk. I will listen to what you want to say

I had no conversation with Beck for 2 days. I had been hoping that my stern words would generate some interest in him providing finance for himself. And, wanting to think this would happen. I was in despair when it did not, and I was unable to believe the worst even though it was the correct decision. The conversation and chats would therefore continue and just maybe he will arrange some funding for himself.

Me: 13/10/2010

Hi babe, have been trying all day to get funds for you. I came close but sadly no one will lend me anymore cash, will chat tonight at work

kisses

Me: 14/10/2010

Hi babe. Now I'm here have to go for a pee back 2 mins.

Beck:

How are you doing?

Me:

Hi babe, what are your events for today? I have some things to find out tomorrow and discuss with you. It does not involve money, it is about misinformation that either you have received or I have been told too. So I can chat at midnight (4 hours time) I have heaps to tell you wish you were here have to have a shower and dinner.

Beck: Okay babe

Me:

Sorry, I just opened an attachment that shut my computer down, back now.

Beck:

Okay

Me:

I will tell you later tonight, what I found out (or maybe I have the wrong info) but at the moment Josh and I are planning a Christmas BBQ in the house early December we have never met each other's friends and already talking about what we are serving, obviously you won't need an invite you will be here.

Beck:

Yes babe

Me:

And we can use your culinary skills too. Is Kate with you?

Beck:

She's not here now, she will be here soon, so what do you want to tell me!

Me:

I have been advised today by different guys (2 in fact) that you don't need to have all the cash to be counted by immigration at the airport or wherever. Apparently several tourists have been robbed in the past and the Australian government has been challenged by this. I know I would not carry that much. One of the guys I drive with is English and has done already what you are attempting to do. He only showed a bank statement. I know my ATM card will work around the world in several countries. So maybe, somewhere one of us is getting miss information. The other issue is that sponsorship is still okay which means that if I can confirm this with Canberra tomorrow you can catch a flight during the week. I have to go and eat and shower. I will chat with you later about 3 hours Bye for now Honey.

Me: 14/10/2010

Yes my love I am home, sorry for the delay

Beck:

OK have been waiting here with Kate

Me:

Sorry I got to work about 45 minutes ago but I had things to do with changeover first but okay now. I gather you two have been talking?

Beck:

Okay babe, yes we have been talking

Me:

Have you come up with any solution?

Beck;

We don't see any way we can get the money from here Kate has one idea, she said why don't you go for the first loan?

Me:

They wouldn't give me either loan because I have not had my second job (that is the one driving) for 12 months .Both companies did not offer me any money in the end. Yes they were interested in taking the car if I defaulted. I had an appointment with one company at 11am tomorrow but they rang me back this afternoon and told me no., because of the job situation.

Beck:

You mean those companies are not willing to give you any loan?

Me:

Yes, that is correct. That is why I sent you the message from my phone as soon as I knew they are not even going to consolidate my car loan with an increase at first that is what they offered but the loan was not approved, that is what I meant by F@%$k

Beck:

So what about the company that asked you to come tomorrow?

Me:

That is the same company I made the appointment with first, and they rang me back to tell me the loan was not approved

Beck:

Okay babe

Me:

So I do not need to come in at 11am.

Beck:

Kate said, why don't you go for the car loan, since I will be bringing the money back

Me:

There is no car loan that is what I was trying to do but that is the company that said no to coming in at 11am.

Beck:

Okay babe you should go ahead and do that babe

Me:

Do what? I don't understand.

Beck:

I think they want you to have the loan with your car

Me:

No they said no as I said, because I have not had my second job for 12 months they will not grant me a loan on this job because it is under the minimum requirement so there is no problem, there is no money being offered at all. I thought you might be considering other options like changing your visa to a tourist visa or making enquiries if you can use the visa later, or reapply later as we are not able to come up with the funds

Beck:

My Visa cannot be change, because I have a working visa already.

Me:

That is what I had said earlier, it is up to you what you decide to do. I understand and I don't know of a solution

Beck:

Babe, Kate daddy is the only option I have

Me:

We are back to square one.

Beck:

Now I am so frustrated right now.

Me:

I am really sorry honey. I have tried several times for you, there are levels of requirement here in these finance companies in order to lend money, and I do not meet the requirement.

Beck:

I know you have tried a lot for me, and I will never disappoint you in this life

Me:

I know

Beck:

I believe you my dear

Me:

This is a challenge and we will overcome it somehow, remember a couple of days ago I said I believe in destiny and a reason for things happening?

Beck:

Yes I know babe

Me:

Well, hopefully this will become clear to us soon and that will mean the solution has been found

Beck:

Yes I remember my love

Me:

I know that does not help us now and I know we are both disappointed

Beck:

Yes babe. You always give me hope I will always love you to the end.

Me:

And you to me honey and there is still always a place here for you with me

Beck:

God will never disappoint us babe

Me:

I hope he can sort this out my luck at winning the lottery is not to good either

Beck:

Yes babe I believe in God.

Me:

Then you can ask him for help, and I will call on the laws of metaphysical energy to intervene, let's see if that will help us. I think for your own sake as I said earlier you do not want to upset Kate's dad, so maybe wait a while before you receive the 1500 pounds. The last thing you need is for him to distrust you but that's just a suggestion honey.

Beck:

I pray so babe Kate she's not really happy about everything that's happened

Me:

I am so sorry I could not make this happen today. That is my last hope

Beck:

Kate is here seeing everything you have written

Me:

That's fine

Beck:

She said she will try to convince her daddy to hold the money till next week

Me:

Does that make it any better for you?

Beck:

I don't really know

Me:

I guess all you can do is stall and hope for a miracle, maybe donate a kidney

Beck:

I will pray for that

Me:

So will I, we will be destined to chat for a while longer I think rather than be ready yet. But I think we should keep chatting to each other

Beck:

Hum, I am so frustrated now, not really happy

Me:

Me neither. Did you get the plaster off your hand yesterday?

Beck:

Yes I did my love

Me:

Well that is something good at least. I know it's not the right answer but that is good anyway

Beck: Yes babe

Me:

I think the best thing to do is not be too frustrated it will only compound and it won't change anything

Beck:

Thankyou my love

Me:

I believe there will be a change but I don't know how or when, what do you want to do now?

Beck:

I don't know what to do my love

Me:

Hum, I think the first thing is don't worry although that is going to be hard as all that is on both of our minds is the current situation

Beck:

Yes my love

Me:

Should I let you go and talk to Kate?... Has your mum

got any answer? Just another suggestion, that's all. I forgot to say hello to Kate "Hello Kate"

Beck:

My mummy was sick a little bit she don't get any answer. She said hi.

Me:

Hi, I am sorry to hear that your mum is sick, hope she recovers soon

Beck:

She said you shouldn't bother, that she understands its' fine

Me: Thankyou

Beck:

I have to go now

Me:

Bye my love

Beck:

Am so crazy about everything that's happened to us now

Me:

I know honey

Beck:

Alright, bye for now

Me:

I will calm down, but it does not mean there is a short term answer

Beck:

I love you from the bottom of my heart

Me:

I love you always too.

Beck:

Kisses

Me:

So there is always a place for you with me   kisses   bye

Beck:

Bye

Me: 15/10/2010

Hi babe, on line now finished all chores so far and enjoying my chocolate doughnut and coffee. How has your day been?

Beck:

Kate is here, she knows everything,

Me:

Hi! Kate love the information I got today is from one of the guys I drive with he is a Pommy and has been here for 5 years, he came in on a work visa as well and said all he did was show the account balance, he for one would not carry that much cash, come to think of it neither would I.

Beck:

That was then 5 years back. Babe Kate said hi to you

Me:

As this is a requirement of the Australian Government, not yours I will ring Canberra and ask the story

Beck:

No problem, you can go ahead and do that. That's how they do it now.

Me:

Yes, maybe it is but I don't see why anybody would have to carry that much cash it's asking for trouble and it has already happened to you, so I will see what they say maybe you have been given the wrong information, it does happen particularly with government departments. Then there is also the situation that you may be a relative coming to stay with a great aunt or whoever, Why would you pay 3000 pounds to do that, even if you had a working visa

Beck:

Babe the money will not be taken from me

Me:

Something does not sound right to me so I will check what I can on line tonight and call them tomorrow because really, you should be here by now and this would certainly help if there is something that can be done

Beck:

They just want me to meet up with their requirements since I have the working visa.

Me:

We don't know if we don't ask

Beck:

Kate said that's what they want so that immigration will not disturb me

Me:

Yes I know they do honey, but I am not convinced that all the people that work in Australia House or the airport can even count properly so they have no need to check all your cash I know they are that dumb here. Who do you have to show the cash to?

Beck:

Okay, but I have to meet up here, hope you understand I don't want to have any problems during my departure

Me:

I know that honey all I am going to do is ask here in Australia over the phone I still don't believe it has to be in cash

Beck:

Yes you go ahead and ask

Me:

Is it alright with you if they ask me for any details that I say you are coming to live with me?

Beck:

Yes do that

Me:

That is really the whole purpose of the exercise thanks it won't be a hassle I am only asking them questions

Beck:

But I know what I am saying because immigration here, are a crazy a lot

Me:

I am very cynical, I don't trust government agencies for anything I agree with you they are really bad here so bad in fact they have law suits against them totalling millions of dollars here in Australia

Beck:

Okay

Me:

They have already been charged with discrimination here. Do you remember the date you got your visa? I know it was a Wednesday but I have to look back through the emails to find the date

Beck:

I don't, I think its 3 weeks ago ok

Me:

That should be enough

Beck:

Ok

Me:

It seems longer sometimes

Beck: Yes

Me:

What are you going to do with Kate's father, tell him you don't want it yet? I should have an answer tomorrow and can send you the answer before you wake up. It's up to you of course.

Beck:

We can't tell him like that babe

Me:

Okay, that's not an issue as I said it's up to you what you do.

Beck:

Kate will tell him that we don't need it this week

Me:

Yes, that's a better idea.

Beck:

Babe, don't say it's up to me is both of us.

Me:

I didn't mean you had to say my literal statement anyway

Beck:

Ok

Me:

Yes I know it's up to both of us, what I meant by that is, you know what is best with Kate's Father I don't so, I should leave that up to you. I just did not word it properly. Is Kate still there with you?

Beck:

Okay babe, yes she's still here.

Me:

Good I hope she understands what I meant I am not trying to say anything wrong

Beck:

She understands

Me:

Good, is mum feeling better?

Beck:

Yes she's getting better

Me:

Good. Tomorrow I have an interview for another job, I don't know what I will do if I have to leave here. This is a good job I guess I will have to see what happens first.

Beck:

Okay, wish you good luck

Me:

I guess I better let you get on with your day now. Josh and I have decided the Christmas party is the last week in November he wants to make up invites, as long as he pays me for the printer ink that's okay. If you are with us by the time we do the invites, your name will be on them too.

Beck:

Okay babe

Me:

Hopefully honey I will have some news tomorrow. Keep smiling. I still love you Kisses Bye for now

Beck:

I love you byeee

CHAPTER 8

THE FRIEND

It is a fact that when you marry you sometimes feel like you have married the Mother in Law as well. There is a similar "Bonus" here where I seem to have inherited his best friend, (maybe his only friend) a single mother with at least 2 children no doubt also unemployed. She reads every message and already wants to come and stay before we have the finances sorted. She would be classed as the typical "Fag Hag" but as she was going to get married later in the year this status would change. Hopefully that also means no trip to visit us as part of the honeymoon. Then I am inheriting the best friend and the husband. I am yet to see what role she will play in this game.

Me: 16/10/2010

Hi babe I'm Home

Beck:

How are you my love

Me:

My phone does not show if you are online and I have been out with my German Friends

Beck:

Oh Okay

Me:

Do I need to say hello Kate? Well hello Kate

Beck:

Yes babe

Me:

I have been in contact with the immigration office today

Beck:

So what is the news?

Me:

As per usual when anything involves a politician to make a sensible decision we can forget it. What I was told is that even with my name and you staying you will need $5000. This now is automatically less than 3000 pounds, they also told me that you will not be asked for this proof at Heathrow and you do not physically need the cash the words that were used were "As this has nothing to do with the British Government, this is a requirement by the Australian Government you MAY be asked for proof of finances which means you put the bank statement with your passport. This I got from Canberra today that means it is possible to create accounts and move money

Beck:

Okay

Me:

The guy I spoke to was not an idiot I was ready for that. I also have a local London number for you to call with a company that help with this process as far as advice is concerned 01925451195.email info@visaforaustralia. co.uk I have got a whole lot of info on your visa half of which I already knew, and when you get here we need to talk about where you want to spend the regional 3 mandatory months. I think given your qualifications in hospitality you should do the Whitsundays. You won't get anywhere in the world closer to that than paradise. Anyway, this is all early stages yet. I guess I'd better let you say something

Beck:

Okay babe I wish you to know that I have 2 years working visa not tourist visa

Me:

The other issue I found out is that you have 12 months to use the visa subclass 417

Beck:

The immigration here want me to hold $5000 which will not be taken from me

Me:

Correct

Beck:

I want you to know that immigration here are very crazy a lot

Me:

As they are here, the words used today (and this is from Canberra) is "Evidence of the Funds" you can actually attach a bank statement as you pass through. I was told today "No one at Heathrow is Concerned with what you have.

Beck:

Some may be jealous that I am leaving the UK to work in AUS so they will really disturb me during my departure and I don't want them to cancel my visa

Me:

It is when you arrive at Kingsford Smith they may check

Beck:

Heathrow will check me as well babe.

Me:

Then I suggest you sort something out for yourself. I am not getting involved any further, you want to come then come, I am going to get bored very soon with this

Beck:

You want to start upset again

Me:

This dilemma of yours, we seem to have a constant issue of 1500 pounds that is dragging on. You should have 1500 pounds from Kate's Dad available, then, you should also have 1500 pounds from your mum from the bank loan correct me if I am wrong..

Beck:

Have you forgot that my mummy haven't pay the 1500 loan back

Me:

What about the original amount that would have been put into her bank account?

Beck

I told you she's retired from work she's living on a government basis

Me:

Okay then I will spell it out for you. If you are interested in us you get here ASAP on your own funds now, because this has gone on for 4 weeks and I am getting BORED.

You know there is a place here for you but I am not going to chat online anymore every night with the woe of Beck Hill's finances

Beck:

What do you mean by that?

Me:

I have better things to do this time babe

Beck:

You want to start again?

Me:

The choice is yours, not mine

Beck:

That's how you got me upset last time

Me:

So what about me! You should have been here by now and just to remind you I have outlaid $4500 on you already with no result, so how do you think I feel! Thanks for considering that

Beck:

Are you putting the blame on me now?

Me:

Absolutely yes, because you lost what I gave you

Beck:

You are making me feel guilty after all has happened to me

Me:

Good, then maybe you will finally think of how I feel because you have never asked me

Beck:

This is not fair John

Me:

No, this is not fair I don't know why you would think that sweetheart.

Beck:

You are making going crazy now.

Me;

All I am saying is that we are not going to resolve anything anymore over 1500 pounds, you know I can't give it to you and you know you can't get it. I have told you it will be sometime to save this, and then the airfare charges. We are like a couple of puppies chasing our tails that is what I am saying, you need to do something for yourself here, remember your comments were "I will not let you down" I can send that particular email chat back to you if you wish

Beck:

My love but you know I am doing my best as I can

Me:

And so have I so what does that prove. Nothing!!!

Beck:

I am frustrated already, and you putting the blame on me

Me:

The reason I put the blame on you honey is easy and I am comfortable with my soul in doing so. Firstly, I gave you all the money you required and am STILL suffering for that because you did not give it back. Thanks for asking how I have been able to pay visa, the car payment, vet bills and rent, by the way which is what you let me down with so, yes, I am comfortable with blaming you. I am guilt free and I have been true to my word. And secondly that by the way is something you read in my original profile

Beck:

Crying!!

Me:

Would you like me to remind you what you wrote? It is here in front of me.

Beck: (sob)

Me:

Let me see, this is for Kate. This is the first line of his profile. " I want someone that is ready to trust" next line "I don't want time wasters" third line....

Beck:
Okay it's me now Kate

Me:

third line "I want someone who can decide on his own" do you want me to continue Kate?

Kate:
John pls you shouldn't make him cry

Me:

Crying is guilt Kate I am not a fool. I want to love this man and be with this man I chose him and I thought all would be fine

Kate:

John I understand how you really feel about everything. Because you have been spending a lot to bring him there

Me:

I want a strong man to be part of my life and help me in my affairs if he cannot do this then I have wasted money and now I am wasting my time? What do you think? Have I wasted my time Kate? Yes I have given him all my available cash, you got it. I have no more available cash. I thought he wanted to be part of my life. There are preserved funds that would look after him when I am gone, but I don't know that he is the right guy anymore

Kate:

John pls you have to be patient with him. You did not waist your money everything will be fine soon I have the faith. I thought my daddy would give me all the money but he accept to give me half alone

Me:

You said "To be with me forever" I said to you "Until the end of time" There are preserved funds that are not available to me to look after my next of kin. That I had hoped would be you

Kate:

I believe everything happens for a reason John

Me:

Kate honey thankyou for helping him out I really appreciate it. I am sorry I cannot refund you Beck, I want you to know I am a genuine guy. I don't think that needs approval I have delivered as promised, it is his turn to do that now.

Kate:

Yes I know John, but you don't need to argue with him

on this issue. We just have to look for way out, that's what we need to do John

Me;

Okay, then can you please tell me 2 things Firstly, how is he going to fund himself and secondly, how soon do both of you think he will be financial?

Kate:

As you can see I have been trying for him and I will not stop.

Me:

Believe me Kate I did not mean to make him cry

Kate:

So I don't want you to "feed up" at this time

Me:

It is not in my makeup as a person and if he were here he would know that

Kate:

You just have to continue trying. We need to do this together John

Me:

I cannot find anymore cash

Kate:

Pls John I don't want you to do that to him. Pls. do it for the sake of me John

Me:

Honey, have you or Beck considered what you are doing to me? I would like to maybe meet this man and kiss him we would obviously have a whole lot of things to understand and explore together, and I am anxious to do this but I am not, believing it is closer yet that is all.

Kate:

I understand you John so let's make it work so he can arrive at your place soon. He always told me he can't wait to do that with you

Me:

Thankyou Kate

Kate:

You are welcome John that's why I told you, you shouldn't give up. You need to try more for him as I am doing.

Me:

I don't know whether you have read the email from yesterday. I think it was where I was looking for close accommodation for you when you arrive to visit, Beck said we had time and not to worry at the moment.

Kate:

Yes he told me everything

Me:

I look forward to meeting you too Kate, maybe you will get the urge to migrate. The politics here are shit and so are the politicians

Kate:

Lol. Thankyou John same here

Me:

The weather here is something you read about in a Novel and the cost of living is lower

Kate:

Okay John

Me:

This City has been rated the best city internationally 2 years running

Kate:

Really!

Me:

Yes really, we are not built on a creek like London or Melbourne. We have the most amazing harbour and until you are part of it you can never understand. I am offering all this to him as my partner that is all I want

Kate:

He wants it as well John so you don't need to be upset with him again let's Make it work out, together.

Me:

When you come here yourself you will be amazed as the plane banks over the Sydney Opera House to make its final approach into KSA. You look at the pics in the mags, but there is nothing like this harbour in the world. I am a local boy and I am proud of it.

Kate:

Lol ahahah okay John

Me:

Is he okay now?

Kate:

Yes you have to talk to him now

Me:

I am aching for you to be here Beck. I hope it is soon is that you back honey?

Beck:

yes babe. Yes is me

Me:

Sweetheart I never intended to make you cry I just wish

you would have considered my feelings. Have you read what I wrote to Kate?

Beck:

Yes I did

Me:

Good. My offer for all I have to look after you when I am not around still stands, if you are my partner only. This choice I cannot make for you sweetheart

Beck:

Thank you, my love. I have promise to spend the rest of my life with you but I know everything will be soon

Me:

Thank you. I want you too that would be good

Beck:

Am happy to hear that from you

Me:

I haven't won any money or lotteries yet. But I do keep trying every week.

Beck:

Babe I know you have tried for me a lot. But I don't want you to stop I know we will make a good couple soon

Me:

I want to love you Beck, I want to hold you. I want us to make a good couple soon, and yesterday would have been better. I do give you permission to remove me as your Screen saver if you want to .I can't imagine I am a pretty sight that large. Its' okay to put something else up if you want

Beck:

Even if you do so I will never remove it because I love it the way it is

Me:

I will keep you up on my wall however, Thanks honey.

Beck:

Thankyou my love

Me:

Beck I am sorry if I upset you that was not my intention. I am anxious now for us together, I went out tonight with my German friends, we discussed their problems with a lover, and mine

Beck:

Okay

Me:

They are the only sensible friends I have as far as our

situation is concerned and they are comforting. They are dying to meet you

Beck:

I see

Me:

I have also told them about Kate. Beck they are fine and they have no part in tonight's discussion because they didn't even know I was going to be chatting with you tonight. The other thing you will learn about me is I am not a good liar I have never had much of a reason to be.

Beck:

Okay babe. You just have to be very careful my love

Me:

Yes I know that we have agreed, and that has not changed. Decisions like that one require both of us to decide

Beck:

Okay babe

Me:

Love you if it is alright with you

Beck:

I love you too

Me:

I would like to have dinner it is after midnight here. Friday I sleep late because of nightshift and I don't eat at normal times

Beck:

Okay no problem babe

Me:

Thanks honey, I will say goodnight to both of you kisses to you Beck

Beck:

Kisses my love

Me: Bye

Beck:

Love you from the bottom of my heart

Me:

I love you from the bottom of my heart and I love hearing you tell me it every time

Beck:

Bye

Me:

I will love you until the end of time   bye.

Me: 18/10/2011

Hi babe I am home

Beck:

How are you my love I miss you so much

Me:

I tried to send a message from my phone but it failed

Beck:

Oh ok

Me:

I miss you too honey. Tonight I ran into a friend I had not seen for 10 years, the sad part is he had to ask that question where is XXX? Anyway I just wanted to let you know that.

Sweetheart that is true my friend who I have had no track of for 10 years, it was like we never parted he has a Scottish boyfriend now, who is delightful and we as a couple have been invited to stay with them on the Gold Coast next year. I told them about you because they were concerned about me being a widow and did not know about my partner's demise.

Beck:

Okay yes babe, so what is their comment about me?

Me:

They are happy for me that I have found someone.

I told you I would be careful I need to be for myself anyway and I know these guys know nothing as it was a surprise. That is why I am later home than intended as I was talking to them. Is everything okay with you?

Beck:

Yes babe

Me:

I had four offers tonight from desperate pathetic guys all asking if I was single I said no my partner is at the moment in London

Beck:

Okay babe am happy to hear that thankyou so much for that.

Me:

Do you remember the TV series "Are you Being Served" We watch a drag show every Sunday night at the club of the series, maybe you are too young, anyway that doesn't matter. Are you alone?

Beck:

Yes babe

Me:

So what are you wearing?

Beck:

Shorts

Me:

And that is all?

Beck:

Yes

Me:

Good, because I am now getting naked; take them off!

Beck:

Babe I am at the sitting room

Me:

So you said you were alone

Beck:

Yes! My mummy is in her room she may come out any moment. Hope you understand

Me:

Sorry I didn't think about that. I was hoping for you know

Beck:

Yes babe I know

Me:

Yes I understand, but at the moment I am naked with a hard on hope you understand.

Beck:

Yes babe I do, you make me hard just now

Me:

Good because if you were alone, and the Pc was private I would say "take your shorts off now lick two fingers and slowly rub them around you arse.

Beck:

Babe I will have to go inside my room to do that

Me:

I know that now

Beck:

But I wouldn't be able to see what you are writing again

Me:

I didn't realize your Pc was in public space, mine is not

Beck:

Yes public place

Me:

Honey its' okay I am naked and horny and I wanted to share my pleasure with you its' okay sweetheart

Beck:

Okay babe

Me:

I will just look at your pic on the wall, think of you and blow all over the screen

Beck:

Thankyou my love, I am looking at your pic now on my Pc and it is making me horny again

Me:

Likewise I would be grateful of anymore pics you want to send honey. By the way tonight I just let my best friend Rupert know you are not a Nigerian Scammer, which is something he has in his head. I know it sounds funny I did not put that thought there

Beck:

Hahahaha is that what he has on in his head?

Me:

Yes, but not after tonight

Beck:

Okay babe

Me:

That is because I told him I contacted Immigration hey sweetheart, I am curious about something with you I think you originally mentioned it in our first contact, what I want to know

Beck:

What is that babe!

Me:

What does "Beck" mean? John means sent by god but I cannot find Beck as a name

Beck:

Lol, I don't really know

Me:

Sorry lol is fine I was just curious. Josh my flatmate's sister is pregnant.

Beck:

Really?

Me:

and he was telling me what he has to sit through with the sister and names and meanings. That is the only reason I asked. I think I'm about to blow a load again, one minute

Beck:

Okay babe

Me:

#%*$&%@   I am sorry about that, you are fucking hot, on my wall and I am horny

Beck:

Lol okay babe

Me:

So that is the problem sorted now, what are you doing today? (Moment) cumming again #%*$&%@

Beck:

I will be going to the gym very soon

Me:

Hm! Sorry about that, but that was you again on my wall, I had to wipe the computer screen this time. I'm glad you are going back to the gym

Beck:

Okay babe

Me:

I want a hot, tight body when you arrive your body that is I will work out for free at work when I know you are coming

Beck:

okay babe

Me:

Are you still wearing only shorts?

Beck:

Yes babe

Me:

and, no jocks?

Beck:

I will have to change before I go to the gym. You know today is the first day I will resume the gym again, but I cannot pull any weight because if my hand. I just have to do the jogging

Me:

I was wondering about that I think I even asked you that when your hand was still bandaged. I want you to have tight nipples when you arrive so you need to do bench presses as soon as you can

Beck:

The doctor advised me to do this

Me:

That's okay but later you can obviously start bench presses again. I have blown my load twice over you already I am hungry for you right now

Beck:

hahaha

Me:

I am sharing how I feel with you. I am deadly serious
Beck I want to tie you up and fuck you

Beck:

Don't worry babe, I know I will arrive soon I can't wait
to suck your cock babe

Me:

Yes I know honey that does not help my immediate
feeling I am going again no juice left that is how horny
you make me #%*$&%@

Beck:

Ok I love you

Me;

I want to know when you are alone in the flat and we
can have cybersex

Beck:

Okay babe

Me:

I want to chat to you when you are naked, hard and alone

Beck:

Okay babe

Me:

So does that mean you will let me know the time?

Beck:

Yes I will let you know when I am alone

Me:

Good because we will be doing the same thing at the same time as I tell you to do them. Are you fine with that?

Beck:

Yes babe

Me:

Thanks

Beck:

Babe I got to go now

Me:

I'm not hard anymore obviously after that little display

Beck:

I will chat with you later, I love you   kisses

Me:

Yes you're right I am talking crap now I will chat later honey love you. I must go to bed now, catch up later kisses

As you read through the previous pages you will notice that there is no intention of Beck being interested in what I have to say. His only concern is for me to acquire more cash for him. There is no compassion or care from the chat text and I was aware of this at the time. I realized I would get no response to any criticism, and again I needed to know the outcome

CHAPTER 9

THE REFINANCE

Beck: 19/10/2010

My love how are you. Are you there?

Me:

Yes hi honey

Beck:

How are you?

Me:

I am great now that I am talking to you I am sorry about yesterday at work. The computer has come back but the boss has totally disabled Google. I can use the internet and view my email but I will leave this to one of the other Concierges to complain about. It may be fixed by tomorrow night it may not

Beck:

Oh okay babe

Me:

If it is not I will chat to you on the bosses Pc

Beck:

Okay babe

Me:

I was checking on my phone if you were online and when you were I was cooking dinner

Beck:

Okay my love

Me:

How was your first day back at Gym?

Beck:

Very hectic, I was just doing lite one

Me:

Don't overdo it

Beck:

Yes I don't

Me:

Even if your hand has healed it has been several weeks

and that means slow again to build up. I used to do gym 3 or 4 nights a week when I was younger and I liked the way I looked and felt.

Beck:
Okay babe

Me:
But I will be happy to work out with you and I may be able to offer you one night a week free at the gym at work. It closes at 11pm there so it only gives you Mondays at the moment

Beck:
Lol okay babe

Me.
Is Kate with you?

Beck:
No she's not here yet

Me:
Is your mother there?

Beck:
Yes in her room

Me:
F@%#k

Beck:

why babe

Me:

Because you know what I was going to ask don't you. So what are you wearing

Beck:

Yes I know babe don't worry we will do that this week

Me:

I hope so honey I am so wanting to

Beck:

I know, we will this week

Me:

Thanks babe. Did you receive the pic I just sent of Sydney Harbor? That was taken from the bridge not by me. In fact I think Microsoft own it

Beck:

I haven't babe, when did you send it?

Me:

I sent you an email about 40mins ago, I will send it again later. It is in my sent folder so I assumed it went

Beck:

Okay babe

Me:

No matter I will send it again. Is your mum feeling better?

Beck:

Yes babe thank you

Me:

You know at the moment I have the most burning desire to go to London but it can't happen now as you know

Beck::

Yes, I know babe

Me:

After Xxxxxx died I wasn't sure if I wanted to go anywhere because I was on my own. Now I want to go everywhere, that is a task to set aside for now.

Beck:

okay babe

Me:

We have to get you sorted first

Beck:

Yes babe

Me:

You seem in high spirits and happy I am glad for that

Beck:

Yes I just can't wait to be with you

Me:

Likewise, just keep working on it keep selling a sob story and your good looks.

Beck:

Okay babe

Me:

And it will happen I have seen it so many times in the past. It even worked for me a long time ago, and that was not while I was a commercial boy.

Beck:

Okay babe

Me:

Oops! I don't think I told you about that forget it please, thanks. I have joined a metaphysical craft group and I have been invited to my first party on Halloween. I am looking forward to it

Beck:

When?

Me:

8;00pm October 31st. in a suburb not far away I am not

sure what to wear yet all I know is no shoes allowed, but I don't know what outfit.

Beck:

Okay

Me:

I also have to bring a plate of food so the witches are fed. No one said anything about nose of Turk or eye of Newt but then it is not Macbeth

Beck:

Okay

Me:

I will tell you about it after the event. It is not a sexual thing it is a religious night and it is mixed company, so none of "that" even though there are a number of gay guys in the group. You know how you feel about your Christianity well this is my release into energy and belief. the same as yours but I just see it differently.

Beck:

Yes okay babe

Me:

I was brought up strict Anglican, and my parents were both Sunday school teachers but it did not rub off with me all the hypocrisy and bigotry, so I found my own universal energy. I believe in God but I just channel it through science and energy, that's all

Beck:

really?

Me:

Honey I used to be a CEBS leader and take the kids on camps on the weekends. That stands for (Church of England Boys Society) I was also a scout leader with underprivileged kids, and belonged to a church fellowship for 6 years. I do accept and respect your Christianity as I would hope you do mine

Beck:

Wow, you haven't told me this before.

Me:

I guess there are still things for us both to say

Beck:

Okay babe yes babe a lot

Me:

I was a member of the Church choir and the school choir. I have performed in school plays and done a nude photo shoot for an international calendar back in 1992.

Beck:

Okay babe

Me:

I don't even have any pics of that, but I saw the finished product, funny thing at the time was I didn't want a copy of the calendar. It was more the fun of taking my clothes off with other guys I had never met. It was the most amazing feeling. I think that is why I did the Spencer Tunic photo shoot at the Sydney Opera House this year. I have that photo framed now. I am not shy is what I am saying here.

Beck: Okay

Me:

Some other things I have never told you about me, I was in the School Cadets and the Cadet Band where I played the trumpet and our school came third in the interschool band competition. I have also been in a Pipe Band for 7 years (no longer) where I played bagpipes and I also learned the guitar and piano a long time ago. My mother being a country girl taught myself and my next brother how to ride a horse.

Beck:

Okay

Me:

I have previously been a member of the international group Apex who work for charities. also sadly, the Masons that I quickly dispelled from because of their beliefs. I hope by now the chewing gum has fallen out of your mouth. That is all true and one day I will prove it to you if you so desire. I remember also as a child my mother took myself and my next youngest brother to learn ice skating and we were taught by an Eastern European Olympic Champion. I do not remember her name I can't even skate anymore because there is nowhere to do it and you forget when you don't use something

Beck:

Okay

Me:

I also went through the Village People phase and learned to roller skate (totally different to ice skating) but I have not done that for 15 years, however that is redeemable as the rink still exists and still has Gayskate on Tuesdays. Maybe I should get you into this

Beck:

lol okay

Me:

You now know a hell of a lot more about me

Beck:

Yes babe

Me:

I enjoyed playing in bands I enjoyed the military precision in the Cadets too. something you would not know about, but when I left school in year 12 I may have had to register for national service and could have ended up fighting America's War in Vietnam .some of my fellow pupils never came home. The only reason I did not have to register was a change of government. So I am a lucky man.

Beck:

Ok babe Good to hear that

Me:

I guess that tells you a bit more about me and maybe why I have the ideals I do I am a very honest and loyal man Beck I am genuine but you have found that out already

I do not like to mention the next line because it sounds like I am bragging

Beck:

Lol hahahaha I know you are honest to me

Me:

The Drum Major in the pipe band and 2 other Drum Majors from other pipe Bands were all ex WW11 soldiers and said that it would be an honour to have me in the trenches beside them there is no greater honour than that yes babe I am honest to you sometimes I lose my head as you have found out

Beck:

Yes I know that

Me:

But I think I'm okay and I won't lose my head with you again

Beck:

Yes u are babe

Me:

remember I promised thanks babe love you heaps

Beck:

Yes babe I will always love you to the end of the life babe

Me:

say hello to Kate for me but she will probably read this anyway

Beck:

Ok babe

Me:

maybe she will have comfort in reading the rest about me as far as your safety is concerned

Beck:

Yes babe you got it

Me:

me too sweetheart and we will meet one day that is now destiny

Beck:

My love why don't you help me with the remaining 1500 so I can arrive by ending of this month

Me:

Because I don't have it I also have to still cover back rent because of what you could not return and at the end of this month I am going back to one job as my driving job will close for Christmas so that also means I do not have any reserve to call on so even If I did have any spare I need it now for survival here I have to find another job I am not financial otherwise and I need to have a roof over my head to that is now my situation I did not want to tell you this but since you asked I thought you should know I am spending every night now applying for jobs I am like you not getting very far you know what it is like that is why you are coming in the first place you are lucky you had someone to help you I do not and I do not want to leave working at RHP but it is only 3 shifts a week so I will go back to full time 9-5 if I have to. I need a job returning minimum \$50K which I am capable of it is just finding the right one this week I had an interview but have not heard anymore yet that is my problem that is also why I want you here to help me out you know what it is like yourself at the moment the roof is still here and I am coping but if I get any cash I need to hang onto it for survival it is my survival we are talking about here and nothing will stand in the way of that You will need to look elsewhere love I also have a party to pay for here end of November, I told you about that too and there are ongoing Vet bills for Cindy's hip now you know everything there is to tell I better leave you with all of this for yourself to think about you see I have problems too now

Beck:

Babe I understand you a lot but if you have any help you can render for me pls don't hesitate remember I will be there with the money

Me:

Yes I know that but I am not going to be able to help you for quite a while, if I don't get a second job by Christmas. I will have to sell the car and there won't be any spare for you it is all allocated I cannot make you understand love I am not able to help you further and I do not know when I will be able too my survival is my survival plus the dog she is to old to deserve anything else

Beck:

It's ok

Me:

my visa is still pretty full and I have to find money to pay that offer just remember I am missing money you could not return that has impacted on everything I think you should try elsewhere if you can I will let you go you are thinking now bye honey chat later kisses

Beck:

ok babe I love you Bye   Kisses

Me:

Honey I have just received an email from immigration that I sent them addressed to you I will now forward this to you

Beck:

Ok babe

Me:

this is from Canberra and I have just received it bye love

Me: 20/10/2010

Hi Babe it is now 10pm here I am leaving for work in 15 mins

I will chat on line in 2 hours maybe earlier I will have changeover to do first. Hi babe I have missed you I am at wok now I will try you later otherwise tomorrow I sent you an email earlier but it does not appear to have gone sorry about that

Me: 22/10/2010

Hi Beck I am here now

Beck:

How are you?

Me:

I am fine sorry I am late it's a busy night at work I have compactor duty on Thursday that makes it later to be on line and I have 2 men crawling around the ducting cleaning the outlet fans none of them are cute

Beck:

Ok babe

Me:

are you going to gym?

Beck:

No

Me:

this is a rest day then

Beck:

Yes babe I am feeling so tired

Me:

I remember one day on the one day off build up on the day off after you break the muscle tissue down during the workout you're not used to being back at the gym yet

Beck:

Yes babe

Me:

are you still doing lightweights or is your hand able to bench press again ?

Beck:

I can't do light weight

Me:

then I guess you have to build it up slowly as your hand gets stronger

Beck:

Just light jogging

Me:

That's okay at least your balls will bounce around (lol) we have had the most wonderful Spring Day today

Beck:

Lol

Me:

I will need to go to the beach tomorrow as Saturday is cool and Sunday rain

Beck:

Oh really Ok babe

Me:

we have had some unusual weather pattern over the past 7 days even mid spring snow in the mountains that is very rare and flooding due to rain in Southern NSW

Beck:

Ok babe

Me:

I guess I better let you get on with your day I have a number of jobs to apply for and some new ones to check out

Beck:

Ok babe I love you I will chat with you later   Kisses

Me:

Kisses chat later I love you too

Beck:

Bye

Me: 23/10/2010

hi babe I am here waiting for you where are you ?

*I had received the following email from Beck on the morning of October 24*th *he was unhappy with my advice that I could no longer help him any further financially. He did remain on line and we continued to chat shortly after*

Beck:

My love how are you doing? Sorry I missed you online is just that I am not feeling good with all the crash is happened to us hope you understand me my love, hope to chat with you soon. Kisses

Me: 24/10/2010

Hi Babe I am here

Beck:

how are you doing my love?

Me:

I have just got out of bed I had no idea it was so late, I guess I needed the sleep how are you? It is a rainy day here today

Beck:

am not that good just woke up now to check my mail

Me:

Do you have the flu?

Beck:

nop babe just about this money stuff because I think about it a lot

Me:

I heard on the news about the UK having to reduce expenditure by 10 percent nationally to cut the national budget by 30 percent that will affect your benefit

Beck: yes babe

Me:

I thought about that last night and Josh mentioned it too.

It might mean the government will reduce the amount required to enter Australia

Beck:

that doesn't have anything to do with that

Me:

No I know it doesn't but they might change the rules to keep travel abundant have you been told what will happen to your situation yet? It appears at the moment that we are the only Western country that is stable and our dollar is expected to be more than the US Greenback very soon

Beck:

yes I think so babe

Me:

there is no need for you to worry yet let's wait and seer what the final offer is the Government here was going to do all sorts of cutbacks most of them never happened. Please do not get upset with the situation I know I am no more financial here but if I were you would be out of there you know that It will only make you sick if you worry honey I am still chasing my tale financially at the moment

Beck:

ok babe my love I have to go back to bed right now because its midnight here,

Me:

Sure honey I need a shower and breakfast Love you heaps babe kisses bye

Beck:

love you too bye kisses

Me: 25/10/2010

Hi babe! How are you?

Beck:

I am fine and you my love?

Me:

I am glad to hear you are good so I am fine too is there any news and government cut backs yet?

Beck:

no any news babe

Me:

you know what they say no news is good news I am having a busy day here so I may have to go away for a short time I will let you know. Are you going to Gym?

Beck:

I don't know yet it depends on my moods

Me:

you are not allowed to have moods they are bad, be happy my love

Beck:

ok babe

Me:

Trust me you will feel better that way worrying about what you cannot change is no good I have read up on this and am currently still reading the subject back 1 moment back now

Do you have a camera on your PC?

Beck:

I don't have I am using old model PC

Me:

I Thought maybe we could do video chat I don't have one either. What is the weather like there? we are having a cool spell with rain all week I went to the beach on Friday that was the only good day we had this is unusual weather for here in October. back 1 minute

Beck:

Weather for here is not steady but we don't have rain here

Me:

back now is it cold there yet?

Beck:

not that much

Me:

good if it's not cold you won't feel that bad

Beck:

but am so worried about what is happened to us

Me:

Honey what has happened has happened. If you can find a way to leave and come here you will find it If you have to stay and endure the 30 percent decrease yes it means plans for us are now

Different, there is no point getting sick or upset about it sometimes life takes strange turns. We still have the opportunity at the moment that things will work out as time goes on we will know we cannot be together as a couple I hope that time does not arrive it is only guessing at the moment even if that does happen you will always have a place in my heart I cannot simply stop loving someone that someone is you

Beck:

thank you my love

Me:

I am keeping myself happy here irrespective of the fact I am not financial I know I will catch up and irrespective of the fact you are not here with me please be happy honey you are a young good looking guy that should be plenty to be happy about and it might be a long way away 25000kms to be exact but someone loves you Me

Beck:

ok

Me:

I hope you are smiling now

Beck:

am happy to hear that from you my love

Me:

Good are you still promised the 2000 pounds or has that now changed with the UK economy? 1 minute

Beck:

I am still promised

Me:

back now, good see there is still something positive at the moment I am not going to be financial for you obviously for a while but all is not lost yet and I want to see you as much as you want to leave the UK

Beck:

ok babe

Me:

we just have to be resourceful and have faith have you just got out of bed for the emails I think I will send you an email with some pics of here and my home that might help put a smile on your pretty face

Beck:

ok thank you my love

Me:

I have to go honey there are thing I need to do I will see if you are on line when I get home in 4 hours if not no problem I will chat with you tomorrow afternoon after I have finished driving take care honey I love you kisses

Beck:

ok babe I love you from the bottom of my heart Kisses

Me:

bye for now

Me:

Hi babe sorry for the delay I was having dinner and Josh was pissed so it took a while how are you? The time here is 9:00pm I will check this screen every 5 mins. to see if you are there Honey chat to me

Beck:

Hi babe sorry I was not here how are you babe

Me:

hi babe, are you there? I will just drink my wine and wait

Beck:

yes I am here my love am here babe

Me:

Hi we are together now I hope gosh I left the chocolates downstairs never mind are you there? Beck where are you?

Beck:

I am here babe I go to the kitchen just now

Me:

Sorry I had a problem and lost the chat line but okay now I don't know if this is going to come to anything

Beck:

Ok

Me:

but I was contacted today about a loan I had previously applied for I don't want you to get excited as I don't know anything yet I have to fill out some forms and fax them from work tomorrow night is only for $1600

Beck:

ok babe

Me:

now based on the exchange rate being .60p I will need more but there is no guarantee on anything yet that is the best news i have tonight honey

Beck:

ok babe

Me:

I can tell you that it will be at least a week if anything happens

Beck:

oh ok babe you know I have no option than to wait

Me:

would you be able to go at short notice?

Beck:

yes babe

Me:

cool as I said please don't get excited I have not been approved yet is Kate with you?

Beck:

she is not here my love I really love all the pic you sent to me I just can't wait to be there with you

Me:

that's fine no doubt she will see this in due course

Beck:

yeah she will see

Me:

you won't believe how much of a broken branch I am standing on for us to be together I won't have an answer for you tomorrow night when we chat and I don't know exactly when if at all funds MIGHT be available

I also want you to promise me now that if I am refused you will not get in a mood I will have done my best.......
Well!

Beck:

I promise babe

Me:

Thankyou did you go to Gym yesterday? last time we chatted you were not sure and I encouraged you to go

Beck:

nop I think I will go today

Me:

love that with you (nop)

Beck:

brb babe

Me:

I am laughing at that now

Beck:

I went to toilet

Me:

I'm going for chocolate brb 3 secs ......back now I realize it was not a pee now (LOL) that was just a term I think you are feeling in better spirits today

Beck:

ok babe

Me:

so have you looked at the pictures I sent you yesterday they are this house my parents in the courtyard and the cars I drive in convoy

Beck:

yes babe I really love those pics very nice

Me:

there is also a photo of the view from the lobby of the RHP where I work

Beck:

I love them so much babe

Me:

It is to give you an idea sometimes we have all sorts of vision in our head and when we finally see something we are perplexed because it is not as we imagined so this is to avoid that problem

Beck:

ok babe

Me:

I would prefer the house to be in full Victorian Grandeur but the times and situation today do not permit this, Still it's not bad for 1886

Beck:

Ok

Me:

I am going to log off honey I have delivered all the best info I can. Just don't get excited yet yes I want you here yes I love you and we will chat tomorrow....Kisses honey

Beck:

ok babe I love you bye for now

Me:

bye

Me: 27/10/2010

Hi babe.

Beck:

How are you doing my love?

Me:

I am here at work watching a horror movie

Beck:

Oh ok

Me:

Have you just got back from the gym? I missed you online earlier

Beck:

I haven't gone to gym yet I was sleeping I am very tired today

Me:

That is because you have too much spare time, I find the same thing especially when I was only working 3 days a week

Beck:

Okay, babe. Kate has made the money to 2000 pounds I am looking for 1000 pounds only

Me:

You know what I was thinking today/

Beck:

What!

Me:

If you get a refund on the airline ticket and buy one with Air Asia you will only pay 600 pounds that means you have another 350 pounds available. The English guy that drives with us told me that's what his brother paid recently to come here, anyway that's good news. However you still need 1000 pounds and I am still struggling because I lost my returnable money I don't even get paid that much a fortnight so you still have to look elsewhere, I am not even at the saving stage yet and I don't have this month's car payment on time. What about some short term work is that possible even if you don't like it. You can go as soon as you have the 1000 pounds.

Beck:

I can't do any job for now I am not in the position.

Me:

What about saving your unemployment benefit for a month or so, or maybe your mother can pawn her wedding ring (or something) and we can send the money straight back.—just an idea!

Beck:

Babe, we don't have any option here again, if we have

I will not bother you again, but we have looked where we can to get money... no way just try to understand.

Me:

I do, and I can't help you either just remember, I lost money I still have to sort that out

Beck:

I know that

Me:

I am not fully recovered yet

Beck:

But remember I will bring the money back as I am coming

Me:

That doesn't help me I haven't got it to give you anyway

Beck:

Okay

Me:

I am really sorry but that is like trying to get blood out of a stone, there isn't any that is why I am worried and I wanted you here so things can be put right. If you take the option of the cheaper airline that means you only have to find 600 pounds

Beck:

My airline money will not be refund babe

Me:

Remember, you don't need any money here until you are working, it will also cost me more and Josh will pay less. You are right some tickets do not transfer money easily or even at all. I was hoping that was not going to be the case. Did Kate's father agree to give you another 500 pounds?

Beck:

No, Kate borrowed it from her cousin

Me:

I must thank Kate "Thanks Kate" I asked my brother, but he has just bought a new motorbike and spent what he had as well as borrowed more. Is the cousin looking to visit you here as well?

Beck:

No

Me:

I think everybody is doing what they can for you

Beck:

Yes babe, I just can't wait to be there now

Me:

I can't wait either, there is so much going on here now in this city, I hope you are here before Christmas. I still have that issue to deal with too, buying Christmas presents and paying for the party. My driving job will probably only last until the end of term in early December .and then I am screwed if I don't have another job

Beck:

Babe I want to be there ending of this month or early next month

Me:

So that would be good, we could include you on the Christmas party invite but you are still short 1000 pounds, .that has to come from somewhere. I thought of turning prostitute for you but they only want young boys I have visions of me as a skeleton stuck to a light post with a dead spider in a web that is running from my shoulder to the light pole, I can picture it now. haha…. I am still buying lottery tickets but no luck yet. Is Kate with you?

Beck:

No she not here

Me:

Oh okay. It would be easy if she could convince her dad for the rest that would be so easy

Beck:

She has tried her best on that

Me:

Yes I know that, it was just a comment. Can we sell your mother as a slave? (lol)

Beck:

Hahahaha (lol)

Me:

Don't let her see that I don't want to be a hated son in law before I get started

Beck:

Babe why can't you borrow money from your work mate?

Me:

Because they get paid less than I do, one of them wanted to help me out but they are fulltime employees and are paid a much lower rate per hour, that is why I work as a casual, I could not live on what they earn. As for the guys in the driving job they are only working 3 days a week so they are struggling too. I look after them but are not able to at the moment (they know how much I have given you), and my rich friends have already said "No" but they are more than happy to let us stay with them in the weekend cottage on the river or the other one in Port Stephens. It is not anyone else's problem anyway. Have you got anything you can sell that will give you the money? This must be very frustrating for you, it is for me I am wanting to be together now really

Beck:

Babe I don't have any option again I swear

Me:

Hmm I am not able to give you any anyway. I cannot sell the car I need that and I cannot ask my friend Rupertt, he does not know everything, and he would stop being my friend if he did.

Beck:

I think you should use the car to borrow money

Me:

We tried that twice remember, check the chats from last week. The answer was I had not had my driving job for 12 months so I was ineligible for a loan. I suppose you want me to sell a kidney?

Beck:

No don't do that my love.

Me:

Good, thank you I hadn't planned on it, also unlike Kate I don't talk to or see my cousins (unless it's at funerals) and none of them leave us anything anyway. We have never had much to do with either side of the family, my mother hates her brother. Beck if I had anything to spare, (or could get any), I would do so for you. I hope you understand that it is just not easy and not possible now. I know you are looking forward to coming, and I am looking forward to it too, but I also need a roof over both our heads when you arrive honey, and that is taking all the cash at the moment. I am still behind in the rent, I have caught up a little now but not fully and Josh does not know. He is very good to me and I must do the same to him.I guess this is in the "I can't think anymore tonight" pile. I will leave you with the thought, maybe something will happen or a change of luck. I think you should keep praying if that's what you do something will turn up, I don't know when, just have some faith and believe in your ideals. Concentrate you energy on us and be positive about it that is the best I can say at the moment. I love you, I want to be with you and I know you feel the same. kisses

CHAPTER 10

THE DIAMOND

The point of lure was now going to be realized. Beck was going to offer something that in most cases was too good to refuse, something of great value and rarity. He was hoping this would dispel any doubts I had and to make sure I found the extra funding for him. In fact the funding happened prior to me knowing of the new find. I was not happy about this new acquisition, where had it come from? Why, was it only mentioned now and above all I would now be eager to supply total funding. I believe this is genuine and now changes our relationship and maybe his immigration status, but as yet I had no knowledge as to exactly what he was bringing with him. As the chats progress I realize there are likely to be problems this I know from experience. From this chapter onwards the subject matter of the Chats changes, they will now be more dramatic.

There was now a third party and I began to receive desperate phone calls in the early hours of the morning.

Me: 28/10/2010

hi babe I am here

Beck:

how are you doing?

Me:

I am fine have you just woken up?

Beck:

yes babe I am planning to go to gym

Me:

that's good you haven't been for a couple of days

Beck:

ok babe so how are you doing?

Me:

I am here not feeling tired not bad at all actually I only have 4 and a half hours of this shift to go are you just jogging at the gym again ?

Beck:

ok babe yes babe

Me:

when will you be able to lift weights again ? Has the doctor given you a clearance date yet?

Beck:

in a couples of weeks

Me:

Cool

Beck:

Not cleared yet I think before a month

Me:

there are a lot of fine bones in your hand they take time to knit

Beck:

ok babe

Me:

I have been going over the contract that was sent to me and I am not happy with it so I don't think I can possibly use these people sorry I know that isn't what you wanted to hear

Beck:

Ok

Me:

do you want me to let you get ready to go to Gym ? I can chat later if you wish another 4 hours or so

Beck:

ok babe I have to dress up for gym now I want you to tell me the contract before I leave

Me:

cool take care have a good jog kisses bye

Beck:

Am here my love

Me:

hi babe

Beck:

My love, how are you?

Me:

I am fine are you okay?

Beck:

Yes babe and you Ok

Me:

I thought I might have upset you yesterday I didn't mean to if I did I am feeling a bit sad about us

Beck:

Why?

Me:

last night I read all your previous emails to me from the first one I smiled and was happy with all the lovely things you said

Beck:

Ok babe

Me:

I wanted to be close to you so I read all the emails not the chats only the emails

Beck:

Ok babe

Me:

I am really sorry that we are apart because of 1000 pounds there is so much going on here and so many jobs available for you right now I don't want you to miss out and it's funny I miss you but I've never met you

Beck:

You know I love you so much Babe I can't wait to meet you and start a new life

Me:

I love you to honey very much, when I was going to meet you from the airport I still have memories of the moment that never was

Beck:

I want to be there and work for you

Me:

I know it might be a while but I have now thought that while it would be wonderful I want to talk to you in person soon will you agree to that Just to hear your voice I know my heart will pound and my skin tingle ......that first Hi Babe what do you say?

Beck:

Yes babe, I have been thinking of you every time in my life I can't wait to be in your arms

Me:

I'm glad you have. You know the company I was dealing with over the past couple of days is dodgy but legal I have pre approval of $1600 that would be about 940 pounds there are two problems with that company

Beck:

??????

Me:

If I miss one payment they will charge me 48 percent interest for the remainder of the loan and the entire period is 12 months

Beck:

Ok babe

Me:

As I have told you my driving job will stop in Mid December when College breaks up and won't resume until mid-January I have to pay this during that period with one job only

Beck:

Ok babe

Me:

The other problem is how do we pay everyone back when you arrive if I have to have this back from you straight away as does Kate's dad and cousin.

Beck:

Yes you will have the money back from me as soon as I arrive and I will start a job over there so we can pay for our needs babe

Me:

If I go ahead with this I will need a commitment from you that you will be on the flight I can't lose any more money!

Beck:

Yes babe Go ahead and do that

Me:

I would like to have you here by the Christmas party Josh is putting on in December

Beck:

I will be in the next available flight Ok babe

Me:

you may be here earlier if the funds are released and if I chose to go ahead with this Okay!

Beck:

I want to be there soon Babe you don't need to worry again Just go ahead and do that I will ask Kate to tell her father and cousin that we will need the money by next week

Me:

I will be requiring a copy of the booking and flight details from you and I will not be sending the money via Western Union

Beck:

I want to start a new life with you my love

Me:

I will go to my bank as it will be deposited there and get a transfer fee it has to be cheaper than $115 so I will need your bank account details to do this

Beck:

I will send you the copy of the ticket babe

Me:

I know you don't like this but that is the only way this can be done this company are so dodgy I have to do it this way

Beck:

Babe I have promised myself to never ague with you again Western Union is the best Because the money will take 1 to 2 weeks before I will get the money

Me:

Honey I'm not arguing I just need it done this way because I can trace it if they try and be shrewd this company is not even in NSW they are operating from a house on the Gold Coast

Beck:

Nothing will happen to us this time my love

Me:

No I don't think so I bank with the Commonwealth Bank here that might mean nothing to you but they do a lot of transfers with Barclays Just have faith I am happy now that everything is going smoothly I know you bank with Ulster and I'm not sure how long that will take but I am going to get all the information before I do the transfer I have been advised unofficially 2 days but I don't know the charges.

Beck:

That's how it is babe and the bank manager will be asking for a lot of requirements. Babe I have told you to stop telling people about us Because I don't want anyone to play with our feelings

Me:

I haven't said a word honey I'm certainly not going to tell anybody about this venture I will be stoned to death by my friends where did you get that idea

Beck:

Ok babe

Me:

You will need to find out what questions the bank will ask and find out if you can have it fast you will need to send me the copy of the ticket before I send you the money because I don't want to go ahead with this until I know you are booked

Beck:

I just don't want to lose you Ok babe when do you think the money will be approved

Me:

As I mentioned I have pre approval that means in theory I have already got it but they have to check out all my information and then agree.

Beck:

Ok babe

Me:

they of course want the car as security

Beck:

As soon as you get the money I will book my ticket and I will send you the copy

Me:

It should only take 2 days to approve I was going to fax it to them from here at work then I changed my mind

Beck:

Ok babe

Me:

I can mail it but what is the point I can fax it here on Monday

Beck:

Just tell me when its approved so I can book the ticket

Me:

yes that's why I need you to find out when your bank will release it because the flight has to match the release Maybe we can send it to your mum's account if you wish

Beck:

Ok I will find out on Monday

Me:

I would hope that next weekend is fine or next week sometime I think that is something for you to work out once the money is available so will I

Beck:

Ok babe Next week will be fine

Me:

And sweetheart I would still love to chat with you over the weekend

Beck:

Ok babe Yes we will chat tomorrow

Me:

One more thing Remember this is preapproval that means I already have an unsigned cheque for that amount which becomes my receipt if approval is granted But there is a slight possibility it may not be granted I just want you to realize that so you don't get to upset I love you honey Kisses

Beck:

Ok babe

Me:

I am going to go home shortly and sleep on the nude beach all day it's 26 degrees here already at 6:20am bye

Beck:

Bye my love I love you so much   Byee

Me:

Byeee (lol)

Me: 29/10/2010

I am going out for drinks with the Germans, so I will chat with you later today about 10pm. Sydney Time. What I want to say is I need you to go to the bank today and get your answer and the time limit not on Monday. I am still waiting for an email from this company as to whether I will have the money by tomorrow, so I need an answer today. Kisses

Beck: 30/10/2010

How are you doing my love? I got your email late the bank would have closed now. I think I will do that first thing on Monday morning because the bank will not operate tomorrow, hope to chat with you soon. I love you from the bottom of my heart   kisses

Me:

That's okay honey I thought I would give it a try but it was too late, by the time you got the message it is now Saturday morning here and I don't have an answer for you

yet because the bark website is closed for maintenance.
(most frustrating at a time like this). I imagine the funds
are there I will check later. Yesterday I have arranged
for my internet barking account to be set up to transfer
funds internationally to a limit of $2000..The manager
also gave me a help desk card if I need it and the fee is
only $22 not $115. I think you will agree the extra cash
is better in our pockets. If I want the funds transferred
by the bank it will cost $33. He advised me this process
will take 2 days from my end here, and that some banks
in the UK will hold the funds as you said. The manager
is familiar with the Royal Ulster Bank and thinks they
will hold the funds for 24 hours before releasing them.
If the funds are in my account I can transfer them any
time to you but I think it would be better for you to
get the information from your bank first because, that
will affect the ticket date. The time here is 9:15am I
am going to have a shower and walk the dog. I will chat
with you tonight in another 11 hours. I love you baby,
keep smiling.

Me:

Hi Babe

Beck:

how are you my love?

Me:

I am fine and what about you?

Beck:

I am doing good my love!

Me:

I guess you are feeling really good now obviously I do have $1600 in my account for you I think that will work out to 940 pounds

Beck:

ok babe

Me:

but that will depend on the exchange rate, yesterday it was .58p not .62 as it was the week before

Beck:

that makes me really good

Me:

Are you feeling a bit excited now?

Beck:

Yes, babe I am, even Kate is feeling so as well

Me:

is she there with you?

Beck:

yes babe

Me:

Good I want to talk to her please

Beck:

ok babe she can read what you are writing

Me:

Okay, Kate Hi how are you?

Beck:

She's doing good she said and you?

Me:

I have a request of you please I would like you to send me an email when Beck is on the plane and it has left Heathrow then I will know he is on his way

Kate:

Ok

Me:

it will also be good for your email address to be here in this PC because he will want to email you anyway and, as for you young man Ok when you know which city you will be transferring at I would like you to do the same thing that way I know I can meet you.

Beck ok babe

Me:

I don't want to pay for parking at the airport for no reason

Beck:

ok babe I understand you

Me:

Thanks to both of you I guess you have read my email from this morning

Beck:

yes I did I have something to tell you about that

Me:

I won't send you the funds until tomorrow

Beck:

Ok

Me:

I think for your own sake you should confirm with the bank how long they will hold the money I know it will take 2 days here so your airline ticket should allow for those 2 days plus what your bank says I guess if it is only one day then you can purchase your ticket it is up to you what day you want to fly

Beck:

babe Kate say some bank take 1 to 2 weeks before they

will release the money, because it's an international transfer she said her uncle has sent money to her before it takes 2 weeks, but now her uncle is using Western Union to send the money to her

Me:

Well 2 weeks is fine by me I really need you to confirm this with them because if you have an airline ticket and they are holding money and not releasing it then I am sure theywill have complaints I know that some banks do hold money that is why I am asking you to check because as far as an international transfer is concerned this is Cash not a cheque that will take time to clear. The manager at my branch did say he was familiar with Ulster Bank and it should be no more than 2 days so let's see what they say on Monday. If it is 2 weeks then you won't have any problem booking the flight

Beck ok babe

Me

if it is 1 or 2 days you may have to take first available flight later in the week. Are you sure there is nothing else that has been forgotten because as well as wanting you to come. I am in the same situation again. I need to recycle that money and pay most of it back

Beck:

nothing else my love: everything is fine now ok babe

Me:

Good thank god for that I as well as you was so shattered last time I do not want to allow myself to experience that again

Beck:

yes babe that will not happen again

Me:

I would like to be really excited now too but I am going to be strong and not allow it until you arrive

Beck:

ok babe I can't wait to see you by next week I will be very glad

Me:

So will I but I ask that you respect my needs because of this company that funded me they were helpful in the fact that no one else would lend me money you know what it's like but they are legally dodgy so I want to deal with banks in case of a problem I am a cautious man

Beck:

ok babe

Me:

but that is a good quality, thanks honey

Beck:

I understand there will not be any problem my love

Me:

the other thing that occurred to me is if you bank does want to hold the funds for 2 weeks if you were to tell them you have purchased an airline ticket for tomorrow and you need to take the money with you there would surely be some consideration. This situation must have arisen before and somewhere there will be a precedent in place already. I want to ask you a question totally unrelated and that is do you prefer your man to be clean shaven or have a 2 day stubble?

Beck:

I love my man to be shaved, babe me and Kate are thinking you should get the money to me by Western Union that will be faster and we would not have any delay so I can book the ticket asap.

Me:

If I have to go to court then I stand a better chance if the receiving and sending was via a bank I used to work for a legal firm and I picked up all sorts of valuable info that is one of those gems

Beck:

Ahahahahaha my love pls. don't have any negative thoughts in your mind again

Me:

Honey that is not negative that is the truth I can even prove I worked there when you arrive I will show you my resume

Beck:

I will arrive to your place safety nothing will happen to us this time you know I can't wait to be with you there I know what we have been going through since all these days I want to be there and start a new life with you I need to start work when I arrive there, you know my mummy still owes the bank because of me, you don't need to worry let's make it work so I can arrive by next week nothing will happen to us this time

Me:

You will probably still be able to arrive next week that is what I was thinking anyway even with the bank transfer Josh is away next weekend so It would be good for you to arrive later next week I will leave that up to you If there is a problem at the last minute Western Union will be the only option but then you will not get 940 pounds because $115 is the sending fee

Me: 31/10/2010

Hi honey, why don't you just get a ticket for a flight that arrives next Saturday, morning it would be good if possible then we can decide how to spend the money. Are you happy with that?

Beck:

Okay I will do that and I will get back to you   kisses.

Me: 1/11/2010

Thanks honey. I want you here as much as you yourself do. For me it is important for you to be here next weekend at the latest or a weekend flight is okay. I look forward to the flight tomorrow and the bank information. Honey I want to know as soon as possible the flight details. I love you, be with me next weekend. Kisses.

Forwarded flight details confirmation London – Sydney (YOFRL1) one way GBP1025.87 Fri 5 Nov 10 17:30 London Heathrow Airport UK 19:55 Amsterdam Schiphol Airport Netherlands Class economy Flight number KL1026 Fri 5 Nov 10 21:00 Amsterdam Schiphol Netherlands – 16:15 Singapore Changi Singapore class economy Flight number KL0835 The waiting time until the next flight is 3h 50m Sat 6 Nov 10 20:05 Singapore Changi – Sydney KSA Australia class economy flight number QF 0320

Me: 2/11/2010

Hi babe that is a mouthful to look at, some of those email links do not open. Anyway I presume you are arriving on the Sunday morning at 6:50am because you are leaving Singapore at 20:05 and flying against time, so that should make it Sunday morning is that right? What did the bank say I will check the email at 7:30am tomorrow, otherwise I will be driving I have a new phone as of yesterday so I can read the emails better on now from there. We still have 4 days to get things organized. Tell me when you want the money because remember I can only draw $1000 per day. At the moment it is sitting in my investment account, I can move it to send it. I will try and chat with you sometime tomorrow evening Sydney time I guess you are really busy now getting organized. Chat later kisses

Me:

Hi babe I didn't know you were online I have been reading your email

Beck:

Am online

Me:

yes sorry about that I sent an email because I didn't think you were there How are you feeling?

Beck:

Am feeling good babe and have been waiting for you for so long

Me:

me too am I right with your arrival time as Sunday morning?

Beck:

I will arrive on Saturday babe

Me:

Oh Okay that is better

Beck:

Kate is here babe

Me:

I was reading the time and thinking Sunday but the time they have listed is local Sydney time then I will be there to meet you of course are you still doing 2 cases? Hi Kate.......

Beck:

Which cases is that my love. She said hello

Me:

Your luggage, are they large cases? I only have a Getz hope they will fit

Beck:

Yes babe only 2

Me:

cool no worries what is happening with the money am I transferring it or not what did the bank say

Beck:

Babe me and Kate went to the bank and the bank advised us to receive by Western Union

Me:

I guess you will need this by Friday at the latest. Okay I don't know what the current rate is last week it was .58p

Beck:

Ok

Me:

if it is lower you will get less I can send this on Wednesday I think

Beck:

Ok I understand

Me:

I will retrieve half the cash tomorrow

Beck:

Why not tomorrow my love

Me:

It might actually be Thursday here when I send it but time is on my side for that

Beck:

Ok I understand

Me:

Because I can only get $1000 per day and I need $1600 that is the regulations here

Beck:

Oh I remember babe

Me:

I was going to get some out today but I wanted to wait and hear from you

Beck:

Oh I remember babe Ok babe

Me:

so I will get $500 tomorrow morning that is okay because you will be asleep and the same on Wednesday by the time you get it, it should still be Wednesday

Beck:

Ok babe

Me:

There will be a shortfall on the 1000 pounds but as yet we don't know how much last week it was 60 pounds

Beck:

Tomorrow is Tuesday at your place?

Me:

yes

Beck:

At least you will withdraw the money on Tuesday and

Wednesday then you will send it on Wednesday is that fine with you?

Me:

Yes it has now just gone to Tuesday morning

Beck:

Ok

Me:

it will be sent late afternoon here when I have finished driving for the day

Beck:

It means you will withdraw today and tomorrow

Yes remember you are half a day behind so that gives me the advantage the post office is across the street from where I park the car

Beck:

Yes babe how is Josh? Hope you have told him I will arrive on Saturday Ok babe

Me:

I have mentioned there is a slight possibility because I didn't have the details in any case he is away this weekend with his dog that will be good for us

Beck:

Ok babe Wow

Me:

he goes away one weekend every month

Beck:

That will be very good babe

Me:

he goes to his sisters place to cook and clean for her she has two little kids

Beck:

Ok

Me:

Don't worry honey I am aware of the time factor

Beck:

Ok

Me:

once I send the money it takes about half an hour for you to receive it but it might take me a bit longer to send you the collection number

Beck:

Kate will email you as long as I am in the plane Ok babe you can do that on your phone

Me:

That's great has she got my email address?

Beck:

I will give it to her

Cool

Beck:

You can email the information to me from your phone

Me:

Yes I guess I can from my phone but I won't promise because I only bought it yesterday and am not that good at operating it properly but I will certainly try. I will also give you the expected weather forecast so you know what clothing to have as cabin baggage on arrival

Beck:

Ok babe that's good

Me:

Maybe, you are a bit more knowledgeable with android phones than me. I have never had one before

Beck:

Ok babe

Me:

I only set Gmail up in the phone today

Beck:

Ok

Me:

That's fine I will chat with you tomorrow honey lots of love to you and a big thankyou to Kate

Beck:

Ok babe Thank you so much

Me:

I will go to bed I have an early start I love you heaps

Beck:

I love you from the bottom of my heart Kisses

Me:

I am holding back on my feelings at the moment until I get that email from Kate

Beck:

You will babe Byeee

Bye

Me: 02/11/2010

hi Honey today I have half of the funds with me tomorrow I will send the full amount to you

I sent a message from my new phone to you today and that did work so I can email the MTCN number tomorrow you might not be online tonight to chat to and I am about to pull this PC to pieces to install hardware Honey your fight is arriving in Sydney on

Sunday morning not Saturday that is not a problem I am telling you so you aren't confused on arrival Take care chat tomorrow at work kisses

Me:

Hi babe I am here did you receive the email I sent?

Beck:

How are you my love. Yes babe I got it.

Me:

How are you feeling today, Hi Kate

Beck:

Am feeling so great

Me:

sorry for not being on line I had to install new hardware okay now, me too feeling great

Beck:

Ok babe

Me:

I will send the money tomorrow I don't' know how much it will be yet I will ask for 940 pounds and see how much that costs me

Beck:

Am feeling so good my love Kate is missing me already

Me:

I wondered if Kate was starting to feel that way you two are obviously so close

Beck:

Seriously babe

Me:

I know that is why I think she will be here to see you as soon as she can

Yeah she will by next year

Me:

I think that when you get here and pay back her dad she will use the same case and be here asap

Beck:

You know I need to work first to earn money

Me:

I know that I have a bill to give you too

Beck:

Yes babe

Me:

Let's get you settled and we can look for work I have a profile set up for me that emails me jobs every day we can use that for you too

Beck:

Ok babe

Me:

I told Josh you will be here on Sunday he will be away until late. He is fine

Beck:

Ok babe that's good

Me: I have just been rostered on for Christmas Day I am not happy because it is not my shift but the money will be very good for the day

Beck:

Ok babe

Me:

Anyway, these are things I can talk to you about later

Beck:

Ok

Me:

so far this week you have better weather than Sydney it is rain here for the next 4 days at the moment but that can change

Ok babe

Me:

you realize you are landing on Sunday?

Beck:

Yes babe

Me:

that should make more parking available at the international terminal anyway

Beck:

Ok babe

Me:

I will be there anyway babe

Beck:

Ok my love

Me:

is there any special diet you need for dinner I can cook for us I just need to know what you don't eat I guess after airline food you will be hungry

Beck:

I will be fine babe

Me:

Okay, is Kate with you?

Beck:

Yes

Me:

good, that is why I said hello I am familiar with the situation now

Beck:

She said hi

Me:

how is your mum with your leaving? Oh Hi Kate

She's feeling happy

Me:

Good

Beck:

Kate said you are taking me from her (Lol)

Me:

I can tell you we have both cleaned the house because it's like we have a guest. Kate my dear I am not taking this man from you I am simply loving him

Beck: (Kate)

Good She said yes she know that you truly love me

Me:

Kate he is still yours as well I think he will be chatting with you every night I will look after him for you until you get here then I might not let him go .Is she going to Heathrow with you?

Beck:

Yes she's going with me

Me:

I figured as much. Kate please don't have to many tears he still loves you he is just going to be further away

Beck: (Kate) Ok

Me:

I am glad she is going with you maybe you need someone to look after you until you are on the plane

Beck:

Yes

Me:

remember to see if you can get you phone unlocked before you leave that way we can get a Sim card cheaper and use it straight away

Beck:

She will email you as soon as I board the plane

Beck:

Ok babe

Me:

We had a very big internationally renowned race here today the Melbourne Cup I was hoping to make lots but I lost $6. I only spent $6 anyway

Beck:

Ok babe

Me:

So I will send you info tomorrow from my phone it will be in your in box when you wake up

Beck:

Ok babe

Me:

I will chat with you tomorrow night at work if you wish I can be online at midnight

Beck:

Ok babe

Me:

at the moment I have a screaming headache and will retire early

Beck:

Hope to chat with you soon Oh sorry my love

Me:

me too honey I think it's the situation of something finally happening with us that's all   Kisses

Beck:

I love you from the bottom of my heartKisses. Yes babe bye

Me:

Bye

Beck:

I know God have a reason for everything

Beck:

I love you too

Me:

I guess this has been part of our destiny with each other we have now known each other for 10 weeks and we have experienced emotions and trust with each other during this time

Beck:

Yes babe

Me:

I am still here through that and so are you so we will start a new life together and Kate will still always be part of that life

Beck:

Yes babe I can't wait to be there

Me:

I am looking forward to our first meet. I am trying to suppress the feeling but it isn't easy I know you will have a good life here honey and there will be new experiences too

Beck:

Yes babe I know that

Me:

Yes that is why you contacted me in the first place remember what you said

Beck:

Lol yeah babe

Me:

"distance is not a problem for the right man"

Beck:

Yes

Me:

I hope to be the right man Babe I will warn you now I tend to cuddle my man in bed to help me sleep

Beck:

You are the right man for me John. Yes babe

Me:

Thanks honey that is what I want. Us, and the end of time is a long way off

Beck:

Yes babe

Me:

I need to go to bed honey I love you chat tomorrow bye kisses

Beck:

Ok Bye babe

Me   3/11/2010

Hi honey, The MTCN number is 393322486! 950 pounds sent 20 mins. ago chat tonight.

Beck:

babe how are you doing?

Me:

I am here babe

Beck:

My love, how are you? Babe the MTCN number you sent to me doesn't complete

Me:

hi honey I am here I have just got home I sent the info from my phone and just checked it on the PC the last digit should be 1

Beck:
Yes

Me:

the number is 3933224861

Beck:
Oh ok

Me:

Sorry, I was on the road driving when I did this and I didn't realize that the last digit was an exclamation mark total 950 pounds that is all I had the money for

Beck:
Ok babe

Me:

it is not even 6 am in London you must have figured out the time I get home and got up early the exchange rate

today was .59p one p better than last week I am really
sorry about that I had no idea the number was wrong

Beck:

Ok babe

Me:

I sent that off this morning at 9:30 am

Beck:

I see

Me:

I did not want to have so much cash on me

Beck:

Ok

Me:

I figured you would have gone to the bank yesterday now
you will have to go today so now everything is complete
I have $80 to live on until Sunday maybe I should look
at prostitution (lol)

Beck:

Lol Don't babe

Me:

I will let you go back to bed now and chat at midnight.
Don't worry I won't turn to prostitution

Beck:

Ok babe

Me:

Sorry honey   Kisses

Beck:

Bye for now   Kisses

Me: bye

Beck: 04/11/2010

babe how are you doing?

Me:

I am here babe

Beck:

hi babe

Me:

hi babe

Beck:

how are you my love?

Me:

I am fine I am feeling a little different how about you?

-

Beck:

am doing great I am feeling so happy

Me:

that's good I'm sorry I missed you on line last night I have been on line all night waiting but that's okay I guess you are really busy getting last minute things organized

Beck:

yes babe you got it

Me:

yep that's what I thought

Beck:

babe do you know why I am feeling so happy?

Me:

as a suggestion it would be a good idea to include forms of ID in your baggage you will need to open a bank account and they are done on a point system where you need to have 100 points to open an account and a passport is not enough as one form I can sort you out in the short term but they can be opened in a day and I can go with you in Monday if you wish

Beck:

Ok babe, ok I will my love I have good news to share with you

Me:

that is really good what is that?

Beck:

babe I know this will change our life to good, my mummy want to <u>inherit</u> her diamond to me which is worth 100,000 pounds

Me:

What do you mean by that?

Beck:

she wants to <u>inherit</u> her diamond for me she wants to give me her diamond

Me:

Wow what is the diamond a ring or a rare diamond with specific facets that is a lot of money honey, I don't know what to say

Beck:

raw diamond which is worth 100 thousand pounds she said she will think about it maybe she will give it to me if I am coming on Friday. I will beg her to give it to me she loves me so much 'I know she will give it to me

Me:

What about your mum that is an incredible thing to do she certainly must love you I know you are worth loving. Where did she get the diamond?

Beck:

she inherit the diamond from her parent

Me:

If you come with it don't tell anyone, except I don't know if it needs declaring at this end Wow thankyou to your mother

Beck:

ok babe I only tell Kate she is very happy

Me:

Did you know about this or was it a surprise I am sure she is very happy

Beck:

It's a surprise babe

Me:

Tell her I promise to look after you and love you until the end of time Wow what a surprise that is

Beck:

I am very very happy now babe

Me:

Does Kate know about this you have every right to be happy babe

Beck:

I told her this evening she was very happy

Me:

This is an amazing thing to have happened I am happy
for you to honey

Beck:

babe I know the diamond can change our life for real
my mummy told me that she has been keeping it for
my future

Me:

It can change our life forever that is true. You now have
a new future and I am glad to be part of it. It will be
your decision what you do with this I would personally
place it in a vault at the bank until you decide, what a
way to start a future with me I am so honoured

Beck:

That's good babe I am very glad to hear that with you
babe

Me:

I guess there was something in our destiny after all honey

Beck:

yes babe

Me:

I am not going to be able to sleep easily today when is the last time I will be able to chat with you before you fly I think it will be this time tomorrow Do you want me to be online tonight which will put it about 9am for you or will you be too busy?

Beck:

That will be fine babe

Me:

Cool I will chat with you then tonight your time 9:00 am there are a couple of things to let you know like the latest weather details for Sunday morning. Have you got everything organized?

Beck:

yes babe

Me:

You must be busy and I am going to go home shortly say thanks to your mum and say hello to Kate I will chat later Kisses bye

Beck:

bye my love kisses

Me:

Hi babe I am here as I said how are you feeling today?

So now you are having a shower and soaping yourself up right? Beck Honey where are you!

Beck:

My love, sorry I was not here

Me:

Hi babe

Beck:

how are you doing?

Me:

really happy I can't explain the feeling but it is good

Beck:

yes babe same here

Me:

I want to ask you this rock stone (diamond) are you intending to bring it with you because that is not a good idea you will have to declare it and that means paying duty on it possibly at 25percent

Beck:

brb babe

Me:

okay are you there? Honey I have to go and eat dinner I have just taken it out of the oven I can come back in 30

mins send me an email if this is convenient otherwise
let me know when I can chat if you are too busy I will
send you an email with what I was going to say I am
going to stay on line but will be downstairs

Beck:

ok I will be online soon babe

Me:

cool I am okay with that give me another 30 mins please
Honey I will try around midnight tonight love you kisses

Me: 5/11/2010

Hi babe I will be home @ 10:30pm do not declare the
stone unless it is written on the declaration Love you
kisses

Beck:

How are you doing? babe Okay I will put the diamond
in my pocket babe I still have 7 hours before I will leave
for the airport I will check you online soon. I will chat
with you before I leave for airport   kisses

Me: 6/11/2010

Honey I have to go to bed, have a safe trip. I will see
you on Sunday and be careful with the X- ray Machines.
If you are carrying the stone wrap your hand around
it to cover it up, see you soon' And so my darling our
journey together has begun and in the morning we will

be as one. All my love to you I give with my heart and soul for as long as I live.

The Subject field reads "CONGRATULATION" the email is from Kate and reads

Kate:

Hello John, this is Kate I'm just back from the airport, I want to inform you that Beck is on his flight already he's on his way to your place now

Kate Sincerely

Me:

Thankyou Kate, our journey begins I will see you next year and I promise you I will look after him.

CHAPTER 11

THE KIDNAPPING

*It is Saturday, and I spend time making room for my new guest in the house. It takes about 2 hours to rearrange shelf and storage space. I empty one set of bedside drawers and one set of cupboard draws and create a personal shelf space for him. I drive to the liquor outlet and buy one dozen **Becks** beer in cans I do not even know if he will drink them but I decided to use the name from the carton for his shelving in the bedroom, I drink one can and fashioned the empty into a bud vase for one of the bunch of flowers that I have also purchased. (These of course were corn flowers as his favourite colour was blue). I had lined the top of his dresser with the rest of the Becks carton it did not concern me if it was too over top it was easily removed I just wanted the first impression.*

Sunday Morning has finally arrived and I cannot help feeling excited and eager to leave for the airport. The flight was due in at 6:35am and did arrive on time. I knew he had about 2 hours to clear Customs I also did not want to pay excessive airport parking. I arrive at the terminal and buy a coffee and proceed to view the arrivals board. I proceed to the correct gate and take up a vantage point close to the doorway. I am remembering now his words to me "I will know you" I had in any event told him in a prior email what I would be wearing. I looked around at all the identity signs being displayed and was thinking perhaps I should have carried a sign saying BECK.

As the passengers began entering I was eagerly checking all the single young men and the time regularly. After about an hour I decided to make enquiries (was he still in immigration because of the diamond?).it is common procedure worldwide for airlines not to divulge passenger information to the public, so I decided to go to the customs desk and enquire if he was still in the quarantine area. The lady on the customs desk did exactly what I had wanted, she rang immigration passenger arrivals and confirmed there was no one named Beck Hill still awaiting clearance and that all passengers from flight QF35 had been processed. I left the customs office.

*It was at this point I received an international call the voice on the other end said "**Mr John Osborne my name is Scott van Bowman from the International Diamond Council and I am calling on behalf of Mr. Beck Hill. We sent you an email to which you did not reply**"This email had in fact been captured in my Junk mail folder and asked If I knew of a person named Beck Hill He was very hard to hear as I was still in the arrivals lounge, of course this was now causing me concern and as I was walking back to the car alone it occurred to me I have heard that voice before was this the same voice as* *the officer from the Australian Consulate in London who had previously contacted me advising they have granted Beck Hill a two year work visa. On returning home I opened the email it included an attachment a letter written on what seemed to be official letterhead from the International Diamond Council in Amsterdam (IDC) these attachments follow.*

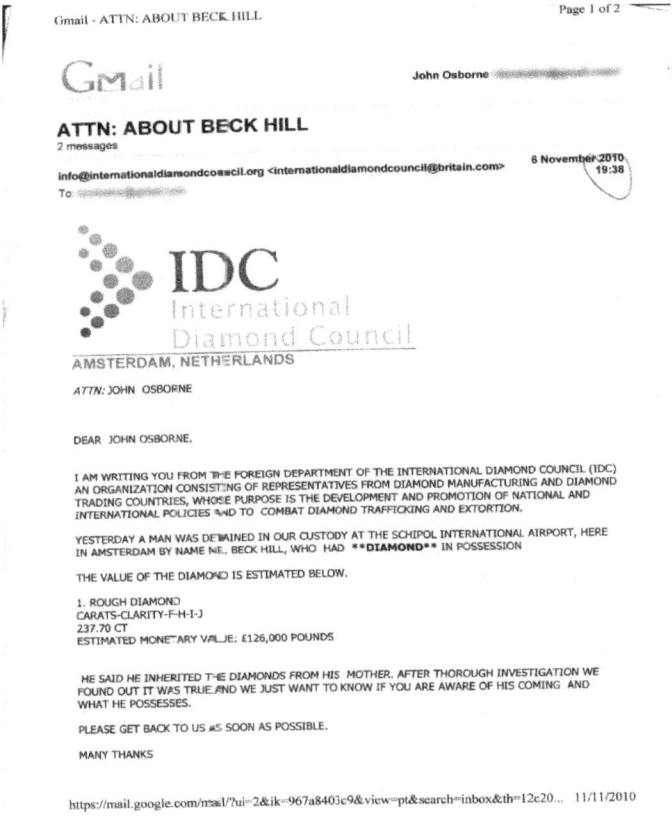

Gmail - ATTN: ABOUT BECK HILL

Page 1 of 2

Gmail

John Osborne

ATTN: ABOUT BECK HILL

2 messages

info@internationaldiamondcouncil.org <internationaldiamondcouncil@britain.com>

To:

8 November 2010
19:38

IDC
International
Diamond Council

AMSTERDAM, NETHERLANDS

ATTN: JOHN OSBORNE

DEAR JOHN OSBORNE,

I AM WRITING YOU FROM THE FOREIGN DEPARTMENT OF THE INTERNATIONAL DIAMOND COUNCIL (IDC) AN ORGANIZATION CONSISTING OF REPRESENTATIVES FROM DIAMOND MANUFACTURING AND DIAMOND TRADING COUNTRIES, WHOSE PURPOSE IS THE DEVELOPMENT AND PROMOTION OF NATIONAL AND INTERNATIONAL POLICIES AND TO COMBAT DIAMOND TRAFFICKING AND EXTORTION.

YESTERDAY A MAN WAS DETAINED IN OUR CUSTODY AT THE SCHIPOL INTERNATIONAL AIRPORT, HERE IN AMSTERDAM BY NAME ME.. BECK HILL, WHO HAD **DIAMOND** IN POSSESSION

THE VALUE OF THE DIAMOND IS ESTIMATED BELOW.

1. ROUGH DIAMOND
CARATS-CLARITY-F-H-I-J
237.70 CT
ESTIMATED MONETARY VALUE: £126,000 POUNDS

HE SAID HE INHERITED THE DIAMONDS FROM HIS MOTHER. AFTER THOROUGH INVESTIGATION WE FOUND OUT IT WAS TRUE AND WE JUST WANT TO KNOW IF YOU ARE AWARE OF HIS COMING AND WHAT HE POSSESSES.

PLEASE GET BACK TO US AS SOON AS POSSIBLE.

MANY THANKS

https://mail.google.com/mail/?ui=2&ik=967a8403c9&view=pt&search=inbox&th=12c20... 11/11/2010

Me: 7/10/2010

Kate, this is John. I don't know whether you know Beck did not arrive. I had a call from the International Diamond Council on my cell phone. I think the call is from the UK concerning Beck from someone by the name of Scott Van Bowman, or Scott Bowman. I missed the call he said he would call back, and for me to check my email for further instructions. I have not received any email from these people so I don't know what is going on, maybe you can sort it out. Regards John in Sydney

The situation was grave (well at least I thought it was) I was not intending to pay any money on principle. I was annoyed with Beck because I had given him all the necessary information concerning importation of such an item, I had done the research and found out the need for a Kimberly Certificate. I had even spoken with Australian Customs. I was increasingly more annoyed with Kate's responses, I was not seeing support from her and with each email reply I received from her I felt she was not only involved in this SCAM but implicating herself further. The next email I send to Kate straight after receiving the phone call from Scott Van Bowman. I was extremely angry.

Me:

As your email address has now been deleted I will send this to Kate's as she is obviously not as intelligent and "running with the boys" so to speak how many of you are there in this group?

There is you and Kate and the (Black?) guy that keeps ringing my mobile reading a prearranged speech. Your clue to me was diamond my clue to you was "I have worked with Customs". BTW both of you are bad spellers particularly Kate. We speak well in the Colony. This will also be an indication if you have both closed the email address sites down by now and Beck (if that's your name), you won't get bashed selling "cocaine" if you don't interfere with their individual territory

John

Gmail

John Osborne

1500 POUNDS

info@internationaldiamondcouncil.org <iinternationaldiamondcouncil@gmail.com>
To: John Osborne

8 November 2010
01:28

IDC
International
Diamond Council
AMSTERDAM, NETHERLANDS.

DEAR JOHN OSBORNE,

THE AMOUNT FOR THE CERTIFICATE IS 1500 POUNDS.

PAYMENT CAN BE MADE VIA WESTERN UNION.

ALL PAYMENT SHOULD BE MADE TO

RECEIVER'S NAME: ADAM WINKELMAN

LOCATION: LONDON, UNITED KINGDOM

IT IS NOT OUR DUTY TO HELP HIM SELL THE DIAMOND, THE DIAMOND IS BECK HILL'S PROPERTY AND HE DECIDE ON WHAT TO DO WITH IT.

THE CERTIFICATE IS REQUIRED AND IMPORTANT. ONCE PAYMENT IS CONFIRMED, THE CERTIFICATE WILL BE ISSUED AND BECK HILL WILL HAVE ALL THE RIGHTS ON THE DIAMOND AND WILL BE THE BONAFIDE AND RIGHTFUL OWNER OF THE SAID DIAMOND.

GET BACK TO US AS SOON AS POSSIBLE

MANY THANKS
SCOTT VAN BOMEN
IDC

Me: to info@internationaldiamondcouncil. org. 8/12/2010 Thankyou, are you aware he should have 3000gbp with him this is money I sent him as a requirement to enter Australia .I have proof with Western Union receipts, this is what he received. Tell him I give him permission to use that money if he has it to release him.

Thankyou. Mr. Van Bowman.

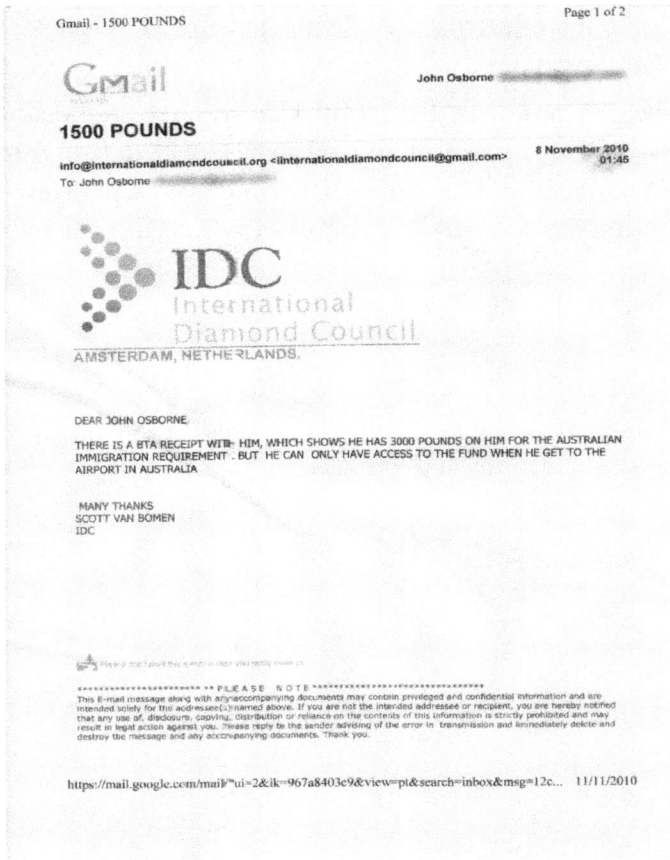

Page 1 of 2

Gmail

John Osborne

1500 POUNDS

info@internationaldiamondcouncil.org <iinternationaldiamondcouncil@gmail.com>
To: John Osborne

8 November 2010
01:45

IDC
International
Diamond Council

AMSTERDAM, NETHERLANDS.

DEAR JOHN OSBORNE,

THERE IS A BTA RECEIPT WITH HIM, WHICH SHOWS HE HAS 3000 POUNDS ON HIM FOR THE AUSTRALIAN IMMIGRATION REQUIREMENT . BUT HE CAN ONLY HAVE ACCESS TO THE FUND WHEN HE GET TO THE AIRPORT IN AUSTRALIA

MANY THANKS
SCOTT VAN BOMEN
IDC

https://mail.google.com/mail/?ui=2&ik=967a8403c9&view=pt&search=inbox&msg=12c...   11/11/2010

Me to info@internationaldiamondcouncil.org

8/11/2010 Thankyou Sir

I am sorry to worry you but this is something I do not know. I have contacted his best friend in London for help her email address is ktcollins24@gmail.com

Regards, Thankyou for your time and help John Osborne

Me to <u>info@internationaldiamondcouncil.org</u> Dear Mr. Van Bowman

Please advise Mr. Beck Hill I do not have the ready cash for this payment and will not be able to find this amount easily. The stone needs GST of 10% paid on it on entry into Australia in any case, so it needs to be sold

Regards John Osborne

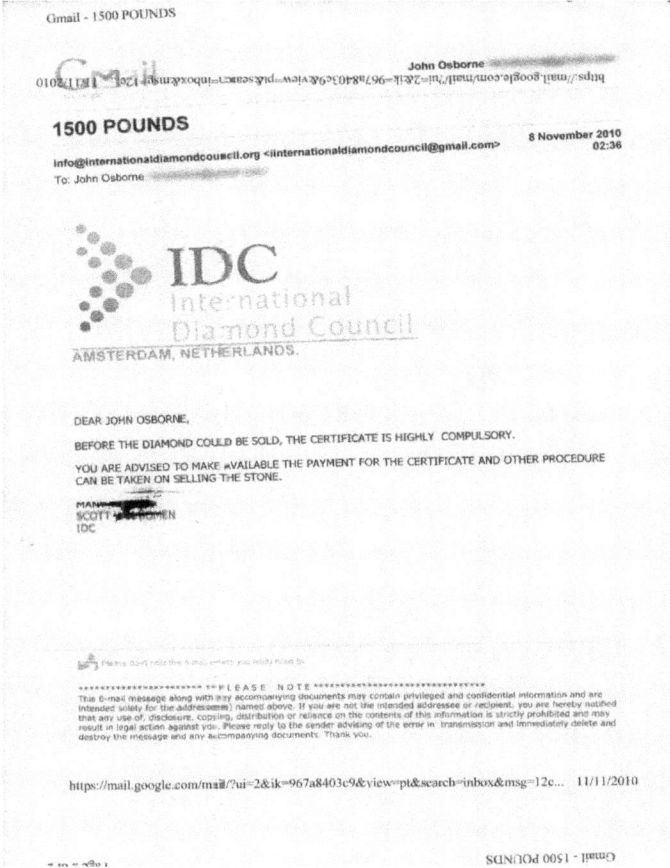

Me to info@internationaldiamondcouncil.org

Dear Mr. Van Bowman can you please advise me how much time I have to pay 1500 pounds before you send Beck to trial

Thankyou John Osborne

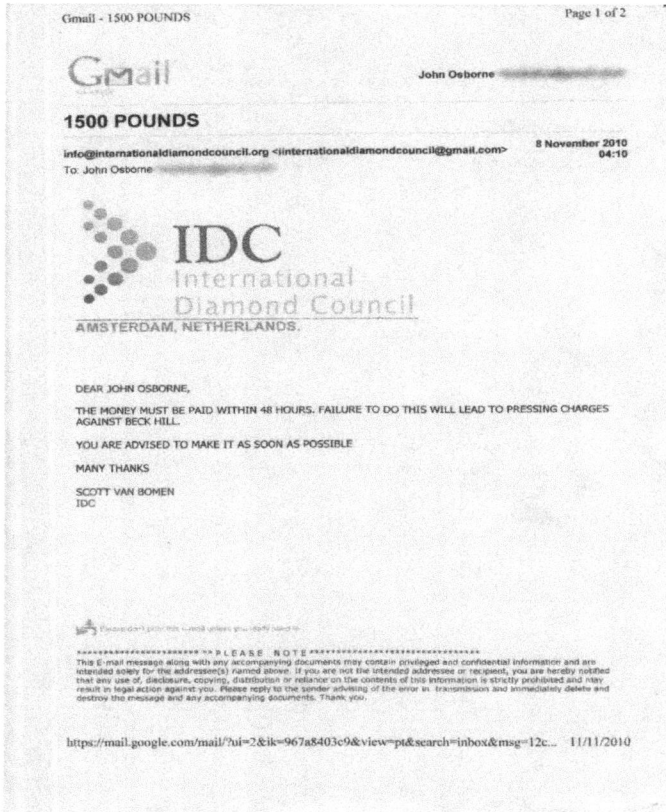

Gmail - 1500 POUNDS   Page 1 of 2

Gmail   John Osborne

1500 POUNDS

info@internationaldiamondcouncil.org <internationaldiamondcouncil@gmail.com>   8 November 2010
To: John Osborne   04:10

IDC
International
Diamond Council
AMSTERDAM, NETHERLANDS.

DEAR JOHN OSBORNE,

THE MONEY MUST BE PAID WITHIN 48 HOURS. FAILURE TO DO THIS WILL LEAD TO PRESSING CHARGES AGAINST BECK HILL.

YOU ARE ADVISED TO MAKE IT AS SOON AS POSSIBLE

MANY THANKS

SCOTT VAN BOMEN
IDC

*********************** PLEASE NOTE ***********************
This E-mail message along with any accompanying documents may contain privileged and confidential information and are intended solely for the addressee(s) named above. If you are not the intended addressee or recipient, you are hereby notified that any use of, disclosure, copying, distribution or reliance on the contents of this information is strictly prohibited and may result in legal action against you. Please reply to the sender advising of the error in transmission and immediately delete and destroy the message and any accompanying documents. Thank you.

https://mail.google.com/mail/?ui=2&ik=967a8403c9&view=pt&search=inbox&msg=12c...   11/11/2010

Me to info@internationaldiamondcouncil.org Dear Mr. Van Bowman

Do I advise you of the Western Union MTC number when I send the money, and as there is a time difference can you allow for that.

Thankyou John Osborne

Gmail - 1500 POUNDS

1500 POUNDS

info@internationaldiamondcouncil.org <iinternationaldiamondcouncil@gmail.com>
To: John Osborne

8 November 2010
04:26

IDC
International
Diamond Council
AMSTERDAM, NETHERLANDS.

DEAR JOHN OSBORNE,

EMAIL THE MONEY TRANSFER INFORMATION AS SOON AS PAYMENT IS EFFECTED.

MONEY SHOULD BE MADE VIA WESTERN UNION TO

RECEIVER'S NAME: ADAM WINKELMAN

LOCATION: LONDON, UNITED KINGDOM

MANY THANKS
SCOTT VAN BOMEN
IDC

************************* **FLEASE NOTE *********************************
This E-mail message along with any accompanying documents may contain privileged and confidential information and are
intended solely for the addressees' named above. If you are not the intended addressee or recipient, you are hereby notified

https://mail.google.com/mail/?ui=2&ik=967a8403c9&view=pt&search=inbox&msg=12c...   11/11/2010

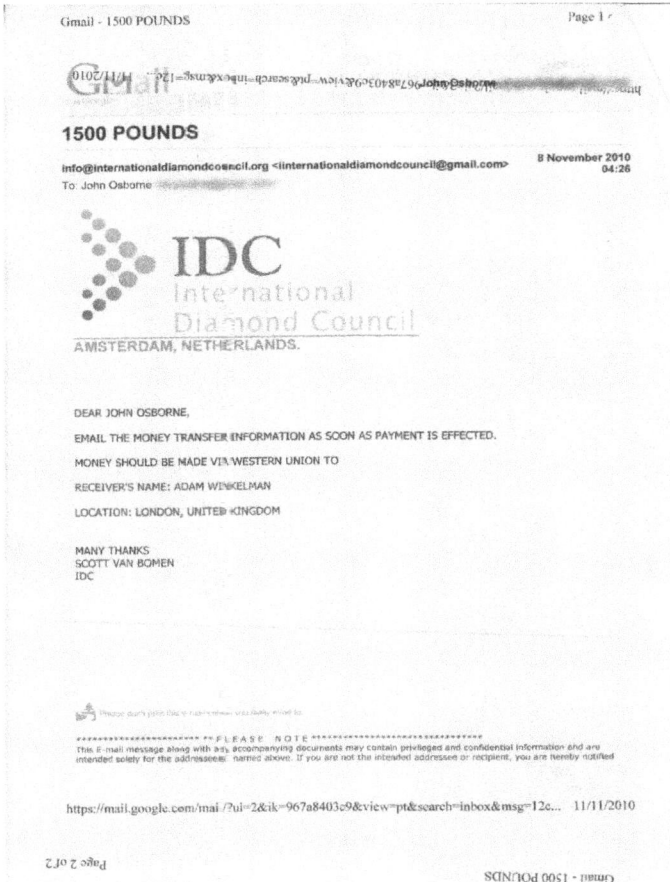

Me to info@internationaldiamondcouncil.org

Thankyou. It is 4:00am here at the moment so this may
be another day away Thanks John Osborne

*I now needed to explore which options were available to
me, how do I proceed now! Who is Adam Winkleman?,
and why does he need 1500 pounds wired to him in London*

when Beck is in custody in Amsterdam. Is he with the British Mine Authority that supposedly affected Beck's arrest or.is he a diamond merchant in the High Street

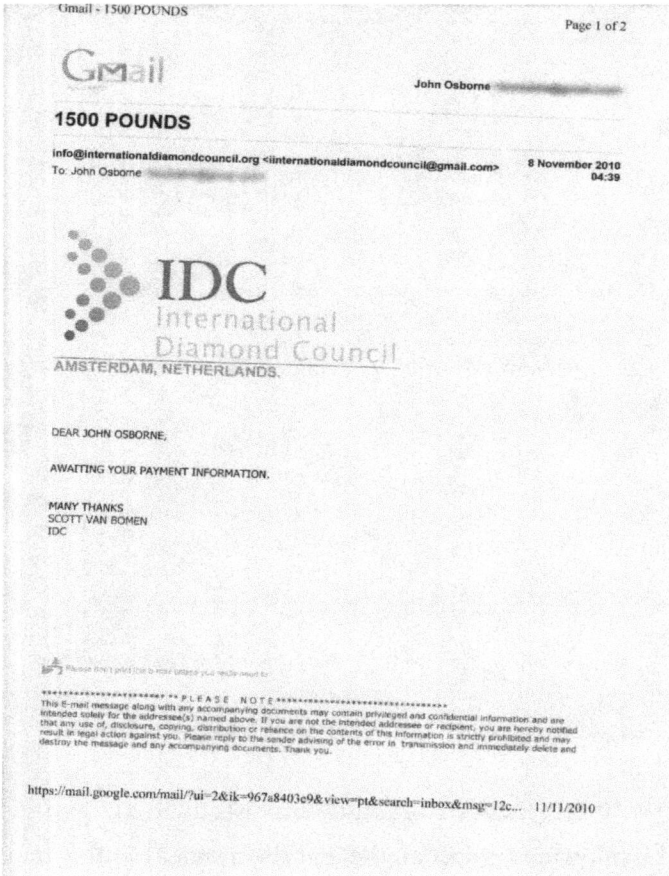

Me to ktcollins24@gmail.com Hi Kate

My source of the funding to release Beck is not convinced this genuine. I am not convinced this is genuine. To start with there is no such organization as The British Mine

Authority and he is emailing via a separate website. If Scott Van Bowman is an officer with the IDC it will be tomorrow before any results are known as this is being checked now. There is a possibility Beck will have to be charged which means the end before the beginning to our relationship. My source of funding is also a dear friend and businessman and he has also noticed that the man in London to whom the money is to be paid, is not listed in the London phone book. So this does not sound good for Beck at all at the moment. Regards John

Kate: (ktcollins24@gmail.com)

John I just wish I could come up with the money, but there is no way, no luck from dad. I'm afraid if we can't come up with the money Beck will be in trouble. I have done my findings and I see it is genuine. We just have to do all we can to get Beck out of this.

Me:

I don't know why they did not call his mum does he always get in this much trouble? I am not going to get involved with him if he keeps this up. I don't think I can help, my friend is checking all the details as there are some things wrong with these messages. We are waiting on a reply from the company as to the authentication of Scott Van Bowman

Me:

Hi Kate, Beck has just rung me (8:00pm) he is still very upset, he is crying and hard to understand, My contact will not supply the funds for his release now Beck will be charged. I don't know what that will mean. I have other parties investigating this as well at the moment and there is no way we need to pay $1600 pounds, the certificate he requires is a Kimberly Certificate which costs 25 pounds for a diamond that size. That is anywhere in the EU. Even Australia requires the same certificate. He needed to have the certificate before he travelled with the diamond, I told him that. The Certificate can be obtained from the foreign and commonwealth office Government Diamond Office Room W3 135 King Charles Street London SW142AA it is called a Kimberley Certificate for the export of raw diamonds around the EU. I am very sad, for I suggested that he use the 3000gbp he has to come to Australia, but that is only accessible when he arrives here which may now not happen. His only crime is travelling with this diamond without the certificate. This matter needs to be referred to London, I can do nothing here. They already admit he owns the diamond. My contact is waiting on information back from the IDC and the identity of Scott Van Bowman. I have alerted the AFP (Australian Federal Police) here but not given Beck's name. Someone is trying to scam some money here and we at this point believe it is someone in the IDC. I don't know if paying for the certificate and sending it to him will help, but maybe you can call the diamond office on 020-7008 6903/5797 or email Goo@gnet.gov.uk. My colleges are waiting on information at the moment but there is no way an organization like that would request a Western Union transfer to London with the MTCN number to a third party, (themselves). I hope this helps him and you. I don't know what is going to happen now. Regards John

Kate: (ktcollins24@gmail.com) Hi are you there?

Me

Hi Kate, I was at work and have just got home. He is very upset and I think with me too. I was not able to help anymore. I don't know what will happen now, I would appreciate an update when you find out he may have to go home.

Me: 9/11/2010

Hi Kate, sorry I missed you if you were online may check later .I have a question for you do you know who this man is in these photographs, is it really Beck? I'm not sure they are all the same person.

I have attached all of the photos of Beck he sent me.There is no proof that Kate has ever seen what he sent me and I was hoping for clarification that this is truly Beck. Certainly I cannot supply any payment, but I would like to have his identity confirmed Sadly Kate does not respond to this request, I also have the feeling that she is somehow involved possibly another member of the scam group. As his best friend she is not terribly upset with his arrest and certainly is lying when she says "I have done my findings and I see it is Genuine". My friend whom I asked to help is a businessman and commodity trader who goes to Amsterdam he is the one who supplied me the information and checking the verification of Scott Van Bowman

Gmail

John Osborne

1500 POUNDS

info@internationaldiamondcouncil.org <iinternationaldiamondcouncil@gmail.com>
To: John Osborne

9 November 2010
08:59

IDC
International
Diamond Council

AMSTERDAM, NETHERLANDS.

DEAR JOHN OSBORNE,

WE ARE STILL WAITING FOR YOUR PAYMENT. WE WILL NOT RELEASE BECK HILL UNTIL THIS IS FULFIL.
AND IN THE NEXT 24 HOURS BECK HILL WILL FACE THE CHARGES PRESSED AGAINST HIM.

MANY THANKS
SCOTT VAN BOMEN
IDC

Please don't print this e-mail unless you really need to

*************************** **P L E A S E   N O T E***********************************

CHAPTER 12

THE RANSOM

The next contact from Scott Van Bowman is 13th November .Beck has now been in custody 8 days. The email received from Scott Van Bowman at the IDC dated November 8th allows 48 hours for payment to be effected, today was November 13th. I obviously was the target for the extra funding they were trying emotional Blackmail and in any event I do not have any credit at my disposal. I do not sleep easily at night and receive several phone calls from Beck at 4;00 am on consecutive days, these are of course not on night shift roster days and the only time there is any personal contact. The first phone call is nothing more than heavy sobbing and cannot be understood, subsequent phone calls, reveal a voice with dual accent while there was a notable English accent there is also another accent, that I am not able to determine, so Beck was withholding information about himself from me.

Regardless of not having any finance and regardless of being suspicious of a scam with several players I was intending to obtain something for the expenditure I have already out laid.so I pursue an avenue of trying to obtain credit and after several unsuccessful attempts and the desperate phone calls I seek help from friends of mine that may lend me the cash. I was extremely embarrassed in so doing but now I had someone else able to help check the credibility of the situation. I supplied them all of the IDC emails knowing that they would start checking immediately. They are cautious businessmen and do not part with money easily.

Kate: 10/11/2010

How are you? John are you there? We need to chat please

Me:

Hi Kate I am here and I want to talk but I am hurting really bad too you know. I am sorry Kate I should have asked you how are you coping, my apologies.

Kate:

It's okay have been waiting here for long time I don't really like all the emails you sent to me because you make me feel down a lot and you don't even care about Beck anymore, you care about your friends and your money now because Beck got to this problem because of the love he have for you and it seems like you don't appreciate him again you know Beck is not happy where he is now he really need our help, are you there? Beck is really frustrated right now, you don't need to listen to your friends' advice because they may be jealous of you, since you are having Beck with his diamond…John, you need to sit down and think about this, you need to take decision on your own, because Beck has been crying for help a lot. I have tried all my best but no way yet. Please John you need to do something about this. Remember how much Beck loves you. Hope to read from you soon.

Me:

Yes I am here that might be fine what you have just said but you have told me nothing in that conversation, I want to know where he is and what is happening.I do not have Beck as you know and he cannot bring that diamond into Australia without paying 10% VAT. I told him that before he left the UK. I have worked in the industry for long enough. What is the name of the institution where Beck is being held, and when is the court date? Kate I would like to know what is going on with Beck, remember I took a loan out for him.

The reason I do not want to report this straight away is because I don't want to ruin his chance of making a new life here if that is what he truly wants, but I have no proof and I am also hurting pretty bad but to hear him crying and begging me for help was never part of any deal to bring this man into my life, but it hurts me because I have feelings for this guy.

Kate:

Beck is in Amsterdam and the man who asked for 1500 pounds is willing to help us out of this even Beck's mummy she's really sick now because of this issue I'm here in their home now. Beck is really hurting a lot I haven't told him that his mummy is not feeling fine because I don't want him to hurt himself more.

Me:

Thanks Kate, all I am after is the truth I am not sure either whether he is in Amsterdam but I will tell you what I know

Kate:

He is there John

Me:

Yes that is possible I guess that means he was on his way to meet me but until now I have had no idea.

Kate:

Yes he was on his way to meet you. I sent you an email that he already boarded the plane

Me:

For the past 3 days at 4:00 am I have had a call from Beck on my cell phone, it only lasts for one minute and he is crying. As we have never spoken (something that I had previously requested us to do) I could not understand him he was crying too much and that made me upset.

Kate:

John, Beck is really hurting where he is and I am so scared.... I don't want him to hurt himself. That's why

I don't want to tell him about his mummy she's really bad John that's why I am here in their place.

Me:

Yes that's a good idea.

Kate:

I know you really love him, but he always warned you not to listen to your friend's comments about your relationship. You know Beck can never play with your feelings John

Me:

I was wondering if that might happen, but again I had to establish if it was real. I want you to know Kate I meant every word of what I said to this man when I said "I will love you till the end of time" but I have been treated very badly by him and now that he is under arrest in Amsterdam I did not create this situation and I do not have anymore money to help. I would like to know why the guy in Amsterdam is willing to help out because I have reasons to believe that this is not the police that are holding him. He did say to me on his last call that he is going to court, so who is this guy now. Once you have been charged it is not likely to be reversed. Do you know of a man called Scott Van Bowmen I have been speaking with him!

Kate:

You know he really loves you for who you are and he is willing to start a new life with you. He hasn't been charged John but they said if we cannot pay the 1600 pounds he will be charged by next week

It seems now everyone is claiming commission what was a fee of 1500 pounds is now 1600 pounds I cannot help but think are there other people in this chain all intending to add 100 pounds and I have broken the link.

Me:

I cannot help, I spoke with this guy about selling the diamond and /or using the 3000 pounds he has on him that he needs to come here to Australia. (if that is true). Scott Van Bowman told me that the 3000 pounds is tied up in a receipt, only accessible when he arrives here, that may be true I don't know, I said to him "sell the diamond"

Kate:

Yes Beck told me that

Me:

He said it cannot be sold until there is an ownership certificate. I told him I didn't believe him the only certificate needed is the information I have already sent to you.

Kate:

John, don't let them sell the diamond because Beck's mummy told me the diamond was worth over 200,000 pounds

(now… the price of the diamond has increased by 74,000 pounds in 10 minutes conversation)

Me

The value of the diamond keeps increasing, first it was 100,000 pounds the fake documentation from the IDC states 126,000 pounds.

What I understand from Beck is that his mum inherited the diamond from her mother.

Kate:

Yes is inherit diamond

Me:

So this is an antique heirloom that should have its own paperwork outside the Kimberly Contract? So why was I told to send 1500 pounds, which is now 1600 pounds to Adam Winkleman in London, and, send the MTCN number for Western Union to Scott Van Bowman in Amsterdam. Do you have any idea? I think Beck is caught up in something sinister. Because as soon as I mentioned to Scott Van Bowman that I had lawyers on the case they stopped asking me for money. That tells me that as yet the proper authorities do not have Beck in custody. But that is not my feeling because of how he is calling me for help. I would like him to call me and pass me on the guard or officer that is with him while he is talking to me. Has he called you?

Please pass this on if he has

Kate:

Okay I will do that we just need to help him out of this John, that's very important

Me:

Kate, there is nothing I can do financially that is why I am prepared to bring this to the attention of the AFP (Australian Federal Police) but I do not want to ruin his chance of coming here so that is why as yet I have not and that is why too I wanted to chat with you. Has anybody in Amsterdam told you what the charges are against Beck? Because it seems that if he was going to be charged he would have been by now. That!!! is very suspicious, I'm sure you would agree.

Kate:

Yes I do but it's like they want to help him out that's why he hasn't been charged now.

Me:

Yes that is it exactly, someone on the take there. I don't think he's in police custody

I think he's in the custody of an organization that does consist of one Black man that goes by the name of Scott Van Bowman for this purpose. You see he does not exist as an employee with the IDC. We have checked that here is Australia. What I want to suggest to you is to let him be charged, because there is no charge. They are only after money this will bring the bandits under scrutiny and they will flee. That is what I have thought all along because, Kate if he had been arrested in Amsterdam his mother would have got a call and all of this matter would not have come to my email address. That is guaranteed I have even been to Amsterdam previously.

What I am saying here and I have no one with me, nor does anyone know of this yet is that SOMETHING is WRONG and we need to alert the authorities (police) in Amsterdam which by the way now because of me is classified as an International incident. I don't know if Beck could tell you but the first email I got from Scot Van Bowmen was about my instructions for receiving a diamond. The message went into my spam box so I did not know it was there and Beck had been in custody 24 hours before. Scott Van Bowman called me to tell me to look in my in box. That message came while I was at the airport waiting for Beck

Kate:

Okay

Me:

They told me 48 hours then Beck called and said they will charge him. Then the next night when he called he said he was going to court. If he has done nothing wrong he should be cleared. I am telling you this because I don't know if you are aware of it.

Kate:

I just don't want Beck to be hurt. Please you need to think about this John.

Me:

I don't want him to be hurt either Kate but he has $5000 of my money and a raw diamond supposedly worth 200,000 pounds I would think any judge would be able to arrange for any payment to be taken from one of those sources, so you see Kate he is actually richer than you or I at the moment. Does he have the diamond or have they taken it from him?

Kate:

I think the best way is follow their instruction because they own Beck now he has the diamond

Me:

No I can stop that I will proceed with my plan and go to the AFP, because he is not going to come here I want my money back, like everyone else. That is sad for him. I also believe that the robbery of the first money sent has something to do with this issue, don't you?

Kate:

I don't John go ahead and do what you had in mind but I am just concerned about Beck a lot

Me:

I want him released as much as you do and we are both concerned. Has anybody told you when he will be released? Do you agree with me that we can help him legally, we cannot keep paying money Kate this is how these bastards work.

Kate:

They want the money so they can release him

Me:

Bullshit. Why does it have to be paid to Adam Winkleman (a jeweler not in the London phone book because that has been checked) and why would an organization like the IDC an International Diamond Trading House use Western Union. I don't think so.

Kate:

John, try, understand anything from overseas has to go through Western Union

Me:

Why would this diamond, that his mother got from her mother need a certificate from Adam Winkleman, who probably, wasn't born when the diamond was mined, also are you aware, they told me Beck was arrested at Schiphol Airport by the British Mining Authority well question 1 is what would the British Mining Authority be doing at Schiphol unless there was a tip off and question 2, do they have the power to arrest anyone, and above all the last question is how come there is no record of the existence of this organization. You see I have done some checking too. That is why I think we should alert the authorities

Kate:

Yeah you said it right but they may want to hurt him that's why we need to let this go.

Me:

That occurred to me as well no we won't I won't let this go. I want these Bastards NOW and I want to do it if possible without ruining Beck's chances of his work visa here but Kate, you need to go to the police sweetheart please for his mum's sake as well as his. Don't let them terrorize you. I will back you up from this end, and report the crime here. For Beck's sake, there is no guarantee they will let him go anyway

Kate:

John I am not gonna do that with you because whenever I spoke with Beck he always beg for help, so I don't want anyone to hurt him please don't do that don't let anybody hurt him I know what I am saying please John

Me:

Okay that's fine but that is what they want you to do I am not so sure. I don't want him hurt either, what do you suggest then? You know, if the money is paid (not by me anymore) they will only want more and more, and we still don't know what the payment is for

Kate:

They will not want more John just try to understand if the money is paid they will release him.

Me:

No I am sorry this is Bullshit. Did you receive an email with the IDC Logo From anyone? or Scott Van Bowmen?

Kate:

Nop

Me:

Well I did and the interesting thing with it is there are no contact details of any kind on the Letterhead, this is a cut and paste job. I can forward it to you if you wish. So now we have the IDC: being used for identity fraud as well. What has he done to get himself into this situation? Has anyone told you anything? The only crime I see him having committed is leaving the UK without the Kimberley Certificate This is one of my fields of expertise Kate. I told him about this before he left for the airport. So to me if he is going to be charged it will only be for travelling without this permit. The way to find out is to contact the Dutch Embassy and ask what the circumstances are and if they ask for the name give it to them if they can find nothing, then he is in more trouble than we thought. because no one knows he is being held it's like being kidnapped. What do these people want, and how do they know about the diamond when he was a transit passenger at Schiphol. He should not have alerted anybody because he would not have gone through the X ray unit so there is something really wrong, how long will it go on? Will they release him ever? But how come he went through the X ray unit at Heathrow with the diamond in his pocket but was arrested by a nonexistent organization at Schiphol inside the transit barrier that's an inside job, maybe someone Beck spoke to, perhaps you would have an idea

Kate:

I don't have any idea

Me:

How else would anyone know about the diamond? Would you like me to forward you all the emails I have received from the IDC?

Kate:

Yes you can do that John I have to go now to pick my kids up from school but we have to do something about it. I don't like the idea of reporting it to the police because this may link to hurt Beck.

Me:

You know when I sent an email to Scott Van Bowmen and said I had my lawyers on the case, the IDC stopped sending me emails which is more to the point why.

Kate:

I think it better we give them what they want so they can let him go

Me:

That is what they want you to do absolutely not! If you

are concerned for him you will alert the authorities, maybe they are thinking as far as you are concerned you are a woman on her own she will do what they want don't give in. Are you happy for me to go to the Dutch Consulate here? I will be relying on you for support you know. I can start the process at work tonight I have 8 hours to kill

Kate:

I don't want you to do that I am not happy with that John

Me:

Okay we need to get him out but I will not pay money he has enough with the diamond, what else do we do? Does your father know what has happened? How did Beck get himself into this in the first place someone was out to get this from him, Who? Kate this is really serious he needs help as we both agree. This is ransom they are after you know that don't you. There is therefore a kidnapping situation and you need to go to the police

Kate:

They will hurt him if we do that John. Please I don't want that to happen to him

Me:

They might kill him if we don't We don't want that to happen either. If you care for him (and I know you do) you must let them know, they are experts

Kate:

We just need to pay them the money so they can release him

Me:

As I said, once I started threatening them with lawyers they backed off straight away never! I will not give in, to many questions remained unanswered. Thankyou for helping me, we need to work together and help him. I have to go to work now I can chat with you tomorrow and send you any information I have received when you want it.

Kate:

Okay

Me:

I have not slept well for 4 nights over this. I will chat to you later Kate thankyou. Just to mention I have been sending Beck a lot of emails I have had to get my feelings out, if you have his password maybe you need to read them and clear them. Thanks Kate Bye

My friends whom I had asked to help have contacted me advising that Scott Van Bowman does not exist. They have perused all the documentation I sent them and have found many anomalies with the text. They are confirming to me this is a scam and I now have to let Kate know.

Me

Good afternoon Kate.

I am sorry to annoy you but you are the only contact I have now and as you are in contact with Beck I guess you can relay the message to him. He did not call last night but then as I am not able and not going to help I guess he won't. What I want to say is this. "Yesterday you told me I had Beck and the diamond, so I am thinking you honestly believe he is still going to come to Australia: you can pass on to him if he ever really intended to or, left London I will have a place for him" But I don't believe this is so I don't know if your father and your cousin gave him money to come here. The person that claims to be Scott Van Bowman said he had a receipt cashable in Australia only for $5000. Again I don't know if this is true. You have read all the emails and know what we have said to each other, including him saying he will not let me down. I don't know why you would think I should fund his diamond SCAM, but clearly this is linked to the previous bashing and theft of the initial cash, again My Money. During all of this he has given me nothing but false hope. He professes to be a Christian, but is not living by their code and he has not even considered my feelings at all at any time. From where I stand this is NOTHING BUT A SCAM.from the start and so I need to report it as an international diamond smuggling ring, and give his name to the Australian Federal Police. Who deal with these issues As he has $6000 of my money I have the right to do this, and I have 4 Western Union Receipts all requiring an ID for collection. So there is something traceable after all. I have even asked you questions that you have not replied to again making me think there is something you are protecting so perhaps I should include your email address, of course this will be linked to a gmail account that will be traced back from your end. I don't even know if his real name is Beck or yours is Kate, or even if you really were going to come here and see him. Is he being charged with something that may prevent him from coming? So before I report everything to the AFP I will wait for you to tell me what the Fuck is going on!! This might also be a case of my identity theft that is why I print out all these emails. I even have his original profile from the dating site and when I told him he was not happy. Hopefully my mobile service provider will be able to supply the police with the incoming phone number anyway.

So I will wait 48 hours then I will start proceedings to claim my money back and report everything as a diamond scam and identity theft. This will also involve Adam Winkleman who wanted 1500 pounds for no reason. Remember I have not sighted any diamond so it might actually be a Cocaine ring you are all involved with. Then there is the fraudulent IDC documentation, they have been contacted by separate party with a different email from here advising of this.

So now you know my intentions, I would appreciate something returned, because if he goes to court, and I am contacted I will spill all to the authorities. Clearly there is a group involved, at least one black guy, and one American Guy, (possibly the same guy). All will be revealed

I really do hope he is going to be okay as I really did want to love him. I don't know if he ever intended to love me and that is sad. I have a feeling this is first offence if it exists at all, but let him know that I did not understand much of his conversation because he was crying to heavily on two occasions. He can always ring me and talk to me when he is free he has my details.

Thanks Kate awaiting your reply. John

Kate:

John we need to talk about this, because you are having a bad thought on your mind now. .

Me   11/11/2010

Hi Kate

http://www.smartraveller.gov.au/zw-cgi/view/travelbulletins/international.scams

I just thought you might be interested in this article from an Australian Government bulletin explaining how travelers are kidnapped. Read paragraph 5 maybe Beck is a victim of this. What I have done is send a brief report of the situation (without using his name) to an organization that we report scammers to (the ACCC), because they have advised they will give me the correct government department or independent body that will be able to assist in a matter like this one. I will speak with you later.

398 | J MOREWOOD OSBORNE

Me

Hello Kate I'm sorry we couldn't chat. Do you have any news? It is a week tomorrow. Has he been charged? I would be grateful for any info. If you haven't heard from him maybe the worst has happened these people have the diamond and he has been murdered I don't want to think that but you don't know. How is his mum doing? I have some info that will help. The British Consulate will pay the fee for anyone in this position and you have to pay them back but that will mean his visa will be cancelled.

I am trying to do a deal with Visa Credit Card to see if I can fly there and have enough to pay for the fee but as yet no word from them, .that is why I would like to know where they are holding him. I will try and chat later bye for now

I don't know where the email address to the international diamond council @ Britain has come from The link is broken. Maybe Beck is still in the UK as I have suggested. If Kate is associated with this group then she will be displeased with my actions and undoubtedly see it as an obstacle to overcome. If not she should be grateful for the concern I am showing and the effort I am taking. This should be happening from London but strangely is not why not. I am now giving false information in a bid to secure some answers and will have to wait and see how successful this is going to be

info@internationaldiamondcouncil.
orginternationaldiamondcouncil@britain.com
12/11/2010 Me

Mr. Van Bowman

As you are aware ¯ was unable to arrange funds for Mr. Beck Hill. I am concerned for his safety and whereabouts. I would like to be able to contact him, can you advise the outcome of his fate, and his contact details will he be imprisoned or fined? He has monies owing to me in his PTA which would have paid his 1500 pounds on arrival in Australia. I have a receipt on my person for reclaiming the 3000 pounds from him, can you please provide address or contact details

Regards John Osborne

Me

Kate, I feel sick he will go to jail for three months in 7 days .Can anybody there help him! I have no money. I don't like Scott Van Bowman at all he is a sarcastic prick.

It was a lovely sunny Friday morning when I received the next communication. I had finished nightshift for the week and was lying naked on the sand watching the yachts in the harbour without a care about Beck. I decided to send the previous email spontaneously at that time. This generated the following reply

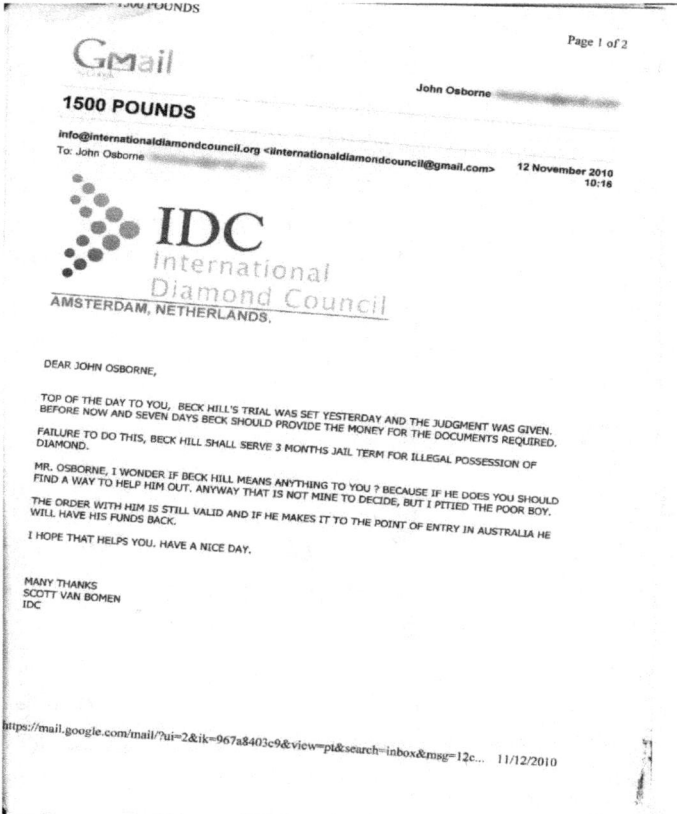

Me to info@internationaldiamondcouncil.org

The British Consulate will pay the funds, that is what they do.. Beck should be told of this

Gmail - 1500 POUNDS

Gmail

John Osborne

1500 POUNDS   12 November 2010 11:06

John Osborne
To: kate collins <ktcollins24@gmail.com>

---------- Forwarded message ----------
From: "John Osborne"
Date: 12/11/2010 10:30 AM
Subject: Fwd: Re: 1500 POUNDS
To: "kate collins" <ktcollins24@gmail.com>

> ---------- Forwarded message ----------
> From: "info@internationaldiamondcouncil.org" <internati...
>
> Date: 08/11/2010 4:36 AM
> Subject: Re: 1500 POUNDS
>
> To: "John Osborne"
>
>

IDC International Diamond Council

> AMSTERDAM, NETHERLANDS
>
>
>
> DEAR JOHN OSBORNE,
>
> AWAITING YOUR PA...

>
>
> SCOTT VAN BOMEN
> IDC
>
>
>

https://mail.google.com/mail/?ui=2&ik=967a8403c9&view=pt&search=inbox&msg=12c...   11/12/2010

Me: 13/11/2010

Kate You or his Mum need to contact the Embassy
immediately'

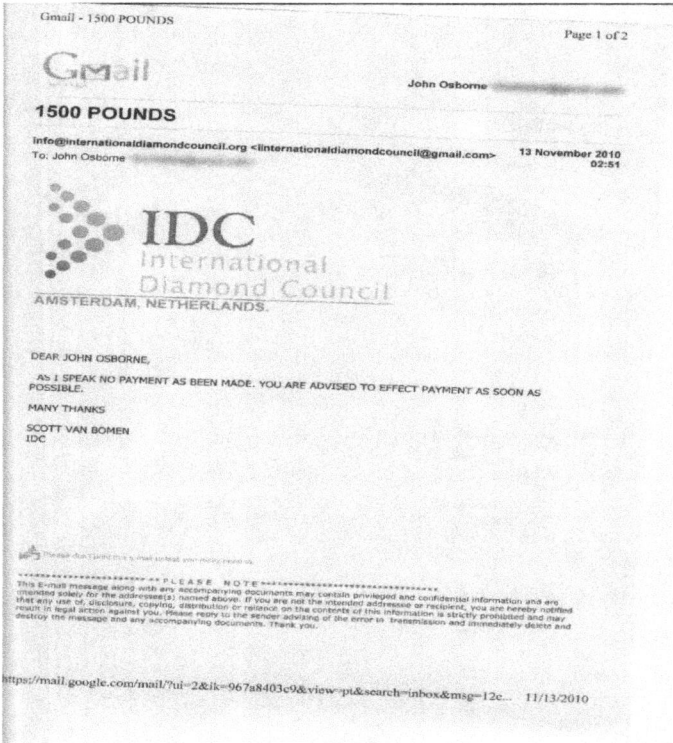

Me to info@internationaldiamondcouncil.org Dear Mr. Bowman

As I mentioned earlier, Beck is a British Tourist travelling abroad with insufficient funds to pay a local fine he knew nothing about. The British Embassy will effect payment when they are advised, and in case you have not advised him I have forwarded the email to his friends and family in London.

From my point of view this is now an international incident and is being treated as such by the authorities here. Investigations are underway here. So at this point Beck will have to do 3 months jail if no one helps him. Does that make it clear enough for you!

Enjoy your day John Osborne

This letter obviously had some effect, it was in the early hours but the phone rang and Beck was on the other end. He did advise me he was going to go to court and I needed to pay the money urgently He was not crying but the speech did seem rehearsed. Sadly my phone was not charged and the conversation was too short. I had made the decision the report the incident to the Police and the Federal Police. In Australia the local police are in charge of handling these situations as advised by the ACCC (Australian Competition and Consumer Commission with who I had previously been in contact.) So early on the Sunday morning I went to my local area command with a written explanation and these emails. A young Female Officer attended to the matter and I took a seat and waited for them to familiarize themselves with the incident, there were two officers reviewing the pages as there was by now a substantial number of emails all around three pages in length.

She reported back to me after 20 minutes to advise that there was nothing they could do, and that this would not even be a matter for the Federal Police, that I should have no more contact with this person.Both the officers reviewing my case were ex Federal Police and they advised the situation. I did in any event complete a fraud report form

I downloaded the faq document concerning this type of scam known as a 419 Scam. I emailed to Kate.

Having been rejected now from almost all avenues I decided to try the only three options left. to tell my story to the television current affairs programs A Current Affair & Toady Tonight, Scotland Yard and the British High Commission. The current affairs programs have website for your story but again sadly I had no reply from them, or Scotland Yard because there website required a report number from the local MET before the webpage would open. I now had no option but to contact to the British High Commission, from whom I did receive a reply advising me to have no further contact with this person who is of "Unsavory Nature". Surprisingly I receive an email from Beck who was sending a message from his email was this Kate? No it was Beck

Me: 16/11/2010

Where are you? I don't know what is going on

Beck:

Am here in Amsterdam.John, what are you doing to me. I was told Kate is very sick now even my mummy.

Please I want you to help me out of this. I beg them before they let me have access to internet. Are you there John?

Me:

Hello Kate. This is John I have just had a call from Beck but my battery was flat I was able to chat with him he told me he begged them to use the internet they give him half an hour but he didn't get to chat much. How are you feeling he tells me you are sick as well he knows his mum is sick too .I guess you told him, how is she doing? He is telling me he was told I would help him actually I gave no such instruction to Scot Van Bowman. I kept writing on the chat line even when Beck was not replying in case he does get the printout or can read it later,

All I know at the moment is he said these people will hurt him: that suggests to me that he has not been detained by the police or any legal authority. I will not pay any money to Adam Winkleman in London. Maybe you have information he was trying to talk to me about.

Anyway I thought I would share this information with you, and I will hear from you if you want to talk. I hope you are feeling better soon.

Beck: 16/11/2010

Hello John, are you there?

Me:

I am here my phone battery died are you there? What the F%#@k is going on Beck?

Beck:

Yes I am here John

Me:

I want a number to call you and I want it now!

Beck:

I don't have a phone with me they only give me phone to call you.

Me:

All I know is (I haven't heard from Kate) your Mother according to Kate is sick, she wasn't going to tell you. The only message I have had is from Scott Van Bowman. Do you know of him? They are allowing you internet access? Are you still there?

Beck:

Yes they allow me babe

Me:

Yes I just received the message on my phone which is charging now, are you reading this? Okay, maybe you can't answer that, it gives me the answer anyway

Beck:

No they are not reading

Me:

Glad they are not. This is what I have done. I have been to the Police and the Federal Police about the situation and shown them the emails. Who is Scott Van Bowman, because this guy is a prick, and if he wants a battle of words with me with the messages he sends, the he has chosen the right person. I have been advised you will be imprisoned on Friday, is that true?

Beck:

Am not aware of that

Me:

One more thing, the IDC (who send me the emails advising you are in custody) is a body of people meeting under the banner of The International Diamond Council Head Office in Antwerp, no official address in Amsterdam. This is a copy and paste job they are using to send emails. I think it's meant to scare me

Beck:

Okay?

Me:

This Scott Van Bowman, who by the way does not have a Dutch Accent and cannot spell SCHIPHOL correctly is an idiot!

If you are in trouble, and you have a PTA receipt for arrival in Australia, why have I not heard from the Dutch Authorities? Have you been charged with anything? Well? Because frankly, obviously I am REALLY PISSED OFF does that help the equation. Okay why don't you just send me a message with what you want to say, there is something more I do remember in one of your emails, and until you or Kate or someone in authority tells me what the FUCK! is going on I don't care. Okay I am still struggling financially because of YOU, and oddly enough I still have the wardrobe space empty for you, but I will change that next weekend.

You know you won't be able to come here now if you have a criminal record. I will let you go you can email the truth and your apologies as soon as you feel like it I am actually going to cook dinner now.. If they allow you to call me, yes I am happy to talk to you and any of the fraudsters in the IDC that want too. Okay love, I will send a message to Kate and see if I get any sense out of her, By the way, but thanks for asking I really was looking forward to us together, so my feelings have been shattered by you again. Sorry Honey but I am angry. I will listen to you when you tell me the truth okay are your 30 minutes up yet? I want someone there in Amsterdam in authority to contact me okay. Are you still there? Hmm, just incase you get to see this, and in case you have not been told, it is your right as a British traveler overseas to go to the British Consulate for them to pay the fee of 1500 pounds. So if there is anybody that is in authority concerning Beck, he has the right to the British Consulate you should all know that.

Your Ref: 1032398
Contact Officer: Emma Corvisy
Contact Phone: 1300 302 502

Australian Competition & Consumer Commission

9 December 2010

GPO Box 3131
Canberra ACT 2601

Mr John Osborne

23 Marcus Clarke Street
Canberra ACT 2601
tel: (02) 6243 1111
fax: (02) 6243 1199
www.accc.gov.au

Dear Mr Osborne,

I refer to your letter of to the Australian Competition and Consumer Commission (ACCC) received 11 November 2010 regarding the possible dating scam you were involved in.

The ACCC cannot give you advice on specific offers; however the correspondence you have received shares the hallmarks of known scams. In such cases the ACCC urges you to **ignore the offer.**

More information on the different types of scams can be found on the ACCC's Scamwatch website (www.scamwatch.gov.au). Additionally the ACCC has produced a publication titled *The Little Black Book of Scams* that provides information about some of the more common scam types.

The information you have provided and other complaints received through our scam watch website greatly assists us to monitor scam trends and take action where appropriate. The analysis of this information also enables the development of targeted educational campaigns and provides valuable information for the ACCC's ongoing cooperation efforts with other government agencies that have a role in scam enforcement and prevention.

Thank you for contacting the ACCC and bringing this to our attention. Should you have any questions in relation to this matter or wish to order a free copy of *The Little Black Book of Scams*, do not hesitate to contact the ACCC on 1300 302 502.

Yours sincerely

Emma Corvisy
Correspondence Officer
ACCC Infocentre

To: The British High Commission
Level 16 Gateway Building

Macquarie Place
Sydney

To whom it may concern

Dear Sir

I am writing to you in the hope that you will be able to assist me or if not advise me on this matter Mt name is john Osborne and I am an Australian Citizen. Who has made arrangements with a British National to visit Australia on a working visa.

While there is possibility of there being a scam involved I am concerned for this man's safety as I am receiving phone calls from him in Amsterdam begging for help and very upset. He left the Uk on Friday November 7th from Heathrow KL1026 at 5;30 pm for Amsterdam. There after a 1 hour lay over to board KI0835 to Singapore and then after a 3hour 50 min lay over to board QF 320 to Sydney due November 7th 06:50.

According to information I am receiving from someone Proclaiming to be with the foreign office of the International Diamond Council in Amsterdam He has been arrested for carrying a very valuable raw diamond a family heirloom without a certificate of ownership, and therefore I a crime .It cannot be sold without this certificate..

While I believe there is the possibility of a scam my friend is only begging me to pay the certificate fee to avoid detention. This I believe would be something the British consul would effectively do. However I am receiving phone calls and now from the international diamond council as well as emails advising me to pay 51500 pounds via Western union to someone in London while the MTCN control number is to be sent to someone in Amsterdam. Last Tuesday and today I have received a short distress call from my friend in London who has then been allowed to contact me via email advising he is being held against his will but not by the Authorities. And he is talking of suicide. I on the other hand am still being req2ested to sent money from a group who will not identify themselves. But have advised they will hold my friend until the money is paid how ever long it takes.

I believe I have been contacted by these people as my address details were with him and used for information on the work visa. I have been advised he still has this visa and a Btu receipt for cash to allow entry into Australia.

The details I have are : : Name Mr.; Beck Hill Address 112 Levita House Camden living with his retired and widowed mother whose name is Sarah. He is 31 years old las at September and was issued a 2 year work visa in early September by Australia House London There is a flight booking reference number YOFRL1 KLM office.

I would I hope you will forward this to your London office for Iinvestigation. I do not have any other contact s or details for Mr. Beck hill ad would be happy to put my mind at rest and that no identity theft has occurred with my details as well

Thankyou John Osborne

http://www.met.police.uk.reporting crime/specific crimes.htm Metropolitan Police

http://www419scam.org/419faqq.htm FAQ doc 419 Scam

www.police.nsw.gov.au NSW Police Service Fraud Report

CHAPTER 13

THE TORMENT

The following letter was written to his "Captors?" I intended to make it clear in this letter that I would not have any guilt and I intended now to walk away from the entire situation. I did not want anymore emails requesting 1500 pounds to Adam Winkleman. The letter is a fabrication on my part and the situation did not occur with me, however the situation is real and did occur to others in that period. It is also intended to let who ever needs to know that I will not put up with any more of this crap, and more importantly that I was not stupid. (This I had to justify to myself after the stupid action of sending monies).I have no way of knowing if in fact Beck really was being held to ransom, or whether there were a group (including Adam Winkleman) enjoying my money in Amsterdam. I had hoped for some resolve for my own satisfaction for the money I had outlaid, but now I was willing to accept I would receive nothing at all,however this did not stop communication requesting payment continuing

Beck:

My love are you there my love?   19/11/2010

Me:

I am here

Beck:

How are you babe!

Me:

Hi Beck I am here what is going on Beck?

Beck:

I am here in Amsterdam babe this people are treating bad babe pls. help me out of this

Me:

Who are these people they are not the police correct? You do know I have absolutely no more money don't you I would have helped you out

Beck:

Babe I think they are not but am suffering a lot here I am I did cried every days

Me:

Has Kate been to the British Consulate? I have been to the police here but they told me it is a matter for the British I have been contacted several times by someone claiming to be from the IDC International Diamond

Council Scott Van Bowman He told me that tomorrow you will go to Jail for 3 months because you do not have an ownership certificate for the diamond is all of that correct?

Beck:

Kate is not feeling fine I haven't talk to her

Me

I have sent her a message to this effect but have had no reply. How long are you allowed to talk today? They told me that you were arrested by the British Mine Authority on arrival in Amsterdam is that correct? Are you there? Are they reading this today?

Beck:

Yes babe they are

Me:

Fine then understand this guys I will get Kate to contact the British Embassy I will Contact the Dutch Embassy here and I will go back to the AFP here as well I know you are all after a cut of his diamond and you are all crooked bastards so I will get it fixed, you can also tell Scott Van Bowman (if that is his real name) that he is a bad speller and I have contacted the only member of the IDC in Amsterdam on his website last week and told him what is happening with the company logo of the IDC His name I think is Erik or Earnest starts with an E. As this is my money you have taken from Beck I am also getting involved Do You pricks understand ME

Beck honey, I will sort this out as much as I can I need Kate to do so as well. Are you going to prison tomorrow? I suspect you have removed Scott Van Bowman already

Beck:

Babe why are you written such things to them? They are treating to kill me now.

Me:

Because they are bastards and I want them to know

Beck:

They don't taken the BTA money from me pls. stop this babe they are seeing everything and they are treating to kill me

Me:

I was told the BTA money has been taken from you. I was also told that you cannot access this money until you come to Australia I was told this By Scott Van Bowman I have an email to prove it. Can you use the BTA money to pay for the certificate?

Beck:

Yes I have access to the BTA money when I come to Australia

Me:

That is what they said

Beck:

The BTA is not here with me

Me:

Where is it in Australia?

Beck:

Airport

Me:

What exactly do you have to pay for? is it an ownership certificate for the diamond that is what I was told but I cannot understand why you would need to send the money to London if the certificate is required in Amsterdam and, how come you got kidnapped at Schiphol and not stopped at Heathrow? in Amsterdam you would be inside the international barrier and not have come through the x ray you see what I mean I smell a rat an inside job from the UK. You should think is there anybody you told before you left home about the diamond. If you were arrested legally you would have been advised that the Embassy will pay the fee, because they WILL here they asked me for your passport number do you know it write it now I can go back to them.

Beck:

Babe I am very tired of this shit I am, I know how I feel, you just need to see how I look now, I am less weight and a lot of crying everyday and I was thinking about my mummy as well. Am so tired with life now I will commit suicide if there's no way out of this solution you are the only one I can count on John remember how much I promise to be with you.

Me:

Yes

Beck:

Remember how much you promise to be there for me

Me:

That is what I am waiting for

Beck:

Babe pls. Just help me out of this

Me:

How? I can't get any money I have asked my rich friends and they said no. I have taken a loan out for you I am paying that I have no cash I am missing you

Beck:

Am not happy at all

Me:

I have not been able to sleep over this for a week I have been worried sick about you. What exactly is the problem is it an ownership certificate for the diamond you require? How long do they intend to keep you prisoner?

Beck:

Babe is time for me to commit suicide

Me:

Please do not what about me

Beck:

Babe I know they want money from us, babe am so tired with life now I am frustrated a lot I just need to be out of this place

Me:

Does any one of the guys watching want to say something to me now?

Beck:

These people are so wicked to me they are not nice at all yes they are here babe they stay at my back

Me:

What are they doing to you

Beck:

I beg them that I need to talk to you they are treating me bad a lot

Me:

Are you being held in a prison? I was told that you were still at Schiphol Airport

Beck:

Yes babe

Me:

Then you did not get charged with any offence yet, that was supposed to be tomorrow

Beck:

My love, pls. don't look me like this you need to do something. Pls. don't let anyone to mock us

Me:

So Does Kate and her father and your mum

Beck:

I don't know about Kate's Father now my mummy is very sick for now and Kate is sick as well

Me:

Honey I have been worried for you all along I even thought that you would get killed over this a week ago

Beck:

John don't you think life is boring to me now?

Me:

Yes darling I do I have been sent emotional blackmail emails by these people

Beck:

Am going crazy now the most people I love in my life are getting sick don't you think something as happened to me, and I am here not happy for a second how do you want me to feel !

Me:

Do you still have the diamond or have they taken it?

Beck:

Babe the diamond is with me they don't take it from me

Me:

Honey can you please tell me what the situation or problem is I still do not have a clear picture

Beck:

Babe I will use this moment to apologize to you, if you are told that I commit suicide you will have to forgive me, because I am not feeling comfortable here.

Me:

Please do not do that Beck this is almost two weeks now how long are they going to keep you?

Beck:

I don't know because this people are ready to keep me for long time they don't even care about me so I think the best is to commit suicide I can't continue like this John you need to know how I am suffering here.

Me:

Are you having regular food and clean clothes daily?

Beck:

I don't babe

Me:

I can't continue like this either Beck that is what they want!

Beck:

That's why am fed up

Me:

Why are they holding you why am I only told what they want to tell me here we could by now have been having a great life together this is going to happen honey you will be okay Beck don't leave me like this don't do anything stupid

Beck:

babe you are the only one I can count on I want you to help me out of this we will sell the diamond and pay all the debt so we can start a new life my love if you don't want me to commit suicide you need to help me out of this

Me:

I have already asked them that, they said the certificate has to be purchased before you can sell the diamond I don't know if that is true. I have a friend here (the one that won't lend me the money) he is a businessman and goes to Amsterdam he said you could still sell it and then buy the certificate

Beck:

Babe we will sell it when I get to Australia that's not the truth, don't mind him

Me:

Okay honey it is just that I have been told all sorts of things and I to have been crying for you and us I still love you Beck but if I say that, they will send me an emotional blackmail email

Beck:

Babe have been crying here as well my love

Me:

Please promise me you will try and hang in

Beck:

Babe I do love you for real you know I can't do without you

Me:

Can you give me any information? So I can go the Consulate anything will help remember I have actually no cash so that is why I cannot help. How much is the fee now.

Beck:

Babe the fee is 1500 pounds I just need to get out of this place

Me:

And is that for a certificate of ownership of the diamond?

Beck:

We will sell the diamond when I get there and we can buy house and start a new life. I mean the money, they want to release me.

Me:

Yes honey, but that is not what I asked, right now sweetheart I need information to sort this out. Does Adam Winkleman in London have a certificate for this diamond? If so why! As I understand it from them this certificate is for Holland only so it should be paid for in Euros locally and, if the IDC were legitimate they would use a Bank not Western Union

Beck:

John I don't understand these people here.

Me:

You see that is the problem with my friends they may have been willing to help me out with a bank transfer but never Western Union. Well you can ask them, that is what they told me and want me to do and I can tell you and them the same thing. No one here will deal with Western Union if this is legitimate that is the main problem to all parties and my friends who were going to help also asked a valid question maybe the people watching can give you an answer the question is how come the diamond needs a certificate if it is a family heirloom! It should have one, and how come money has the be paid to Adam Winkleman in London and the MTCN number given to a man called Scott Van Bowman in Amsterdam?

Beck:

Yes babe they told me that. John we just need to follow these peoples instruction because they are not nice to me, they said I don't have much time to talk to you again. John, pls I want you to help me out here.

Me:

If I was paying the money I would not part with it without an explanation that is why my friend is rich he suspects things and asks the right questions. Honey I cannot help you out financially I am still paying off the loss from the first time. I will have money in March but not before so I need to go to the embassy again. But to all who are reading this my question still stands. Honey, I love you hang in there please.

Beck:

Babe I told you to be careful with your friends about us because I know they don't like me.

Me:

No sweetheart you have got it wrong there is only one friend that will remain suspicious he does with everyone and he does not know most of this. This is natural for anyone to want to know

If I was parting with $3000 I would want to know where, and why, you can't not expect that don't worry honey it is not about us yet hopefully you will be able to prove that or not even have to if you get here. You see Beck also part of the problem is we don't know what is wrong in the first place and to us we can think of all sorts of things maybe you have been told a different story to me, that is why I am telling you what I have been told. Kate told me Scott Van Bowman was trying to help her but I disagree. What has she been told? You see I can't contact her either. If they want money for some certificate why don't they let the consulate pay it for you it does not make sense otherwise, unless everyone else there is in it for themselves, I have thought of that too. I know why you travelled with the diamond sweetheart but I wish you had listened to me and what I said I will leave my phone on and charged in case you are allowed to call me honey Beck honey I am crying now for you

Beck:

Babe I am crying here already is like I don't have a life

anymore these people look like kidnappers to me and I have been suffering a lot

Me:

That is what I thought who are they anyway do you know?

Beck:

But you are not ready to help me financially I think this is the time to commit suicide my love

Me:

That is unfair for you to say I am not ready to help you financially I have spent over $6000 on you already and there were not going to be any more problems when you left for Heathrow this time remember! I would help you out if I had some back!

Beck:

Babe I don't mean to say that I know you have tried a lot for me

Me:

You actually have more than me, you have a diamond worth 1 quarter of a million dollars and 3000 English Pounds I have $95 until Tuesday how fair is that

Beck:

I know, that's why I am begging you to forgive me if

you hear me commit suicide, that's why I told you we will sell the diamond when I get to Australia

Me:

Honey I will not forgive you for taking your own life honey (BRB milkman has arrived)

Beck:

But am so frustrating right now I understand life without you is boring to me babe understand I have promised to spend the rest of my life with you

Me:

Darling I want to ask you a question. Is there some agreement or something we can do with these people to make a deal of some kind so they release you, and we can make some arrangement for payment will that work? I want you too Beck I have been wanting this since we met online now 3 months ago. I am hurting and sad too. Do you think your captors will do a deal, can you ask them do you want me to ask them now? (BRB 2 minutes security problem here at work)

Beck:

They are seeing everything you are saying, they said no you can only make the payment by Western Union

Me:

(Back now) why, can't they give me an answer to that because I have already given you mine as to no way!

Beck:

They said no, they want the money by Western Union

Me:

That is not an answer nor is it any attempt to tell me why. Can you put one of them on the keyboard or can't they type either!

Beck:

Ok wait

Me:

Because quite frankly if you guys are kidnappers 1500 pounds to a foreigner is not any demand for payment.

Beck: (one of the Captors) Is not

Me:

Is not what! Who are you guys anyway?

Beck: (Captors)

We are who we are and your efforts trying to apprehend us is a waste of time you must effect payment before we will release Beck

Me:

Did they get you to write that?

Beck: (Captors) Write what?

Me:

Guys you need to understand one thing I will not be effecting any payment at any time on those terms now or ever so if you are waiting for money you will be waiting a long time as my concern is with Beck

Beck: (Captors)
And Beck will be here for a long time

Me:

My attempts to apprehend you may not be as futile as you think, and no, I don't think so

Beck: (Captors) Ok

Me:

You need the money before that, let's see who has the bluff shall we

Beck: (Captors)
I'm not ready to argue with you

Me:

He will be on record for travelling to Amsterdam and missing his connecting flight

Beck: (Captors)
I think this conversation is getting out of proportion. If you are ready to pay

Me:

All I have to do is convince someone to look at the footage at Schiphol (Spelt correctly) and see if they can identify any of you.

Beck: (Captors) Ok

Me:

I am not going to pay I want to know why you are asking me for the payment anyway

I would have thought his family and friends around him would be the ones to contact not me

Beck: (Captors) It's okay good day

Me:

You are full of shit

Beck: (Captors) Have a good day

Me:

Beck sweetheart, don't worry they can actually talk.

Me: 19/11/2010

Babe I hope you are alright but after all that has happened I need proof. That you are as you say held hostage in Amsterdam. I know you get upset when I ask for this but now it is necessary, remember I have emotions too! I wrote a letter to your kidnappers but never emailed it. It was to express why I would not have guilt for not sending money. It was also something you didn't know about me.

Beck:

What is the problem John, you should be making me happy here

Me:

Do you honestly think that anyone would keep someone chained up like you say for almost a month, knowing that no one is interested in you. Beck I don't know what is going on I keep telling you that

Beck:

I don't know why they are treating me this way

Me:

What are they doing to you now, are you still chained up, are they reading this?

Beck:

They are not reading they don't want me to come online again. They told me that because you are seeing me online and chatting with me, that why you do not take things serious...have begged them to release me that I will send money to them when I get to my destination. They are laughing at me

Me:

They have not sent me any demands and if they don't

want you to come online, then they are never going to get money anyway are they! This is the only communication we have, do you want me to send the letter I wrote to them, telling them why I am not guilty with emotions, I will if you want.

Beck:

Yes you can send it to me babe have been praying to God, to take me out of this because it's only God can help me out.

Me:

If they question you, that is also written into the letter. Have I got time? How long have you got online?

Beck:

I guess 20 mins.

Me:

Honey, can't you give them the diamond to get yourself here! Okay here comes the letter, it will take about that long to type in case they drag you away

Beck:

Ahahahahah John, you know the worth of the diamond, and I don't really know why they are not wanting it.

Me:

Who and why?

Beck:

I don't know John

Me:

Okay, I will start now Beck honey I never even spoke of it to you

Beck:

Okay babe okay.

(letter following)

> Beck, are they listening, gather around gentleman. I will never mention this again
>
> Beck honey I never even talked of it to you in fact if you remember I told you I never went to war (Vietnam). I lied Basically gents I have fulfilled my time of guilt so letting me think he will die in your custody will not work with me.
>
> Beck sweetheart obviously you are involved in some way with this because you would not have been set up if you weren't I don't know how much and I don't care but gentleman when any of can tell me you have seen someone still alive with half their face missing let me know when any of you can tell me you didn't jump out of your skin when you commanding co shot that man to put him out of his misery let me know

You see guys I have a service record.

I am not proud of it I don't talk of it and I don't want to remember it but there was a war between 1969 and 1975 that Australia was involved in Vietnam. I had 9 months service before we were all recalled I hated it I cried I remember the blood spattered when the co shot that guy, I cried I vomited and I was called a sissy because of it. But you receive good counseling after that to take away all pain and guilt.

Beck sweetheart these guys are only after money from me. Which we know is not going to happen If any of you men can stand up and say you have endured that or worse then speak up now. If you don't believe me you can access the Australian war service records 1969-1975. gov.au I think that is the web address.

As of tonight if this ridiculous behaviour continues I will block this address from my email. Beck sweetie I will send Kate another email address for me one I created two days ago in gmail especially for this moment or maybe I will use another one anyway I have several.

I hope one day you keep your promise Beck as I have kept mine (until the end of time is a long time honey) maybe you are a homophobe and out to rip me off I really don't know you have certainly avoided some critical questions that I have asked. And you most certainly have been kidnapped by being recognized. There is another issue.

Gentleman I have one more thing to say Maybe it is the proud British heritage I have in me and the Highland Spirit from my great Grandfather. But as far as you wankers' are concerned My British lives on. And the famous line known the world over spoken by a True Brit in time of need like now " I will fight you on the beaches but I will never surrender"

God Save the Queen Goodbye gentlemen.

Me: (to Kate)

Hi Kate, this is John. I understand you are not well. I hope you are recovering rapidly. I do want to talk to you as a matter of urgency. If you can please find the time thanks John. It concerns Beck he is suicidal. I would appreciate it, thanks

Me (to Beck)

Sweetie, if you get to see this I have just faxed a lot of info to the British Embassy here in Sydney. They have a special fax number for missing persons abroad, love you.

CHAPTER 14

THE LIES

There are now so many lies that are now being told by both Beck, and his Captors (assuming that they exist.) Again, he <u>creates</u> excuses to justify his predicament. I am aware of this and send one abusive email to him. This I did with the hope of getting the truth from someone involved in this scam to tell me the truth. After criticizing him I again show love and care in my messages. I still don't want the game to be up until I have some answers and therefore don't want Beck or anyone else to decide they cannot win and the game is called off. I am now convinced that there is a chain sequence of some sort in place and that Adam Winkleman is for some reason dependant on 1500 pounds. I hope to disrupt this and maybe get some answers because of it. Beck does not seem to be terrified, and 1500 pounds is an insignificant ransom amount for a kidnapping.

Beck: 23/11/2010

Hi John are you there? Why did you wrote such mailed

to me? I am here I am dying and you are not even care for me, its ok I think is time for me to commit suicide byee….

Me:

You know maybe if you told me what is going on I might believe you. I wanted to care for you but you wouldn't let me. The British embassy told me to have nothing to do with you and the situation was dodgy. They told me you should get to the British Embassy in Amsterdam if you need help and that you can use the BTA money.. It would be nice if you considered my feelings for a change, and remember if you ever make it to Sydney

I will give you accommodation it is in my interest to do so. If you want to chat or are allowed to chat how about tonight 8:00pm Sydney time that should be 10am Amsterdam time

Then I will listen to you

Beck:

John

Me:

Yes

Beck:

John what have I done wrong to you? This is not what you promise me you are now turn your back to me wish is unfair, you should know what am going through here

Me:

I just want you to tell me the truth

Beck:

What truth?

Me:

Why you are stuck in Amsterdam a prisoner

Beck:

I thought these people are like kidnappers they only give 15mins to chat with you John

Me:

That is fine but, why are you there in the first place? This is more than a diamond isn't it?

Beck:

I told you is like someone set me up babe

Me:

Yes that makes sense that is what I said to you earlier is it someone in London you spoke to can Kate be trusted? I haven't heard from her and I have left messages. You know, what I was told by the British Consulate is that you can access the BTA money if it is only about 1500 pounds do that then you will be released. You owe it to your mother to do so, are they reading?

Beck:

John I trust Kate so much I don't think she can do that to me, nop they are not reading

Me:

Okay that was just a question but the setup had to come from London obviously they were waiting for you in Amsterdam correct?

Beck:

Yes

Me:

Then you or someone has told someone in London prior to your departure

Beck:

I think so babe, have been thinking who can that be

Me:

Yes that is good to think who but in the mean time you need to get yourself out of there. Are they reading this?

Beck:

No they are not reading. John seriously you need to be in control of your anger sometimes I don't like what you usually wrote to me when you are angry

Me:

I am only writing what I was told by the British Embassy

Beck. They are your countrymen you should arrange with your captors to pay the money from the BTA as I have told you and get yourself out of there okay! If we only have 15 mins then do that. The embassy also told me you need to get to the British Embassy in Amsterdam if you can I have already given them your name so they will know something if you do.

Beck:

Babe I can't I would do that if I can.

Me:

Where are they holding you, what is the place called?

Beck:

I don't really know I don't have freedom here.

Me:

Is it a warehouse or a jail?

Beck:

Not jail is like warehouse John pls I need to go out of this place

Me:

Are you the only prisoner?

Beck: I thank god that they are straight they would have raped me, yes I am John Me:

That is what I wondered. It seems really strange they are

doing all of this for 1500 pounds there is something else Beck what happens in the end if you pay 1500 pounds, maybe they will kill you. I don't want to scare you but is a strong possibility

Beck:

They will not kill me john they will free me

Me:

That is good

Beck:

I have been told that my people want to waste my life because they can't afford to pay 1500 pounds

Me:

I was told the 1500 pounds was for a certificate of ownership for the diamond that is necessary as proof of ownership in Holland, you see we are being told different stories. I was told they will keep you for three months and that you were going to jail and you had a court case pending. Maybe they do intend to keep you for 3 months. They said to me that was the price for the ownership certificate but then who is Adam Winkleman in London that the money has to be paid to, and who is Scott Van Bowman?

Beck:

I don't know babe I thought maybe their partner.

Me:

Yes that makes sense he is the one that calls me. Are you being fed and able to shower etc or have they got you on a chain? Can you chat to me tonight or call me perhaps please

Beck:

After my shower they got me back on chain

Me:

Are you serious?

Beck:

Yes babe they are not here now I am alone here

Me:

And chained up right!

Beck:

My legs now not my hands

Me:

Can't you bend it or break it, what about yelling out HELP! Beck that is a lot of trouble for 1500 pounds

Beck:

They will kill me if I try that John

Me:

How do you know they won't when they are sick of this

game anyway? Do you still have access to your bags and still have the diamond?

Beck:
Yes I have it

Me:
Have they taken your passport?

Beck:
Yes my passport is with them

Me:
Then why haven't they taken the diamond and killed you! It doesn't make sense

Beck:
How do you mean? Do you want them to kill me?

Me:
Are they legal authorities? I don't think so it sounds to me like someone is out to scare you and teach you something, this might be a vendetta.

No honey, I don't want them to kill you but why are they doing all this for 1500 pounds I want you to get out of there tell them you will use the BTA money one of them can go with you to the bank. Is there a window you can throw a note out for help or scream help from it.

Beck:

I am not close to the window at all John you are not in my shoes. That's why you are saying these people are very perfect.

Me:

Yes I know sweetheart but I wouldn't say that is why I am asking

Beck:

I can't even see sunshine here.

Me:

Are you there?

Beck:

Yes am here

Me:

Darling I have to go to work I want to chat but have to go can we talk tonight as I said before

Beck:

Babe I will have to beg them

Me:

I think they will let you go in 3 months, they told me you will be there for a long time okay not to worry whenever you can okay!

Beck:

John I don't think they will let me go

Me:

I thought of that, that is what I meant to say when they get bored they will kill you. What have you done to upset someone to do this, can you think of anyone in particular? If these people are so perfect, you must know someone in London that could look like they belong to this group. This group have sent me emotional emails on International Diamond Council Letterhead that has been copied and pasted to look genuine. Even if someone paid 1500 pounds I don't think they will let you go.

Beck:

These people are bastards

Me:

Yes they are, but if you are in the building on you own can't you try and cause an electrical fire or something to attract attention to yourself I have to go honey I will leave the chat line open okay, will they read this when they come back?

Your mother needs to report this to the authorities. Beck, are you there?

Beck: 25/11/2010

Hello John

Me:

I am here babe are you there Beck?

Beck:

How are you doing? Yes am here my love

Me:

I'm alright honey what about you

Beck:

Pls help me out of here john am not doing good

Me:

Are they reading?

Beck:

No they are not reading, am falling sick now

Me:

Are they feeding you? If they are not reading do they read what you wrote later?

Beck:

Not constantly, yes sometimes they read later sometimes they don't read at all. They feed once in a day

Me:

Okay that is what i wanted to know, and your clothes are no longer clean either are you cold, you have packed summer clothes

Beck:

Yes babe

Me:

Does their PC you are on have in private browsing, because I want to tell you some things that you can do, if it does this.

Beck

Yes go ahead and tell me babe

Me:

Okay you can delete from in private okay so do so at the end of our conversation. I can chat with you on Hotmail if you prefer to I have an account anyway what i want to tell you is this I have run out of all options so, my next step is to put you in as a scammer to current affairs they will check the situation out and that might lead to your release, do you understand what I am doing I want their reporters to investigate so here we have two current affairs programs where people contact them about all sorts of issues including internet scams these shows are aired on prime TV 6:30 pm to 7:30 pm weeknights everyone watches and there have been scam issues before on these shows. I hope they are interested in us because this one is so different now that means if they want to air the show they will want some emails from me and want to know the story they also usually have investigative reporters to check it all out

Beck:

Ok I don't understand, and I don't think that will work out because this people are kidnappers

Me:

Okay no one here will help me. My last call was the British Embassy and I have given them your answer

Beck:

Babe pls I beg you in the name of God I don't want u to do that. This place is killing me John

Me:

Why honey, they might be able to help you all I am thinking of is letting someone find out that you are being held hostage

Beck:

Pls don't put me up as scammer

Me:

Okay if that is what you want but there is a chance of your captors being found out. How long have we got to chat?

Beck:

I think we have 15mins left

Me:

Okay I want to say two things first (and I want an

answer) why don't you use the internet to contact the British Embassy in Amsterdam and ask for help do you want me to find the website and second I want to send you the email I got from the fake International Diamond Council telling me of your fate but I won't send it if you don't want it. I have it in a draft ready to send

Beck:

Babe they can't locate where I am. That's the problem. These people are professional they cannot find out where they keep me this place is under ground

Me:

Okay, you must have some idea are you near the airport can you hear planes?

Beck:

You can send it babe, I will check it next time

Me:

Did they blindfold you when they apprehended you? Did they say anything? There must be something and you should send for help anyway

Beck:

Babe I can't hear anything I don't even know how I got it, here I mean

Me:

Okay when I send it, it actually states a date of your

incarceration and a time period. At the moment I have it figured they will keep you for 3 months from the 18th November that means release in mid to late Feb 2011. I would go online and ask for help you must for yourself let everyone else worry about where you are, you know when they are sick of you and the game they might want to dispose of you. I have not heard from Kate either.

Beck:

Babe why you don't want to help me out here, I know I would have been in your place by now, if you have paid these people

Me:

That is the only way I know of to try and help you I don't have the money I am still paying the back rent also you have missed your connecting flights so you won't get a refund on the airfare I imagine I don't have another fare for you either, why doesn't someone in the UK pay for you

Beck:

But you told me you said, you always have money to fly to UK

Me:

Yes but it is not in my possession and it is only $2000

Babe:

Babe I think they will find my way to your place after you pay them out

Me:

I need $3000 to pay for 1500 pounds my mother in law (from my deceased partner) has this money for me and she will give it to me when I set a date to fly

Beck:

My love you can still look for $1000 to complete the money

Me:

The Embassy told me you can use the BTA money anyway and if these people are who they say then they will have connections to sell your diamond on the black market anyway, have you suggested that to them?

Beck:

Babe I told you I have receipt now, I will only have access to the BTA when I arrive to Australia.

Babe I don't want them to do that because that's all the inheritance I have in my life, and is going to benefit both of us when I arrive to Australia

Me:

Oh okay yes I realize that but is it worth it for your health and life. Can't you try and escape when no one is there that is I assume you are not always chained up

Beck:

I can't babe because they chain me down here I am my legs are chain now and they have camera every where

Me:

What about the warehouse is it deserted or do people work there that can help you

Me:

Oh fuck I forgot about cameras

Beck:

It's deserted

Me:

So this is your jail they told me about

Beck:

Yes babe

Me:

I have just sent you the draft I was talking about, you might want to delete it but then maybe if they know you have what they sent me they will have to think harder to keep you. Have you figured out yet who set you up? Also you will need toiletries shaving cream soap etc. are they providing you with essentials? It looks like a horrible Christmas for us

Beck:

Babe Am like a slave where I am

Me:

But they aren't screwing you that is something good tell

them you want clothes and new bathroom supplies they might get them for you, what are they asking you to do?

Beck:

Have told them that before but they did not correspond to me

Me:

Then you will start to smell and they will have to do something then. Is it cold in Amsterdam now?

Beck:

Babe this place is hell you just need to help me out here don't let me die here

Me:

I have no doubt it is honey that is why I am wanting to try this last avenue to see if they can help us no one here will help me anymore you see.

Beck:

What about the company you take a loan last time

Me:

My friends know I have helped you and know you haven't arrived they think giving me money is a waste of time that is my problem the maximum I could get is the $1500 I used to send 1000 pounds to you I asked them for an increase: because their flyer said up to $3000 but when I rang they said no because I was now too committed, you see I am trying to do what I can that is why I thought of other options instead of the payment.

Beck:

I think because they don't know what is happened here, how I wish they know they would have help

Beck:

Babe the payment is the best option why don't you contact them again

Me:

What about some tools in the warehouse to break the chains are there any available?

Beck:

I told you they have cameras everywhere and they have security around

Me:

The payment might be the best option but it is not available and what proof is there that if it is paid they will release you. I mean you know who they are and what they look like that is not good for you I don't want to scare you Beck but what proof is there that they will let you go!

Beck:

I swear to God john they will release me after the payment. They will.

Me:

Maybe honey that would be great but I have come up against a brick wall here

Beck:

They will

Me:

As far as money goes, I also finish my second job in two weeks for another 2 weeks so I will be short of cash, and then they close for Christmas and I have a party to provide for next week remember. Are there any assets you have at home that can be sold, will they let you speak to mum to arrange something

Beck:

Yes I know maybe but if you try to find way and pay them, remember we still have 3000pound BTA money in Australia

Me:

Do you realise that $3000 is not that easy to come by at the moment and my rich friends will not help out. I really am not able to get any more cash. I will make heaps of cash working full rosters here and the other job but that is not until February and March. that will give me enough to fly and accommodation.

Beck:

I told you mummy is very sick she at the hospital

Me:

What is wrong with her? Have you received the email yet?

Beck:

I don't really know her condition, you there?

Me:

Yes I am here

Beck:

Pls you need to help me out here John you have done a lot of things for me pls. don't let me down this time

Me:

Beck there is no money available to me that is why I want to alert someone attention to your situation it does not mean you are a scammer but they won't be interested in any other form of current affair with our situation. Babe that comment is unfair and it hurts me for you to say that. Everything I do for you every suggestion I offer you block Yes I care but there is nothing I can do. The Embassy is your best bet

Beck: 28/11/2010

Babe

Me:

Hello Beck I wasn't expecting to chat with you on line I am here so where are you? Are you there?

Beck:

Yes babe, am still here at the kidnappers place

Me: I am sending this using my phone I don't believe
you Beck:

WhyJjohn? Where do you think I am why you don't
believe me?

Me:
Because the story is just that a story no one would go to
all that trouble for 1500pounds

Beck:
Meaning?

Me:
If you were only <u>using</u> me you have done a good job

Beck:
John stop it what do you mean? I hate you just now I
see you don't care for me anymore

Me:
There is a lot you are not telling me

Beck:
Its' fine you can let them keep me here and do whatever
they want to use me for

Me:

I wasn't even expecting to hear from you anymore. It's just a game to you isn't it! I trusted you silly me

Beck:

Bye

This next email was written and sent offline I did not want any interruption's from him

Me:

Hello Beck I hope you are holding up okay. As you know I am compiling all our chat emails and attempting to get a book published from them, and as I am typing them all individually into word I am reading our chats to each other. This one really was (I thought) going to make you the man for me, written September 1st by you, we had just met. This is chat number 6 it reads *"Firstly I am so happy that we are communicating with each other. You have said everything all. I really understand every word in your mail, we seem to think alike and that may make it easier to get along fast. These are all important sentiments and issues in a relationship. It is about two halves together making a whole. It is about two total beings joining together. Of course with the best intentions, these are not guaranteed to lead to total everlasting success, but if the motivation is there to begin with, great things are possible. I don't really get attracted to people. I follow my heart and I know it always leads me right, maybe that's why I am writing you. When I like someone I think I can trust the person, because without trust a relationship will never grow. I like being with a caring and honest person, someone we can be happy together. I need my own man, the man I call mine. You know things fall in place when you fall in love, and when you are in love things come so easy. I'm a very caring guy who loves to make his man special. Treat my man like an angel, care for him and treat him right in and out of bed."* there is a bit more to this email, but you finish by saying *"Please take care of yourself and I will hope to read from you soon kisses and hugs"* So Beck, when did you decide to stop treating me nice? I am not finding any trust in our relationship so it will not grow. I need to ask you if you wrote this from your heart or plagiarised it for your own means. Can you give me an honest answer please?

Should I forget about us? I am thinking you are not interested in having a relationship with me anymore. I would be grateful for you honesty and if you are not interested, then I will leave you alone.

With what is happening to you, and your inability to want to help yourself, I feel that my "loving you until the end of time" is turning into an hourglass that will run out. I would be really grateful for your thoughts on this to ease my emotions into a sense of calmness and I accept your decision.

Me:

Hello my love I am here and I am glad you are online I thought you might not want to talk to me anymore are you okay?

Beck:

What is it again?

Me:

What do you mean? What is what again

Beck:

Because you abused me a lot last time we were chatting I think you want to continue abusing me again?

Me:

Honey I am very sorry I was not abusing you when we chatted I was disbelieving you, however I know now that is not true

Beck:

But you don't have to do that

Me:

I want to tell you why please I was reading all the wonderful things that you have written to me and I want to be part of them this situation is not helping either of us and I promise you from this very moment that I will not let it get to me any more

Beck:

Is it? Because I love you so much and I have told you that I can't do without you

Me:

Yes because I am the same way I have just been reading BRB (need to speak to someone)

Beck:

Ok

Me:

Sorry honey back now I am wanting us to be together. I am wanting to do all the things with you, you spoke about. I have been to everyone I can to get help for you and am out in the cold, on my own with that. I believe in you in spite of what I have been told by the consulate and I want the world to know about us. I love Beck Hill and I will never change my mind that it will be until the end of time. That is guaranteed I am sorry I am crying now. I have hurt you in your hour of need. I am unable to financially assist in this situation, and no one believes us, I promise you I will be strong I just want to be able to be with you and I know you want out of the current situation. Please forgive me. I know in your message to me you said there may be arguments: I am embarrassed that I started them.

Beck:

Yes babe your words touch my heart now am crying as well John. I want to spend the rest of my life with you

Me:

Babe I feel as though I am part of you and I have done

for a while. What I am worried about is you, we don't know what is going to happen you know and now I am worried that they will read this and it will make it worse for you. Honey I love you I have wanted to say that for days and now I feel better. I was trying to not let them know that is how I still feel because if they read this the emotional emails will start again to me from them. I think BRB (again)

Beck:

Ok

Me: (Sorry) as I was saying I think you are stronger with this situation than me and it is now my turn to apologise for being weak with this, when you need me strong. Honey I am so very very sorry please forgive me

Beck:

Its ok my love I have forgive you babe

Me:

You know something, I learned about you today reading the emails. As I am typing I learned that you are romantic and sensitive

Beck:

You know I can't do without you and I have promised to start a new life with you thank you babe.

Me:

I know that honey and I know that is what you want as

well as me and I will remain waiting for that to happen because I have a feeling inside me that is that same feeling when we first spoke 3 months ago. The feeling has never died I just doubted my feelings that's what happened are they reading this?

Beck:

No they are not babe

Me:

That is good, have they told you anything?

I picked up last night when we chatted that you are in better spirits than you have been before are they looking after you better?

Beck:

Babe I haven't eat anything for the past 12 hours now, am just sick and tired of here now it's like am feeling sick and I told them I want to go to hospital they did not answer me

Me:

So do you think they want you to die, and that way it is not murder <u>and,</u> they get the diamond is that the game they are playing. Have you got any toiletries or clean clothes have they released the chains? If there is not going to be anyone there over Christmas you will die

Beck:

Nop they haven't release the chain

Me:

What good does that achieve, what happens when you need to go to the toilet and so on how can you sleep chained it means they don't trust you not to escape I know you said it is impossible but rather than dying you should try. I imagine now you also have a beard. What is strange we do not know if you have been reported missing as a tourist from London Maybe, If Kate is better she needs to try and do something. I was told here by the Embassy that it would need to come from the UK or Holland; are you still there

Beck:

Yes am here John

Me:

How long can we chat babe?

Beck:

Less than 30mins I guess

Me:

That's okay do you get fed every day? what do they give you? Okay I understand you are still being treated badly right?

Beck:

I told you not every time babe yes babe

Me:

That is bad, that is why you have lost weight it sounds to me like they are not interested in really looking after you or turning up at all they are losing interest in you that could be good. Have they said anything to you about the situation? I mean this guy Winkleman! is not going to get his money obviously so what is their next move.

Beck:

They said I will die here if they did not get the money

Me:

See I told you that you seemed pretty confident they would let you go if it gets paid but I am not so sure I think someone wants you dead regardless you have to fight for your survival they are going to make you weak with starvation then let you die chained up. Beck that is not going to happen it will all be over another way I think they are all sick of the game now

that is why you are not being fed

Beck:

Babe see they are after this money that's what they want they said they will not release me if they did not see the money

Me:

Do you mean the sale of the diamond or just the 1500 pounds? 1500 pounds is not a lot of money to hold someone hostage for

Beck:

Babe is 1500 pounds they are not after the diamond I don't know why

Me:

But why, that doesn't make sense that is strange too

Beck:

That's why I want to get out of here before they will think of my diamond John

Me:

And why pounds not Euros? And they let you keep the diamond! You saw the email I sent you where Van Bowman says that the diamond can't be sold without the ownership certificate. He told me on the phone that this was the price but if they are crooks then they could sell it on the black market so that puts it back to a specific need for 1500 pounds only why? And who are they working for if they don't want the diamond bye honey, chat whenever we can, sorry I thought they had stopped you talking

Beck:

Am here John

Me:

What do you do all day long have they given you TV to watch in Dutch or some books to read? Hi babe, are you there alone at the moment, what I mean is any security there?

Beck:

Babe they did not give me any book or TV to watch there are security here just looking at me from far

Me:

Okay I see. Do they have cameras on you all the time? And how on earth can you sleep with your ankle chained.

Beck:

Yes babe

Me:

Is there a bed for you, so this warehouse is it empty or are there people getting goods from it that can maybe help you. What is happening from home babe, what about Kate's dad reporting you missing in Amsterdam does anyone care over there? Is your mum out of hospital she can report the situation that still puts us back to the original question what is so important with this 1500 pounds to go to this guy in London? Bye honey

Beck:

Its empty babe

Me:

That is what I thought it must be some government experimental warehouse. Beck someone is out to get you the money is no guarantee for your safety you know what these guys look like. I can send an email to the address I have for them but he comes back with threatening and emotional emails to me and does not agree to anything I say. I even have his voice on tape here they know I am on the other side of the world and cannot do anything. What did they tell you the 1500 pounds was for sweetheart you need to take some risk for you own safety first of all get them somehow to remove the chain hide some clothes in the shower and try then when the chain is off I won't say anymore at the moment okay just in case.

Beck:

Babe that will never work out John

Me:

Neither will the payment because this is where they are not professional, No one here (as in my friends) will lend the money because there is no proof to anyone you are in custody or kidnapped. The only person that gets the ransom email is me. No one in London knows of your situation they are obviously not that desperate for the money otherwise they would let everyone see or at least prove your situation. That means what I said is true it is you they want more than the money who and why, and whoever it is wants you to suffer badly. These guys are not professional kidnappers they are working for someone.

Beck:

Babe I don't even want to know I just want to get out of here

Me:

They won't hassle me more than gmail even fake ones because they won't leave anything substantial for me to go to the police with. I have already done that babe

Beck:

You can tell people another thing to lend money from them if they will not believe us that am in custody

I understand

Beck:

Why don't you go and lend money from your in laws?

Me:

I can't get that money until I have shown here where I am going to fly to, but like anyone

I will not pay money of that amount to something like this. It is absurd! There is no way that money is for what I want. If I don't travel on this money I am a dead man now these people have been told by me already I don't have the money so they are not hassling me anymore. No one, no one at all that I know would waste money as a payment in such a way as this, me included I have given you what I could but it wasn't for no reason, this is just giving money away that is what I mean, these guys are not professional if that is their best effort. Don't worry babe that proves you will be okay no pay no die. Winkleman is not getting his money. In fact I would be more inclined if it comes from London to walk to his shop and hand it to him myself after you release has been <u>arranged</u> this is like blackmail. Scotland Yard needs to be involved now. I can't contact them, sadly it has to be reported to the Met first and you need to include the reference number they give you on the internet page to gain access to the yard but I will look on the net and see what other options I have and if these guys do read this then <u>they need to do better than they currently are</u> no one will pay don't worry honey BRB

(need to help someone) I am here now babe, are you there? Are you there honey? Hi babe I am back now so are you goonies reading this now? Do any of you want to talk to me? How about Scott Van Bowman has he got something to say? Tell him to send me a message but I'm telling you now no one will pay money for this situation, this is in case you are reading this Oh, in case you are wondering I have already been to the British Consulate here they are looking into the matter and have already been helpful to me. Hi babe you are back? I thought they have to talk, no! I was right guess none of you want to speak

Beck:

Mr John we have nothing to tell you we will never beg you to rescue your lover boy

Me: That I already know, but I'm telling you that not even my rich friends will pay. money for this ridiculous venture, you see the IDC does not use Western Union and will not be involved with this situation I cannot do more that I am doing but this clearly is a vendetta against Beck by someone it is not the 1500 pounds

Beck:

You claim that you love him and you can't help him out, don't ever think that we will release him without paying the money. We will not or else he will die here because we don't care about him, good day

Me:

And that is supposed to scare me?

Beck:

We only need the one thousand five hundred pounds to release him that's all

I don't trust you to release him even then and if you want money he has the diamond or you can cancel his BTA receipt the embassy told me that

Me:

Are you there babe?   30/11/2010

Beck:

Yes am here John

Me:

Did they take you away earlier, did you read the last part of our last chat

Beck:

Yes you mean when you were chatting with them?

Me:

Yes well I want to say something but they will read it so I won't. Are they watching now?

Beck:

They want to chat with you

Me:

Okay

Beck: (Captors)

MR JOHN OSBORNE YOU CLAIM THAT YOU LOVE THIS BOY HERE AND YOU ARE NOT READY TO BAIL HIM OUT DON'T THINK WE WILL RELEASE HIM IF YOU DON'T PAY THE MONEY. WE WILL NOT OR ELSE HE WILL DIE HERE WE DON'T CARE ABOUT HIM HE CAN DIE IF HE WANT TO WE HAVE NOTHING TO TELL YOU AGAIN OK.

Me:

Firstly Guys (Captors) Capitals are only for shouting at people

Secondly I don't know whether I told you but the British Embassy told me not to pay any money this is a dodgy operation (their words) and Thirdly, none of my friends (including the rich ones) will even give me money as they see this as a scam. Have they gone away? Well in case you are still waiting for me to say something "you have no idea how silly this is for 1500 pounds that is not even a professional amount" and why, are you asking me when he has family and friends in London that would be able to come up with the money.

Are you there Beck or have I got the goon squad still? *(no answer for several minutes)* now everybody's run away you guys are a pathetic bunch of losers. Losers because If I am the only guy you have to ask for the cash you have got it wrong. There's not even any proof Beck is not in on the scam and for all I know, he could still be in London. I only know that is where he started because that is where I sent the Western Union Money come to think of it that is where you want me so send more Western Union money see what I mean, sorry guys nice try no deal.

READ THAT!

Me:

Are they reading?

Beck:

Yes

Me:

Is that you Beck, or someone else

Beck Yes

Me:

Are you there Beck how do I know it is you! Are they reading?

Beck:

Yes

Me:

They told me they had nothing more to say to me so I will only talk to you. Is that you Beck if you are there what, is the name of my flatmate?

Beck:

Josh

Me:

Okay you have my attention

Beck:

Am here they are looking me far away

Me:

Are they reading all of this?

Beck:

Yes No babe

Me:

There is not much I can say then but I need you to tell me your date of birth, there is a reason for that

Beck:

They are coming now babe

Me:

Okay send it later I want to guess what has happened here, you left London with the diamond and they apprehended you at Schiphol correct! Then they figure I am a rich guy or in any case they want in on some money correct? It doesn't matter what excuse they use and the deal is I pay you walk free, incorrect. Who told them, or how did these guys know about your diamond? Did you tell them about me when they interviewed you, its' okay you can answer that. Babe I have to go to bed I have to work in the morning it's 2:45 am here but you know that anyway

Beck:

Yes John they interview me and I told them about you

Me:

Honey that's okay don't worry, the problem is who knew you were carrying a diamond of that value. Why haven't they contacted anyone in London, are they reading now? Anyway I have contacted Gmail now

Beck:

Gmail! for what?

Me:

So if you see some activity that is strange, that is why. I will get you out of this

Beck:

Don't let Gmail block my account

Me:

The location of where you are now, you don't know you said so no, they won't block it they will investigate and get back to me I intend to sort this out bye honey I have to go to bed.

When you are allowed to chat I will be waiting

CHAPTER 15

THE HOSTAGE

As all chances of us ever meeting are now fading, I decide the only value I have is to keep in contact with Beck if possible. The only avenue I have is to identify him as a scammer, accusing him of this and not knowing where he was located I used some bluff in the hope of obtaining information from him I do have a second Cousin in London but I did not contact him to check out the existence of the original address. I did pursue an avenue of enquiry of my own with any authorities I could do so with and was aware that I may not be contacted by them if they did locate his whereabouts. The question I now needed to ask myself is "how would I prove this is a scam I willingly sent him the funds" Would I even get a reply from him, we were not chatting anymore I was composing emails and sending them, waiting for a reply. There is also the usual question 'How do I know you will be released if I do pay the fee" not even allowing for your arrival in Sydney. (The following letter from Beck has obviously been written or plagiarized by a third party. This level of English is above his capability, so again proof there is more than one person involved.

Me: 4/12/2010

Shortly I will send you a link that lets you view your name on the scammer's website, they have to approve it first but it has been submitted. I am not sure what response I will get from Western Union but I have also sent them information via the tab on their website. My Second Cousin (who lives in London) will check out the Levita House Camden address and email back to me. If you are there and you see a stranger around it might be him. He wants to do this he loves the detective stuff. I thought of sending Scotland Yard an email but they would probably think I was insane doing so from Australia so I didn't bother with that.

This is the most profound shit I have ever come across. You play on people's emotions and take them for granted.

The book is coming along it will be a couple of years, but you will get the name Beck Hill in print, and maybe in the title but not sure of that yet. If so, I'm sure you will agree Beck Hill on the front page on a shelf of every bookstore you walk into is amazing Huh…

I may be in London in July 2012 I doubt you will want to see me but I will put the offer out there now. You underestimated me big time didn't you Bye

Me; to info@internationaldiamondcouncil.org Your time will be up shortly

John Osborne

Me: to Beck

I thought you might like to know I have also contacted ▮▮▮▮ (*the original dating site*) and alerted them. I guess you'd better change your name again.

Me: 7/12/2010

You would have to be the most gutless piece of shit I know you are going to regret doing this to me. I can pay to have you found but I don't know whether you are worth it. I do know Karma will get you because it is a basis for what I believe and it works for me all the time.

You don't even have the guts to reply to me, or maybe even read the emails, you or Kate, is she in this too? Maybe she's your wife. Maybe this email will bounce back as your address is closed.

I have found someone by the name of Becker and another by the name of Ben Hill on the same scammers address list. I guess you are both of them from previous victims, and to think I said

"I will love you till the end of time" Well it is the end of time for you soon. You really are a very nasty person and that idiot, that left his voice imprint, what's his name, Oh! That's right Scott Van Bowman. The same voice as that of the officer that called me from Australia House saying he has granted you a two year work visa. I am now passing this info back to the British Consulate.

Beck:

Ah John, I am highly disappointed in you. Is it because

you can't help me out of this problem, that's why you are prosecuting me with such things. I don't believe you can write this to me. I know most of your friends are giving you bad advice, I wouldn't say more than that.

Me:

My friends have nothing to do with this. I have not heard from you for two weeks, they think it is over, I think you have made a big mistake by not coming. I also don't believe there is a diamond. How can you have no conscience when all I wanted to do was to love you.

Beck:

They don't allow me to come online now all of these days. Is that why you are thinking such things? You make me cry right now, I don't believe this from you John, you know I really love you, and I have promised to spend the rest of my life with you.

Me: 8/12/2010

P.S. I won't change my mind on this unless you come to me. I hope what you say is true Beck, as I do want to love you. The problem I have honey is, I don't believe anyone would go all that trouble for 1500 pounds and that I am the only one that can help you .Beck, my offer is still open for you. I will truly pay .them when you are with me otherwise they get NOTHING! By the way Honey, I really do want to love you but you are not making it easy love n kisses, you are so Hot!

(Beck letter to me) John My Darling

Life is so unpredictable. Changes always come along, in big or small ways. I don't know what happened that this sudden change has turned my world upside down. I don't know exactly what it is, it just hit me, but there is something really special about you.

It might be all the things I see on the surface, the things that everyone notices and admires about you, qualities, capabilities and a wonderful smile obviously connected to a warm and loving heart, these things set you apart from everyone else. But it may also be the big things.... The person you really are that I hope to know more someday. And it might also be the little things....

The way you walk and all your actions. I receive so much joy just being able to see a smile in your eyes, If I ever figure out the magic that makes you so special, I'd probably find out that it's a combination of all these things You are a rare combination of all these special things. You are really amazing.

Inside of me there is place where the sweetest dreams reside, where my highest hopes are kept alive, where my deepest feelings are felt and where my favourite memories are safe and warm. I find that you're on my mind more often than any other thought. Sometimes I bring you there purposely just to make my day brighter. But more often you surprise me and make your own ways into my thoughts. There are even times when I awaken I realize you've been a part of my dreams. Then during the day, when my imagination is free to run, it takes me into your arms and allows me to linger there knowing there's nothing I'd rather do. I know my thoughts are only reflecting the loving hopes of my heart because whenever they wander, they always take me to you.

Only the most special things in my world get to come inside my heart and stay. And now, I realize how deeply my life has been touched by you. John pls don't let me die in pain here I want you to pay these people so they can let me go, remember how you promised me to be there for me anytime any moment, this is the time I need you most in my life pls help me out here.

CRYING

Beck

Me: (letter to Beck)   9/12/2010

Hi Babe

I don't know how long it will be before you can read this but I will wait for your reply. I always enjoy getting an email from you just like 3 months ago when we met. I am so happy you have written those nice things about me and I'm glad you finally realized what I have been saying in my profile. I don't want to sound bombastic but I am a nice guy, I know that and people always tell me that. My partner used to look after me and protect me from silly things that I am doing now, that I would do because I am a nice guy.

I really would like to share those things with you in person. (Maybe one day) I do not intend to say anything bad or nasty about you Beck, I will say I don't know what is going on. I do believe you were on your way to meet me and something went wrong. Do you remember what you said to me in the last email before you caught the flight to Amsterdam? You said "Honey nothing will go wrong this time I will be there' Yes I am upset that did not happen and something has changed that is preventing you from coming and I don't mean currently, I mean ever do you remember one of the questions you asked me on September 1st, you asked me "do you believe you can love from distances" maybe I did not realize then what you meant. Did you mean that you will love me but only from a distance does that mean that you never wanted anything more than that? I don't know I guess I have to love you from a distance now.

Honey I know you might be in some trouble and you have asked me to help you now as this is the time you need it most. I did say I will always be there for you. I am here for you babe but I need some answers to some issues that I do not understand. I am not saying I will pay the 1500 pounds and as you know I don't have it but as I am the paying customer I would not part with any more money without knowing what I am spending it on. Yes I know I have already parted with my money I guess as a waste but when I gave it to you I knew (according to you), what I was buying but this time I do not. Maybe I should cut my losses and forget about the $6211 I have lost so far so to me it seems silly to make the total $7711.

You see Honey, what makes you so sure you will be

released when this amount is paid. If I were in your shoes I would be thinking I don't trust them, they won't let me go I know who they are. In this situation you would be much better off having an exchange with a friend or family member, someone to meet you in Amsterdam, they pay the money the kidnappers release you for that I may consider flying to Amsterdam but I would not turn up alone either. There also arises another question, If they release you, how are you going to get a flight to Australia. You have missed you connection and this would require purchase of another ticket. You would probably be unshaven and have 2 cases of dirty clothes that would attract attention to Customs here if you were carrying a diamond. I know you haven't listened to me before and that is what got you into this mess I guess. You also asked me on the same day September 1st "are you dominant in a relationship" I answered you with "Maybe I will share the dominance if that is going to work". Clearly it will not.

My main concern is this 1500 pounds going to a stranger (maybe another player now) in London. I am more inclined to deliberately deny this Adam Winkleman the funds, I have nothing to lose anymore, it may be fun to see the result. I can no longer be the only person that can pay this money now, you see I was led to believe I was the target and no one else but if they will not allow you online and they do not contact me either (and this has been over a week) then clearly they have moved on to just keeping you hostage. It seems strange to me that after one month in custody you still don't know what it is all about and you don't seem to want to help yourself. I know they might be monitoring you there and I believe they have your password too, they might even read this before you. Now with my new Android phone I am constantly checking if you are online I love it.

What is going to happen to you over Christmas? Do you think these guys will come by and feed you maybe, maybe not. I would start to be concerned now, maybe I want to make you mad so you will come here and slap my face hard or punch me so at least you would be here. Do you remember Greg? Well he stays at my place now about 3 days a week. He will not commit yet to a full relationship, I know he wants one with someone I just have to convince him He doesn't know anything about us at all but he might find out on Saturday, I have the party that you were going to be listed on the invite for happening and some of my friends will want to know what has happened the rest will want to know what it was, including Greg (Don't worry I will tell them it's over) that is better for me also, so I don't look like an idiot. I might even have some of them give me money to recover my losses, don't know yet.

Lately I have been guided by my partner, he is coming to me in my dreams about this situation and he is not saying forget you, he is saying be careful now how I spend money and make sure I know what it is for. You told me I Was stubborn. So my sexy man, get yourself out of this and come and be by my side I know it's time to move our relationship on to another level because we will only be in a stalemate this way, remember I love and I miss you and I would like to meet you and I will wait to hear from you

Hugs and kisses my love Me:

How often will they let you chat? I might be lucky on Saturday and, receive money from one or more of my guests. My love there is something I forgot to say earlier and that is yes I am still always thinking of you being with me soon. Beck, sort this mess out   Kisses

Beck: (letter to me)   10/12/2010

The pain you have caused me is unbearable I cannot sleep I no longer eat, even breathing was difficult in your presence. I wish things were as they originally were, but now I realize that is impossible. I have nothing but insulted your intelligence and questioned your ability which I assure you is unlike any I have witnessed in every possible aspect. Your eyes shine with an amazing radiance, your smile is divine and your image remains cemented in my mind. It is ironic you were my one and only true happiness, though at times you were my only sorrow.

All I can ask for now is your forgiveness though inside I will yearn for so much more. I yearn to embrace your gentle touch, to gaze into your mystifying eyes just one more time and to kiss softly your full red lips. If I had known things would turn out this way I would have changed it all. I can do nothing but apologize for my behavior these feelings were new to me. I had not felt for anyone what I feel for you.

All I ask is please be patient and understanding as these times are difficult and a struggle for me. I am torn between survival and my feelings for you. Life throws us many curves the path may be long and hard but in the end the road widens and life changes for the better.

John, regarding Greg things are hard right now and they seem to just be a big blurry mess. But I don't blame you for any of it. "CRYING " we can be happy together if we work everything out which I think we will. You are everything to me and I love you with all my heart.

Now I must feel this way alone I have pushed you away and spoilt my opportunity if in fact a chance ever existed. Maybe one day our paths will reunite. If this wish is granted all will be different I will treat you how you deserve to be treated and vow I will never cause you harm. Until then I shall suffer the punishment I have dealt myself

Beck "CRYING"

Me: (letter to Beck)

My love, are you saying goodbye? That is sad but I can live with that I would have liked for us to meet and have our lives together but you are right, I did not destroy that opportunity you did. I hope things work out for you and as I said I may be given some money on Saturday at my party that would be enough to sort you out but my asking price would be too hard for you to meet my demands and Scott Van Bowman would not agree so I am not going to offer. It will now just help recover my losses to you. I can forgive you although I do not understand how you end up in this situation in the first place. Did a chance ever exist in the first place? I thought it did, maybe I was wrong. I hope one day it all work out but it's a journey you must take alone. I am not deserting you I just refuse to pay someone for no reason who is attempting to Rip Me Off!

So until then my love I will leave you to search for what you need, I believe it is a big mistake your rejecting me but I guess you have to do what you have to do Bye.

Me: (letter to Beck)

My darling I am sorry for writing another email to you but I have tears welling up now and I need to let my emotions out to you. I feel like I want to ask you a lot of questions the way we did when we first started chatting. I know you might not get to read this for a few days but I have to write it anyway, for myself if not for us. Firstly I want to thank you for telling me in your last email that you did not want to insult my intelligence. I have all along been checking every detail and price possible before I sent you money. They all checked out okay I even sent you more money when you were robbed, that I had to take on face value. I have my own ideas about that and, if am right, it will tell me something about you, if not maybe you will tell me one day. I am not going to tell you what I think. What I would like you tell me is that we can meet one day not too far away. I guess that depends on you and your current situation and I guess it has ruined us ever being together as a couple sadly. I really do need a partner Beck and if Greg is willing to accept a relationship that will be fine for me

As yet we are only casual and as he is staying on Saturday night for the party maybe I can convince him I like him heaps, at the same time if you were to arrive on my doorstep I would not turn you away my commitment remains. You have just told me you know I have that quality in your last email, I know I do. And I have been trying to tell you that for a while, no matter I really do hope you can sort this out for yourself soon because I would like to stay in touch with you. I really am trying to turn this situation of ours into a book in two years' time so far I have 2 chapters written. You could even sell the story to the media I guess. I am going to give you my business email address in case I have to delete this one because of Scott Van Bowman so don't let him see this one. I also want to tell you that none of my friends are giving me their opinion. I have not been telling any of them much lately I have been too embarrassed to do so. Well Babe, take care of yourself and chat to me when you can. At this stage I will be in London July 2012 maybe we can catch up then if not before. I feel better now that I have written this to you and I won't say anymore other than "you will always be in my heart and I am the man you never met that is happy to love you until the end of time.

Bye my love   Kisses

Me

Sweetheart I keep on reading what you wrote to me, all

I can say is yes I believe the chance for us did exist and so want to still be with you, I do forgive you and as I write this to you sobbing I pray we can be together soon, you touched my heart Babe and we have been together 3 months. Please don't throw that away, all my love

Beck: (letter to me) Dear John

As the day fades away and slips into night I find myself once again clinging to my prayers. Every night I pray to God that he will keep you in his arms. I pray that he keeps you out of harm's way until we can finally be together again.

It sometimes seems so unfair that we took longer than the day we were supposed to meet. I realized when you love a soldier you cannot expect anything. You asked me what I want to do about us, well, my sweetheart I do not want us to end.

Just because of the problem I am having now doesn't mean we have to give up hope, if you really love someone, the problem, the time and the distance apart should not make a difference.

I will wait for you. I wouldn't care how long I would have to wait. I would wait forever if that is what it takes! I love you, so you have my answer I feel the same way you do.

I love you John, I have loved you for a very long time and I don't think I'm going to stop loving you anytime soon.

Love always

Me: 11/12/2010

My darling Beck I have read your beautiful message but\I don't think you wrote it or have even read it. I know they have your password so in future every time you reply to me why don't you begin the message with something personal about us you know last time I asked you to tell me the name of my flatmate well next time, and every time tell me something different that only you would know because I am not going to talk to these idiots at all, as for you Beck I can't wait to be with you.

Beck: (letter to me)   13/12/2010

John my darling

It's me not them that's why I will start by saying how was the party on Saturday, and how is Josh going? Sweetie, I miss you and you know how much I love you

I know you don't need another reminder because I tell you a thousand times a day how much I love you, but I do and that's my only way to show you. I love the hundred ways you show me how much you love me, and I know my simple words can never compare. From day one I knew there was something in you that no other man had.

You are the most AMAZING man I have ever known. Thinking back to the strange way we met, how we grew so close in just a few short days, and how you were the first one to show me the meaning of true love, it makes me smile and fall all over for you again.

Baby, you make my heart beat faster each time I think of you and you give me butterflies. You are the one I want to hold for the rest of my life. In your arms is where I belong.

You melt me every time you tell me about the future that you want to spend with me and how we could show the world the real meaning of being in love with the right person

I wish the people around you saw me and accepted us being together, because I don't think I could live a day knowing that you are not in my life. I know that anyone that tried to replace you would only be compared to you in my mind, and I know they could never live up to you in my eyes. Every time I look into your eyes I know that is where I want to live and die. And every time I dream of you I don't want you to let go because that is the only place I feel the safest.

I know when we first got together everyone wanted us apart. They told us that our relationship would never last, and they still tell us that. But we have proven them wrong and I want you to stay in my life forever, as you will in my heart. I know forever is a very long time but it won't be enough time for me to spend with you showing you every day how much I love and care about you.

I hate being far from you knowing that I carry your

love in my heart. I pray that you will carry my love in your heart and I look forward to the day when we can be together.

Sweetie, if you got some money from the party as you told me before I will be very glad to get out of this place. My love if you send the money to them I think you should not give them the information, just tell them the money have been send and the information is with me, so I will only open my email for their Boss to see the information not someone else.

I think that's the good idea so they can allow me to go. The Boss told me already that he will arrange a flight to Australia for me after they got the money, hope to receive good news from you and the information.

What words can describe the sweetest most beautiful part of my life. You are my certainty, my comfort and hope, without you I would be lost. I know we have our ups and downs but if you'll let me in the rest of the time we have, I want to make you feel how you deserve, like a King ,like a Goddess. Each day I hope I can give just a little bliss of what you give me

I love you from the bottom of my heart Tears on my eyes now

Beck: (Me business email address)   14/12/2010
(Subject) pls get back to me asap
John how are you doing? Why I haven't hear from you?

I sent you an email to your gmail account don't know if you got it Hope to hear from you soon

Beck

Me: (Business email address) "This is an automated message"

Thanks for your message I will reply as soon as possible. If the matter is Urgent please call

+612xxx - - - - - or +61xxx- - - - - - -

Regards John Osborne

Me: 15/12/2010

Hi Babe I am sorry I have not replied I have been busy today with work parties and other guys. It is like that here at time of the year, you know Summer Holidays. Anyway I don't have good news. I did not get any money only abuse from the woman who was going to give me the money because she works in finance. I hope you can sort yourself out I really would love to see you soon. Are you still chained up in the warehouse? Kisses

Beck: (letter to me)   18/12/2010

John my Darling

My love for you is endless so tender so hot and complete. I swear to God I want you in my life. I love you more and more with each day passing and it eases me to know as tomorrow approaches that I will love you more than yesterday and tomorrow will be more than today. My love for you cannot be measured by words alone as love does express my true feelings for you.

When I think of our love it reminds me of all the things you are to me. You and only you have given me so much hope and have made me realize how much I want you! You show the true meaning of how a man should treat his partner.

John please accept my heart as your own and listen to both of ours beating as one. You are my reason to live. Without I'm nothing, the years will be a test, but nothing will keep me from loving you or from being by your side. I love you more than you could ever know, you are my world. I just wanted to let you know how much I love all that you are and will be. You're truly my love, my soul mate and my best friend.

For the first time in my life I have something to believe in. You've seen me at my worst and still take me as \I am. I thank God for you every day because I know you're Heaven sent, you are my angel. I love you from now 'til death us do part.

Right now you live far away from me and I really mean its killing me, but I know in my heart we are doing alright. I don't want to lose you to anyone else especially Craig or anything that anyone wants to say about you. I want you to know I love you from the deepest part of my heart I'm always so lost for words when it comes to you, I just wish there was another way we could be together.

I want you and always will and there is nothing that will ever change the way I feel about you… I love you love can make you do things that you never thought possible. It's the place where a part of you will forever be a part me I promise you'll always be in my heart I love you

Love always

Me (letter to Beck)   18/12/2010

It is always nice to hear from you, if this is you talking to me that is you have one vital piece of information incorrect and it has been mentioned my me in several emails lately I want to tell you what is happening in my life because it will affect any relationship I have with Beck. His name is Greg (not Craig). Yes I want a relationship with him but he will not commit to that, in fact he won't say he loves me, maybe he doesn't but he's honest with his feelings and I am so happy knowing that. He is 35 years old from an Italian Father and an Irish Mother. He is 6' 1" tall and has a toned body but does not go to the gym. He has long nipples that stand out through his tee shirt, you do not, nor are you 6' tall. He has large dangly balls and a 9" cock which is bigger than yours and he shaves off all his chest hair and pubes so he is body smooth. He is so Hot! He is an excellent kisser, a great dancer and has a wicked sense of humour like me I already know those things about him you I do not. There is something special about this man on bed, like you he likes it doggy style his big cock hurts more in that position. We discussed the issue of bare backing each other from the start and we are both happy with that, in fact he goes further I allow him to shoot inside me but what is so wonderful is we will fall asleep with him cuddling me while he is still inside me, now you know why I want a relationship with this man.

He likes me tying him up to the bedhead and fucking him. He likes me cumming all over his face and he swallows too. Unfortunately, last Friday he cracked his ankle in two places as part of an old injury and is now on crutches for the nest month. I was hoping to share NYE at a friends with him but he wants to stay home and convalesce. I just have to drive to his place which is an outer suburb to see him. Anyway he is moving back into the city in a couple of months and will be working behind a bar again, somewhere in Oxford St. I hope. He has indicated he might accept my offer to stay here until he gets set up, that means he will have your side of the bed.

If he wants the relationship of course I will say "Yes" as for us (anyway I'm not sure there is us anyway) you never arrived and I am now not sure at what point you changed your mind so it doesn't matter. Personally I think you made a big mistake by not wanting to live here, there are so many opportunities here but I guess you prefer the dodgy lifestyle you have with your accomplices in Europe, that's fine I accept that. Do you want me to say "You won the Game" So you did but you did not win the final attack the last 1500 pounds.

You have given me an exciting time, but then I've paid for it. I am hoping you will give me accommodation at your place in 18 months' time. It will only be a week I have other destinations to go to maybe you want to come to Scotland with me but then you've probably seen that already.

My friend that abused me (and did not give me the money) has rung since to apologize but Rupertt has told my Mother in Law and now she is on the warpath. My Flatmate says I should start a new life in 2011 and I agree. My German friends have told me to "Stop looking for apples under the horse" and start looking for them under the tree. They are right you I met under the horse, it didn't work.

I will help you out if you ever decide to come to Oz but somehow I don't think you do. My feelings for you now are more that of a curiosity to meet you but I would not say no to doing all those romantic things you spoke of. I am up to writing chapter 3 with the story now that's actually the part dated September 6th Beck to John 10:00pm AEST "I will never let you down"

I don't understand your life as it is, sadly maybe you got cold feet thinking about mine I have a good life and great friends. Now that it is summer here there are so many Hot Guys here all just wearing cargo shorts T shirts and thongs (fucking hot). I get hit on for some one nighters and sometimes say yes. I thank you for being able to motivate me and get my writing started, after all you are writing this now Babe not me.

You are free to email or chat with me whenever you

want, a phone call would be nice I'm sure you can afford to make one with that diamond of yours. My sadness, as aspirations with you will pass in time and my finances are growing strong again. I am working on Christmas Day until 3:00pm then I will go to the lunch I have been invited to with friends, I will catch up with Greg before New Year did I mention he also looks hot in a T shirt and cargo shorts. Anyway, I guess you need to take care of yourself and please let me know if I can stay with you on my visit, it will be no more than 5 days I am only away for two weeks in total.

Please pass this message on to Beck Bye for now kisses

CHAPTER 16

THE SCAMMER

It has now been 3 weeks since any communication with each other, I have made a New Year's resolution to put the incident behind me, I know I will wonder what has become of him but that will only be short term and I will prefer not to talk about it. Beck has made several mentions that I should not tell my friends anything perhaps this is the only truth he spoke indicative of knowing in advance how the relationship would finish. It is now a new year and lots of fun things to do.

I feel content that I have been able break the chain in this pyramid letter scam, Adam Winkleman was never going to receive 1500 pounds and someone else maybe Scott van Bowman would not take his step up the pyramid for failing to pay to do so, what did this mean for Beck are they crooks dealing in diamonds? Did he enter a deal to pay 7500 pounds for an uncut raw diamond and was to end up 1500 pounds short? Maybe there were headlines in the local news Headless handless body found floating in canal. One thing is for sure this news would never be heard of in Australia

Perhaps I have been the victim of a diamond scam and there is a group that makes a living from this. I have been told by State and Federal police here in Australia they are not interested in this scam it is not worth it to them to investigate anything less than one million dollars there is just not enough manpower and that I should change my email address and stop communication with this person. I attempted to contact Scotland Yard but their website is unavailable until you provide a reference number from the local Met office, so this group will continue operating.

I had hoped to have a different ending to the one I am writing here. Even a headless body in the canal would have been satisfying and if that were the case there would be some information available get some truth Three weeks have passed into the New Year and I am meeting new people moving on with my life. It is Friday morning January 7th 2011 2:10 am ADST I am working night audit as usual and receive a chat on gmail it is Beck.

Beck: 7/1/2011

Hi

Me:

Hi

Beck:

How are you?

Me:

I am fine and surprised to be hearing from you though

Beck:

Am here in UK now am at the hospital not feeling fine

Me:

Why are you at the hospital?

Beck:

I am feeling serious pain on my chest.

Me:

Have you injured yourself.it could be a heart condition you know

Beck:

The doctor said so.

Me"

Well I guess you will have to slow down a little with your life then

Beck:

Yes I will. How is everything with you over there, and your new man?

Me:

I saw Greg last weekend. We were out all night even with his bad ankle. I won't see him this weekend though and he still won't commit but that's fine I can have him on a casual basis

Beck:

Oh but I thought he is committed already?

Me:

No he is committed to being single but he enjoys being with me

Beck:

Okay

Me:

I want him to want a relationship, but he is not prepared to yet after the last one, anyway I am happy being with him when we are together

Beck:

Okay

Me:

you know you have a strange bunch of colleagues or business associates (if that's what you call them) it's no wonder you have a heart condition you should be somewhere nice and warm.

The weather here is great at the moment, is it snowing there?

Beck:

Yes

Me:

I'm glad it doesn't snow in this city I am built for comfort and warmth I don't like the cold weather.

Beck:

I don't like it as well

Me:

That's why I can only travel through the Northern Hemisphere in summer

Beck:

Okay

Me:

I like Sydney in Summer, the boys are all so sexy not wearing much at all

Beck:

How is Josh?

Me:

He is angry with me at the moment. I let a friend of Greg's stay over he said for a couple of days until he returned to London but he was bull shitting and stole some electronics form the house

Beck:

Really!

Me:

John got a new ipad for |Christmas and was worried it might have been taken too but it is okay. I just have to make sure no one stays over ever again. Greg was so embarrassed and upset over it, then we realized this guy was only a rent boy but the stupid fool had used my computer to logon to his Facebook so he left his profile and email address behind for me to give to the police. Some guys are just sooooo stupid

Beck:

That's very stupid

Me:

Yes, so I sent him a threatening message and told him he'd better leave the state. Josh is after him as well as Greg and the Police.

Beck:

Okay

Me:

I know what Pawn shop he took them to and I have the serial numbers of most of the items, so when they are on sale the police will seize them for me. He also used some profile pics on his Facebook page that were not of him and oddly enough I know the guy whose pics they are so I have told him and given him the email address as well to threaten this prick.

Beck:

That's bullshit

Me:

That's true this guy reckons he was going back to the UK as he has dual citizenship in fact that is bullshit too .My New Year's resolution is " No more men after 2010" except Greg and my ex contacted me to arrange his 30th birthday this Saturday which I did. I even bought him an expensive bottle of Vodka and had gold leaf blended in as his present so I guess that makes me stupid too. I am curious now Beck what ever happened to the diamond?

Beck:

Nothing happen to the Diamond

Me:

Well you should be okay then you don't have to worry about money you can live comfortably.

Beck:

I am not worried

Me:

That's' fine, what about your mother?

Beck:

She's fine

Me:

That's good. So what are you going to do with yourself now? Do you have any plans? a new man perhaps!

Beck:

I don't have any yet

Me:

Yes well winter is not a time for these things anyway. You just need to stay out of harm I guess. Are you back at the gym?

Beck:

Nop

Me:

So when did you leave Amsterdam and those idiots

Beck

end of December.

Me:

It would not have been nice to spend Christmas in a warehouse alone, I told you they would get sick of the whole charade and let you go once they knew no one was interested there was no gain or game in it for them

Beck:

How is ur job?

Me:

My job is fine I am on holidays until nest Tuesday form driving job but I am still here at Hyde Park and I will be working here 5 nights a week for Feb and early March (4 weeks) because one of the other guys is going to Thailand

Beck:

Oh okay

Me:

I will also be driving and working 57 hours per week but this is money for next year's holiday

I am buying currency now, the Aussie $ is 71p at the moment I have bought some for my brother as he is competing in the world titles in Glasgow in 2012 perhaps we will go together. I am training myself to go without alcohol for this entire 4 week period that will be the hardest part of night shift

Beck:

Okay

Me:

The company told me they would get someone to drive for 2 weeks but I said no I don't want anyone driving "My Car" and the guys I drive convoy with don't want a stranger either we all work so well together and they are great guys. I am deadly serious about wanting to meet with you when I get there

Beck:
When are you coming?

Me:
July 2012 but we will also be going on to Scotland and parts of Europe as well. I will only be away from home about 3 weeks not sure exactly what days where, it depends on what day I can get a ticket for the Tattoo. Are you staying back home at your mum's place?

Beck:
Yes

Me:
Say hello to her from me. I guess I'd better go now. I have to deliver the newspapers, you stay out of trouble and away from scams I will no doubt chat with you again at some stage.... Bye.

Beck: 15/1/2011
Hi are you there?

Me:
Yes how are you? Are you out of hospital yet?

Beck:

I am out of hospital now

Me:

I was wondering why my phone was saying Beck Hill, now I know it means you are online with gmail my phone alerts me now. I told you, you will never get rid of me I have spent too much money for nothing for that to happen. I hear there is a lot of snow in London at the moment. … We are all naked here, it is sooo hot 24/7.

Beck:

How are you?

Me:

Hi Beck, what did the doctor say, was it angina, or was it a mild heart attack. I have been dealing with this issue with my dad who turned 82 yesterday.

Babe! Talk to me, I can't bite your head off from 12,000kms away. If you want to know what Scotland Yard said ask me. I learned something that I did not know the Met and Scotland Yard are the same force

Beck:

Is Heart Attack

Me:

I thought so I hope you are okay. How severe was the rating? My dad has had 2 heart attacks 11 years apart we were all told that as it was Angina they may be few

510 | J MOREWOOD OSBORNE

and far but he needs a stent in the Aorta Artery keeps him going.

Hey Beck remember what I said, "maybe you need to slow down now" there is no use you having all that wealth and dying before you can spend it (I am cynical). You know if you don't want to talk to me you can log off and I won't have to waste my time, but well if you are chatting to other people as well it is going to alert me too. Do give my love to Kate I hope her father is not going to kill you with all the money that was "rob". The next comment is yours babe

Beck:

Hum

Me:

Okay

Beck:

Well how is everything with you over there?

Me:

Hot guys hot days, hot weather. I made myself a resolution for New Year "No more men after 2010" I have broken that 3 times (twice with Greg) he has been the only true nice guy I met last year. My Ex has just accused me of everything but he did not get residency I hold the only card for that on paper and now he hates my guts. Oh! Well he wants residency, I am the Australian Citizen he can FUCK OFF! That's how things are with me babe. BTW my tolerance level of acceptance for 2011 is zero please do not let that intimidate you I might do that next year maybe maybe not.

Beck:

Okay, how is Josh anyway?

Me:

He is going away tomorrow he is on summer holidays, everyone here is... He is taking his dog with him for one week then he goes away in 2 weeks without the dog, I told him I will lock after Bella as long as he looks after my dog next year, we both agreed. I only found out last week he has a degree in Psychology, he is a great flatmate and only a plutonic relationship thank God!

Beck, it has been nice chatting to you but as usual you are not saying much I have to go honey. I have just come home from the Shift and I am hungry, Greg did not come out tonight. So I actually came home alone. I only mention this because I am up to writing chapter 3 of your book and it was the day 13/9/2010 and you were upset I brought some guy home. Babe I have to go now would love to chat same time tomorrow

Byeeee.

Beck:

Okay but that doesn't make me happy when you talk about Greg

Me:

Sweetheart, nothing makes you happy you do realize that you could have had everything but that was before the diamond came into play.

Beck:

The diamond is with my mother now

Me:

Interesting thought, the diamond will never give you love and happiness it will get you sex yeah and false love, sweetheart I am happy the diamond is with your mummy, you never listened to what I said in the first place and it caused a lot of grief for you. I was never, at any time, going to pay 1500 pounds to release you and the reason for that is I thought the whole issue was so badly handled by Scott Bowman (if he exists) that there was never any guilt on my part, I never pay for something that is not tangible, and you chained up was not tangible. I know one thing tonight at

least I am talking to the original "Beck".

Beck:

To be honest with you I am not really happy about ur relationship with Greg because that break my heart a lot

Me:

Why are you upset about Greg how can you say that when you never came to be with me and you never considered my feelings and the fact I so much wanted us to work and you had other plans from the start, I was left in solitude by you therefore I took it on my own feelings to make a decision

Beck:

But I never knew things would go that way John.

Me:

What do you mean you never knew things would go that way?

Beck:

Because I don't know everything would be like that, I thought I would have been in ur place for a long time but I don't know that shit is going to happen to me

Me:

Beck I want you to see something from my point of view I believed in you so much I wanted us to work out. I was wrong so obviously, as the situation changed and you were "Double Crossed" (if that's true) I had nowhere else to go. I had 3 relationships in 2010 my ex, Greg and you 2 out of 3 have let me down, Greg has not. I don't know really whether you wanted to love an older man I'm sorry for me you didn't, .but I don't know how much of anything you said is true Beck.

Beck:

John age doesn't really matter to me I have fallen in love with you already

Me:

That is what you said in your profile and incessant email chats, but the fact is you are there and I am here and you have no excuse for us not to be together. Do you have any idea how excited I was to meet you and how happy I was to meet your mother as well you just left me hanging for no reason babe you hurt me, all I wanted was to love you.

Beck

I am sorry my love everything "hurted" me as well

Me:

"until the end of time"(remember?), you know I feel like I want to kiss you now and forgive you but I am not sure that is a good idea. I know that you are now going to be uncomfortable for the rest of your life so I guess what I am saying is when you come to Oz let me know and we can maybe chat. I would still like to hear your side of our relationship if you do.

Beck:

My love I still wanna meet with you for real because am in love with you I don't think I can live without you. John I really wanna spend the rest of my life with you

Me:

All you have to do is get yourself here and I will meet you. Sweetheart I am open to you but now far more cautious all you have to do is arrive, you have all my details

Beck:

But you have to show me care as you did before

Me:

Maybe if you do that I can actually hold you and say "I love you Beck Hill" but not until then.

Beck:

I don't think you still have the love you have for me before, since you have been going out with Greg.

Me:

I don't have the love for us as I had before and it has nothing to do with Greg, it has to do with what I spent on you for an absolute waste of time. Until you feel guilty about that we will not be a couple as much as I may, or may not want to.

BTW

Greg is a really genuine guy. He doesn't SMS me when he is coming to town he comes up behind me and gives me a hug and kiss (something we were going to do remember). All you have to do is get here this time at your expense because I have given you everything, then we can start a life if you have time, otherwise please don't waste mine. I so much wanted to love you.

You know, if you are lost for an answer you start by saying don't you want my thick 81/2 cock up your arse.

BTW you have my address I'm sure you could surprise me if you wanted to love me

Beck:

John, you know I don't have work here and if I come there now I will need only flight fee

Me:

No way babe you've got the diamond you are on your own financially with this. My heart has hardened thanks to you and I am grateful

Beck:

Okay its fine you making me feeling depressed now I guess I have to go now you know I am not feeling good and the doctor has warned me to stop thinking

Me:

I would think the doctor has warned you to stop hanging out with all those suspected criminals. Anytime you want to arrive, when England is in worse shape than it is now you let me know. I think my offer was, and is very good. I am not looking anymore, and Greg will not commit so the only person that has this offer is you babe. I will let you think on that, all you have to do is arrive. As far as I am concerned I have kept my bargain and paid in full Remember I was never going to and never did pay 1500 pounds to release you from bondage and I didn't feel guilty remember (your soldier).

I have to go it is 2:30am, for old time sake I love you kisses

Beck:

I love you too kisses

CHAPTER 17

THE REGRET

I was feeling some contentment after our previous chat I was able to vent upon Beck and I had hoped he would be reduced to tears and as per usual wondered if they would be false. Now the situation has completed a full circle, I lost my money, Beck is a scammer and from this point it is game over. It would be 10 days before I heard from Beck not really expecting to hear from him at all. Then I received the following letter that has been written by a third party again, this is easy to recognize there are no spelling mistakes and the grammar is correct. Their message in this letter is clear it speaks of ongoing commitment and confirms a pyramid scamming operation. This letter is a standard format you would receive from any scam group and perhaps this group has used this several times before, there is even evidence of this in the text. One thing is for certain they are still looking for payment of 1500 pounds to Adam Winkleman. I have to reply in kind with a letter to Beck and this should be farewell.

Beck letter to me   25/1/2011

Dear John

I know that neither one of us had in mind that we would meet someone on the internet and fall in love but it has happened. And for that, I have no regrets in fact it is one of the best things that has ever happened to me in years. For this, and what has happened to us and between us I have you to thank.

For almost the past months you have brought so much joy to me that words can never explain. In the past year, you have brought so much life back into a lifeless body and we have not even met face to face. For almost the past months, I know and realize what it is to LOVE again and to feel loved.

I never thought it would last this long, but it has. This is a clear indication that we have so much in common and we are building on something that is real. I hope we get the chance to see this thing through.

There have been hard times bad times and good times, but with that comes lonely times. We have reached new and higher grounds with what we have shared in the past weeks, and I would do it all over again with you if I had to. I have no regrets

I am sending you this to let you know that I have been sent an angel to be with me, and you are that angel. I STILL LOVE YOU FOR REAL.

Please understand that we have so much to give to each other and I look forward to that day. I believe it is closer now than ever before. It is just that there may be a few more obstacles that we need to clear up and I think you know what I am talking about. Besides that we can and I know we will survive, what I need is flight fee my love.

Love always Beck Osborne

Me Letter to Beck   27/1/2011

Good morning to you babe

Thanks for the nice words in your email last night, maybe you did learn from the experiences last year with us. I certainly did and I wondered if I really had put a spark back into your life after losing a partner. I had hoped that we would, by now be living as a couple, but with a new year comes a new realization, for me and that is you intend to only have an internet relationship and not meet me in person whether I come to London or not for you. I am not quite sure, and I'm not going to guess because what I want to think and what is reality may be far apart. I guess you are out of hospital, and on heart tablets and I guess you are still playing the game.

I also believe you are not born in the UK and that may be of concern to you however rest assured it is not as far as I am concerned. But I am concerned as to why you want me to pay for the airline ticket. I thought you had a diamond worth 126,000 pounds. When we last chatted you asked me for the fare as well. Why don't you sell the diamond in the UK as you can do this easily, it has already got you into so much trouble. I watched the movie "Blood Diamond" last night starring Leonardo Di Caprio it's all true as I said about the Kimberley Contract which 40 nations have signed and I agree. There should be certificates in order to stamp out this barbaric practice in Sierra Leone.

I guess if you really want to be with me you will find a way. I am not in a relationship with Greg, he doesn't want one we are friends and fuck buddies, that is all at the moment but I do have feelings for him. Anyway, enough about him I hope you are able to sort out your obstacles you refer to, I was under the impression everything was fine all you have to do is get yourself here.

Anyway, I will leave you to sort out whatever you have to I must move on with my life. You know where to find me if you want to.

Cheers babe

Beck: 29/1/2011

Hi are u there? John

Me:

Give me 5 minutes I am home only on the toilet

Beck: Ok

Me:

Hi babe I am here now I do have to go to the toilet but

I am at home just stripping off its' 28 deg. Celsius at 12:30am how are you anyway? brb toilet

Beck:

Ok

Me:

I am back now sorry for that I had a big meal out and walked home 5 blocks you know what it's like are you there?

Beck:

Yes babe am here

Me:

How is your health?

Beck:

Getting better babe

Me:

you never told me much about your heart attack is this something that will happen again or is it under control I ask because I am facing this with my daddy.

Beck:

No, is under control now yes you told me then about your daddy

Me:

Cool okay so why do you need airfare?

Beck:

babe believe me I have think everything a lot, and it make me cry every time I remember what happened between us Now I am ready to be there with you

Me:

really?

Beck:

Yeah my love because I always feel that I don't have a life every time I am thinking of it, my love if you really can justify to me, I promise I will be there with you even this coming week

Me:

you know I told you, you will regret not being here but all that aside and I am not going to do that

(I told you so routine) but you have unless I am mistaken a diamond worth 1 quarter of a million dollars

Beck:

But I don't have the flight fee that's the problem I am facing now everyone has change to me in the house

Me:

sell the diamond!

Beck:

My mummy has collected her diamond back Things has change in the house everyone has changed to me

Me:

what do you mean everyone in the house has changed to you?

Beck:

Because of everything that happen. Yes Kate has change to me, you know, the money she borrowed from her daddy John I really want to have you in my life

Me:

I thought you lived with mummy alone

Me:

I tried to contact Kate via her email after you got kidnapped and I never heard another word from her. Isn't she getting married anyway?

Beck:

First week of next month

Me:

I wondered about what was happening with the money from Kate's dad are you invited to the wedding? I would have thought you were to be the best man so who is the guy she is marring?

Beck:

His name is Paul

Me:

do you like him? I mean he is stealing your best friend and you don't make friends easily (according to you)

Beck:

He is nice guy

Beck:

But I don't know what Kate have told him, it seems like he's changed

Me:

you mean about you?

Beck:

yes, they did not do like that before

Me:

Is this since Amsterdam?

Beck:

Yes I guess. Because I didn't hear from her suddenly

Me:

I thought she really liked you, but she didn't help you either in Amsterdam

Beck:

Yeah she does, but I guess is because of the money that she didn't help me

Me:

that is when I tried to contact her, to which I got no reply I am sorry that you have lost a good friend maybe the money she borrowed for you that was to be paid back when you got here, was to use in the wedding. I still am paying a loan I took out for you too.

Beck:

I understand that

Me:

maybe it will do her good to have lost this cash she was also asking me to borrow money for you

Beck:

But john now I really want to be with you now I can even be there this new week

Me:

now she will need to buy a house with Paul and maybe realize cash is a sacred item Sweetheart, darling love, you may want to be with me this week but in the first part of every year after Christmas I have a lot of bills to pay for the year so I don't have available cash now until the end of March and that is for my trip with my brother and Robert next year I will hopefully meet you then if you want to, ,you are still welcome here before hand but it is up to you now to provide for yourself

Me:

I am still here I gather Scott Van Bowman did not pay for your ticket here after I refused to pay him

Beck:

Yes he did not, my mummy arranged flight for me

Me:

you did say he would pay for the ticket if I paid the 1500 pounds (which, I might add is dearer then the airfare, so who did pay for your release in the end/?

Beck:

They just let me go, no one paid for it

Me:

I told you that they would get bored with the whole concept especially when Christmas was coming up and their demanding wives would have wanted them home, no one to feed you none of them wanted a murder charge. I had a strong feeling from the start that they would let you go but I could not tell you that with them reading could I

Beck:

Ok

Me:

anytime you want to be here let me know, you are still welcome to stay

Beck:

Babe you know is only flight fee I need

Me:

please don't ask me for this I don't want to upset you by saying no. I have already paid this remember and have no guilt too remember (your soldier)

Beck:

Ok babe I hear you

Me

Thank you, all you have to do is get yourself here I will take care of the rest that is a fucking good offer to anyone anywhere in the world honey I now have a deep hatred for Western Union too

Beck:

Ok Why?

Me:

well I sent all the cash via western Union and got nothing for it so I contacted them (as I have everyone I can) about the identity of the recipient ie. YOU and they told me that only the police would get that information so I abused them and pointed out that I had paid their wages by sending money with them and I would make sure I told everyone they were dodgy as well, sadly they didn't care

Beck:

Oh I see

Me:

so I will never give them anymore business but then I don't have to anyway that is the truth love you already know I am not an idiot to lie down and accept everything I mean to start with I have to shut up about our Welsh Prime Minister (yes Julia is from Cardiff)

Beck:

Ok

Me:

I wish she would go back to Cardiff she wants to tax us all because of the Brisbane Flood disaster we are all saying go back to Cardiff

Beck:

Really!

Me:

more money. I have to fork out this time for redneck Queenslanders I don't think so, those fools all bought property without getting plans from the council of the 1974 flood line (yes it's happened before)

Beck:

Ok

Me:

these are all new people to Queensland the originals know this and would not build on the canals of Southport and West bank. OMG the dog has just farted I need spray brb

Me:

are you back at the Gym?

Beck:

Not yet

Me:

Beck I have to get a drink and something to eat hopefully you will surprise me and just arrive one day until then I guess we chat if you want to

Kisses

Beck:

Ok

Me:

bye for now thanks for the chat kisses

Beck:

Ok .... Love u

Me:

Love you too! Prove it to me get yourself here

Me: 3/2/2011

Are you there?

Beck:

My love am here, yes I am here

Me:

How are you, Hi I am here too, are you best man at Kate's wedding? What are you doing today, we are in a heatwave here, wish I had cooler weather

Beck:

The wedding was great

Me:

Where is the honeymoon?

Beck:

Somewhere around London you know, Kate is not really being nice with me like before

Me:

I was wondering if Kate would change she has no use for you anymore. I find that happens when people get married. Do you like Paul?

Beck:

Yes I did

Me

I gather you don't like Paul anymore?

Beck:

Yes I like Paul because he is a gentle guy. But Kate has been poisoning his mind. She won't trust anyone anymore she has to make sure her husband stays faithful.

Me:

You are right you know, I thank god I am a Gay man because women, poison their husbands minds I don't think they even try to stay together with their man for long They should be in my situation and lose someone you love after a long period. Death is so final. You don't even want to think about divorce in these circumstances. You mark my words she will change now and maybe destroy Paul in the process. Maybe you have to lose her as a friend she sees other things more important now, no need for your sharing secrets anymore.

Beck:

She is here in the sitting room, do you want to talk to her

Me:

Not really, I sent her emails while you were in Amsterdam, and she never replied, besides it's none of my business you are my friend not her

Beck:

Hmmm just this is true talk from you. The words really touch my heart.

Me:

Well there is nothing much to do here and so many cute boys living in the complex walking in and out sometimes pissed and not wearing much clothing

Beck:

Okay

Me:

I would like a piece of so many of them there are several cute gay boys here as well

Beck:

The weather is cold here

Me:

The weather is cold you say, well I will swap you we have been living in an oven for over a week, at the moment there is light rain but it is 31 deg. outside at 5:45am. I know I will get over

Winter for the four months when we get it, but I would like some respite from the heat now, even the dogs are losing their hair from it. How come you are online so early in the evening?

Beck:

Why?

Me:

No reason, it's just that I usually talk to you earlier than this time. Do you remember I told you I had some items stolen by that queen I let sleep on the lounge? Well I have located them in a pawn shop, the Police have impounded them I will eventually get them back but this will take 59 days, apparently that is how long the court order will take. They want me have him charged, I said yes.

Beck:

Oh yes you told me about it.

Me:

Talk soon babe must go home

Beck:

The words really touch my heart okay my love bye your love still remains in my heart -- Kisses.

Me:

I am sorry my love I have just been alerted you sent me a message. Obviously I have also woken up now and I have just read the remaining words you sent me after I have logged off from our chat earlier, thankyou for the kind words .Are you going to let Kate read the chat we had earlier, she might not like what she will read about herself. I will talk with her if you want me to but what do I really have to say, anyway I guess you are busy so I won't bother you anymore now Bye…

Beck: 14/2/2011

My love happy Val Day

Me:

Hi babe and to you too I haven't had any flowers cards or kisses so I guess this makes you my Valentine wow that's nice

Beck:

How I wish I am with you there. How are you doing?

Me:

That would be nice I would have bought you flowers and published our betrothal in the paper, I guess now I can call you my Valentine.

Beck:

Yeah coz you are my Valentine as well.

Me:

Thanks honey, that's nice, in that case I should say thanks for the flowers

Beck:

Lol thank you too. .Babe I have something to ask you do you have a credit card?

Me:

One day, some day when you least expect it I am going to walk up to you and say "Hi babe" and you will know it is me. I promise you. The challenge will be finding you but that is all part of the chase.

Beck:

I want to be there with you as well, John please answer my question do you have a credit card?

Me:

Yes but it is very full at the moment zzz

Beck:

Full why? How do you mean?

Me:

I mean I don't have much credit available because I have reached my limit and while I am paying it off monthly I am not paying more than the minimum each month. Sometimes I use it in that month so my limit does not decrease by much. I am trying to get rid of it and I am hoping to get rid of $2000 off it with the extra shifts I am doing for the next month I need a supplier with low interest my Visa card is not. Why do you ask?

Beck:

How much is the limit?

Me:

$10,000 that is the problem, I am too old to go back to prostitution to pay it off (lol)

Beck:

To pay it off, what do you mean! Are you owning debt with the credit card?

Me:

Well the more I pay off the card each month the more credit I have available

Beck:

Ok

Me:

It also means that I am paying 22% interest rather than something like 5%

Beck:

So $10,000 is the limit of the card?

Me:

There are banks that offer a low rate on balance transfers I have already tried that

Beck:

Okay babe

Me:

Maybe I should try again, that way I can pay it off faster. The other option was going to be "turn you over to a slave trader" when you arrived to pay my credit card Lol

Beck:

My mummy wanted to receive money through your credit card but it's $20,000

Me:

I don't understand what you mean.

Beck:

Some company wanted to pay my mummy $20,000

Me:

Do you mean your mother has a $20,000 debt?

Beck:

Nop, she wanted to receive money by credit card

Me:

Okay, I hope she is not being cheated by this company this does not sound very trustworthy

Babe:

Is not by cheated, lawyer is involved about this

Me:

which doesn't help you, because any money deposited onto my card will automatically pay the debt before the rest is available. That means the bank get it first.

Beck:

Ok, you know my mummy trusted you a lot she wanted to receive her money from your credit card

Me:

I don't understand why when $10,000 is going to go to the bank

Beck:

She will instruct the company to pay the money 2 times to your account, they will firstly pay

$10,000 and after you get it they will pay the remaining $10,000

Me:

Why, she won't get the full amount in any Case \I can't pay it back

Beck:

Okay, how much will she get?

Me:

The other $10,000

Beck:

Why? She will instruct the company to transfer $10,000 first

Me:

She will get the other $10,000 at the exchange rate for the day of the transaction

Beck:

Ok I understand you now no problem she will understand that

Me:

That makes it less than $10,000

Beck:

Yeah I understand sometime the money exchange rate is low

Me:

That is a big loss Beck. I don't want to be in a situation owing a pensioner money

Beck:

John, the company will transfer the money to you 2 times first $10,000 and 2nd $10,000. John, you don't have to worry okay! My mummy really trusted you with her mind lol, you have charmed her

Me:

I don't know what I said to charm her but if she is expecting $20,000 I can never give her the other $10,000

John I don't really understand what you mean? You mean she will not get the other $10,000?

Me:

If the company is giving her $20,000 and they pay it into my Visa, then the first $10,000 will go to the bank as payment in full for my outstanding balance, yes she will not get the other $10,000

Beck:

Okay if the company pay only $10,000 hope she will get it?

Me:

There might be a problem with that

Beck:

How?

Me:

Because that is the first $10,000 which would be for the bank

Beck:

Why is it like that? If my mummy asks the company to transfer $10,000 this week, and after you get it to us then she will ask the bank to send another $10,000 to you following week.

Me:

You would be better off using a card with more credit available. What about Kate?

Beck:

I told you Kate has changed to us

Me:

Yes that you did say

Beck:

If my mummy ask the company to transfer the money this week and after you get it to us then she will ask the bank to send another $10,000to you the following week

Me:

Why is payment only by credit card, what about direct debit into her account.

Beck:

The company can only transfer the money by credit card

Me:

well sadly I'm not going to offer my card details to an unknown company

ahahahahahaha

Me:

I don't even use my card on the net for safety reasons.

Beck:

John "common" nothing will happen to your card, you don't need to be worrying yourself about this ok? Your card is safe, nothing will happen to it, just help my mummy receive the money pls my love. She really trusted you.

Me:

Not okay, I don't know anything about them and neither do you

Beck:

Yes I "knew" about them the company is genuine and reliable

Me:

I have had many offers from internet companies wanting to offer me a job

Beck:

Oh, this is not offer from the internet babe I understand, the company are not scammers

Me:

One of these job companies asked me immediately for my credit card details for payment of wages. This company was fraudulent. Beck, honey I am not prepared to give my credit card details out at all. Sorry.

Beck:

John, you mean you never trust me or my mummy? Lawyer is involved about this. It's the company my mummy sell the diamond for.so they offer us $20,000 and they will pay remaining $100,000 in 3 months' time

Me:

Oh! That is how you feel I am not going to try and change your mind I would have shared this with you if you were here but not now as you are not.

Beck:

So you don't need to be afraid at all

Me:

I'm not afraid Beck I chose not to accept the offer

:

Why John?

Me:

It is my card and no one else's

Beck:

Yeah I understand but John pls help us you know out of the money I can get a ticket to come over there

Me:

This card is my saviour sometimes I can't go without it

Beck:

Yes I understand the card is very important to you, my love let's make things work out for us

Me:

You can sell the diamond to do that

Beck:

Read my chatting very well we already sell the diamond to the company. They want to pay us

$20,000 they will pay the remaining balance in the next 3 months which is $100,000

Me:

Yes, let's make things work out for us, you have my address. It will only cost you $20 from the airport to the house

Beck:

Oh I get it now that you are angry with me its' fine I have to go now, I will chat with you when you are no longer angry anymore

Me:

So that is why you said $100,000 I thought it was a typing error. Okay I'm not angry Bye...

CHAPTER 18

THE REALITY

If I was supposed to be shocked reading a letter from Beck declaring his love and signed with my name it was a waste of time. I was noticing that my persistence in being firm was paying off and now was his realization. Everything I had said in our chats was true. His captors let him go, no one paid Adam Winkleman, Kate did not trust him anymore and he was still in the same predicament he was at the start of his journey. He was now finding out how much of what has been "chatted" is now happening to him. I surprised at the attempt to hijack my credit card. He has been agreeing that I am correct, yet not able to understand the stupidity of that request. This was clearly a final attempt to pay Adam Winkleman, and Beck was not the originator of this idea. I felt a sense of satisfaction.

Beck: 3/3/2011

Hi

Me:

now you are there

Beck:

how are you babe?

Me:

I have the PC on now

Beck:

oh ok babe

Me:

it is easier than using the phone I have been busy with chapter 6 of the book

Beck:

yes babe

Me:

now 100 pages long

Beck:

which book is that babe?

Me:

the story about you

Beck: why?

Me:

might be a good seller might not be but I have to try I've wanted to write something for years but didn't know what, this is reality I am inspired you may have unleashed a hidden talent in me that remains to be seen

Beck: 10/3/2011

Hi

Me:

Hi beck, how are things with you?

Beck:

can't complain am cool and you?

Me:

Happy now my working hours are back to normal I have my 3 day weekends back

Beck:

really? I am very happy for you

Me:

I have a busy social Saturday this week and can catch up with Greg on Sunday

Beck:

Ok

Me:

I have made a bit of money out of these long extra days over the past month

Beck:

really?

Me:

at 7am tomorrow I Will be over the moon

Beck:

oh ok

Me:

it will be my first weekend free for over a month

Beck:

how I wish am there with you

Me:

How is the weather in London?

Beck:

the weather is cool a bit cold

Me:

it would be nice for you. To be here I know you will like it here

Beck:

yes I want to be there I want to start a new life over there

Me:

I have come to realize there are a lot of local hot guys here you know when you want to start your new life here you already have a place to stay and I'm sure we can get you work

Beck:

that would be very good so I can be able to help when it comes to bills because you will not be the only one paying for the bill

Me:

You would also make Kate jealous

Beck:

ahahahaha, you got it

Me:

you would pay your way I know that

Beck:

she will be very jealous when I arrive there babe you know I don't have money to do that

Me:

maybe she doesn't want to come here if you're not but

if that changes she will ask her daddy for the date and the fare for her and Paul

Beck:

Lol she will not come because she don't like me again

Me:

Don't stress about not being able to afford to come

Beck:

Ok but I think of it every day because I want to be there

Me:

It is very strange to waste a long term relationship. Everyone that comes here wants to stay Australia is a land of opportunities and lots of sun

my love pls help me to come there pls John

Me:

honey the money I have is to be in Scotland next year with my brother

Beck:

My love I will refund it back to you as soon as I get there and find a job pls babe

Me:

That is what you said last time remember

Beck:

babe I promise my word this time

Me:

you should still have some of the money I sent you

Beck:

babe believe me this time I swear I will arrive to your place I don't want to continue like this

Me:

Like what love? I thought you were enjoying travelling through Europe Beck: are u there my love?

Me:

Yes

Beck

Babe I promise to be there this time and I will refund the money back to you when I get a job

Me:

I am using my phone not the pc

Beck:

Kate is mocking me now

Beck:

I need to come over there my love

Beck

I can't stand the shame any longer

Me:

Honey I can't Help you my cash is all organized

My love you need to think of it very well don't lie to your feelings you know you love me very much and I do love you as well

Me:

what about the diamond, or the pta fee I sent you

Beck:

My love, pls don't let people mock us. They have return the diamond back to my mum I promised to be there this time

Me:

what is Kate saying?

Beck:

I want people around you to be surprised. She said you have left me alone She said many things, she said am now single she hardly talks to me I know she hates me now

Me:

No I left you alone when they wanted 1500 pounds they wouldn't' let you talk to me

Beck:

She don't know that you still love me I know she will not be happy if I come to arrive over there

Me:

I know this would probably end up happening you and Kate I mean

Beck:

Because she will not believe that we are still communicating. Don't mind her she's jealous of me

Me:

do you want me to send her a message ?

Beck:

No! she's not nice to me anymore, why do you want to do that babe I want u to just leave her alone

Me:

She will be more jealous of you if you can get yourself here especially if you finance yourself

Beck:

I know she will later regret everything that she's doing now yes babe you got it but you need to help me out John pls Just put the last trust on me and I will surprise you babe

Me:

I can't afford it babe My brother is looking forward to this so am I this will be the holiday I spoke to you about when we first started chatting last September.

The holiday I need as the widow now that it is nearly 4 Years ago I have to travel for myself

Beck:

Babe the holiday is next year I will refund the money back to you before the holiday

Me:

I still would love you to surprise me

Beck:

Babe pls for the sake of love we have for each other

Me:

Sweet heart I cannot repeat last September I don't want to build expectation

Beck:

My love that will never happen to us again I promised you

Me:

Please do not get upset I have now seen how easy it is to lose everything the odds are not good

Beck:

John since you promise to get me job over there I will refund the money to you Pls my love

Me:

I really cannot help honey I tried recycling money before there is too much that can go wrong I also have to use this money for repairs and bills. Sure I would love to love you but you have to do this too

Beck:

Ok

Me:

That is what I mean by surprise me you call me from the airport to come and get you: Besides that's what I have already paid for then I guess it is still maybe we will meet one day. Babe I have to and have a shower and get ready for work I can chat in a few hours from now if you want

Beck:

But I don't have the money to come

Me:

Kisses to you too

Beck:

Kissed too

Me:

Bye for now. Mwah

Beck: 16/3/2011

Hi Babe, how are you?

Me:

I am fine sitting home alone naked before work Josh is
out on a date tonight and another one tomorrow night

Beck:

Really! Oh how I wish I were there with you

Me:

It would be nice for you to be here

Beck:

Yes I know, but I don't have the money to be there

Me:

But I think you need to be here in Winter

Beck:

So I can keep you warm

Me:

After the Summer we have had you would not have
coped; living in an oven and yes babe, you can keep me
warm, two bodies entwined in winter I start from the

bottom and stop in the middle while under the sheets you can feel my tongue on your arse.

Beck:

Yes babe

Me:

Good now I have your attention I have a finger in now loosening you up for deep penetration. Your lips also taste sweet. I think by now your nipples are hard too, and how's that 81/4 inch cock of yours. As you can see I'm horny

Beck:

You make me horny John

Me:

What are you wearing ???

Beck:

Speedo

Me:

Take them off NOW!

Beck:

I can't my mummy is in the sitting room

Me:

I don't care get rid of her now I'm hard I need you to be

hard too now! and naked now! I need for your foreskin to be back

Beck:

Am hard now but understand I can't be naked she will be mad at me

Me:

Don't worry about her now, wet two fingers and slowly poke them in your arse, I am doing the same now

Beck:

Okay am doing it now

Me:

Good! Is there any precum? I am dribbling.

Beck:

Yeah!!! Am cumming now babe

Me:

I am thinking of my cock in your arse I am really hard. Good I am ....

Beck:

Wow I want to feel ur cock in my (ass)

Me:

I want to put it there. That was good, thanks for that babe I will be horny at work all night.

Beck:

Okay my love

Me:

You taste sweet

Beck:

My love I want to feel this in real, pls help me with the flight fee so we can do this together

Me:

Me too Beck a young cute man like you will find a way of getting the fare

Beck:

Babe you know I don't have a job pls help me .I will refund it back to you I promise.

Me:

I think you have just shown your talent, all you need to do is charge for it Darling

Beck:

I will never do that in my life babe and my mummy will hate me for that. John pls help my life am begging you. Pls John I will be there this time

Me:

You know that if you were with me I am an ex rent boy

Beck:

Just put the last trust in me

Me:

Why?

Beck:

Pls. John

Me:

I have already given you my trust

Beck:

Pls babe trust me for the last time pls

Me:

You hurt me by not turning up

Beck:

I am sorry John. I can't wait to be there with you this time

Me:

You need to prove yourself to me love, also I will never use Western Union again.

Beck:

I swear I will be there this time am not happy here.

Me:

I contacted them (Western Union) they told me they could not give me information even though I had given them the money, so on principle I will never give them money again.

Beck:

Oh! Babe

Me:

They can go to hell. No one does that to me.

Beck:

Don't look at their own mistake, do it for the sake of me, tou can use other branches

Me:

No! I will never give them another chance. I hope they go broke. Never again! No one does that to me

Beck:

Okay you can use money gram

Me:

What is Money Gram? Is that a post office money order?

Beck:

Is another service to send money, is like Western Union. You can check it online

Me:

That still doesn't help I don't have the funds available

Beck:

John pls

Me:

I just don't Beck

Beck:

I know you have it. Just help me I will refund it back to you

Me:

No I don't I gave it to my mother in law so I wouldn't spend it

Beck:

You can go and collect it and tell her you need part of the money

Me:

She knows I sent you some money and she wants me to get to Scotland. They will give me the money when they check with the Travel Agent or see proof

Beck:

Babe, you don't want to help me that's why I know you very well

Me:

You see, they care for me

Beck:

Well its fine if you don't want to help me anymore and I will not ask you for help again. Cause things seem like you are not ready to help. You have sealed your mind.

Me:

Okay so if I don't want to help you I really have the right. You have given me Nothing!

Beck:

You have been good to me before. But I know you have been convinced by group of people

Me:

Not silly anymore, I convinced myself when you come up with as many excuses as you did it wasn't necessary to have anyone else tell me anything

Beck:

Okay I will not ask you again

Me:

Good because you will never get anymore from me just you arrive here. I tried to tell you that before, does that mean you will never chat anymore? You know where I am. I have to go to work now Bye.

CHAPTER 19

THE DESPAIR

I of course am glad that Beck is now suffering with realization. Kate does not spend much time with him anymore now that she is married. He is still begging for assistance from me and I suspect his peers are holding him accountable for the 1500 pounds to Adam Winkleman that I never paid, the pyramid still had to evolve and someone has to be held responsible and that has to be Beck as the other members of his group realize also that I will not pay. I am enjoying the power I have now and spending my $6000 wisely on torment.

The diamond has been returned to his mother and I am not aiding him with my credit card details. Prostitution seems a fair and reasonable way to earn the payment and conveniently as I am also extremely horny the internet sex request should open his mind. I realize while I was asking him to perform lewd acts on himself he was probably not physically performing them but then neither was I. This was

566 | J MOREWOOD OSBORNE

*not a problem I just needed his full attention and conformity
and he is in despair.*

Beck: 7/4/2011
Hi

Me:
Hi

Beck:
How are you doing?

Me:
I am fine

Beck:
Long time how is everything with you?

Me:
everyone around me is dead or in hospital last week but
I'm okay so is Josh

Beck:
How do you mean? What happened?

Me:
My next door neighbour died in her sleep she was 61
There were 4 police and 2 Detectives at the house Beck:
When was that?

Me:

2 days ago my other neighbour fell and broke her wrist and now has had a hip replacement.

Me:

The manager of the local pub was hit by a drink driver while on a Pacific Island holiday and airlifted back to Australia for major surgery.

Beck:

U there?

Me:

I'm here at work as usual

Beck:

Ahah

Me:

Quiet night

Beck:

Sorry to hear about this. How is work with you?

Me:

I am doing fine with my 2 jobs all back to normal

Beck:

Oh good to hear that. Well I miss you a lot

Me:

I guess I am comfortable I mean I am earning enough for the lifestyle I am living

Beck:

All is good to hear from you

Me:

and you too

Beck:

Am okay

Me:

it is my poor dog Cindy she is old nearly 12 and apart from being lame with arthritis she is now incontinent I have been angry with her but I must understand. I am taking Greg out for his birthday lunch on the harbour next Saturday and I am going out with the Germans on Friday and with my friends on Sunday evening all is good there. There are a lot of gay guys moving into the neighbourhood into all of the new apartments and they are still building more So Many Men.......

Beck:

Hmmmmm. You are making me jealous now

Me:

I did not mean to make you jealous. Greg is not available to go out with me on Saturday night so we will do lunch hopefully something else afterwards but as for all these gay guys they are all young and cute many of them are couples and there are 2 moving from the street behind us into our street these guys are on Grindr and other pick up sites Josh is overjoyed at the prospect of the one named Tomboy or known as Tim Tam at the pub. Tim Tam because he is "finger licking good" here we have a chocolate biscuit called Tim Tam. Anyway the weather is cooling down to acceptable temperatures now

Beck: 4/5/2011

Are you there?

Me:

Sorry I was taking a shower. It will be too cold later to do so and I have to work tonight

Beck:

Oh okay. How are you doing?

Me:

I guess I am okay

Beck:

It has been a long time

Me:

Yes. Well that is probably because we have nothing to chat about anymore

Beck:

Hmmm

Me:

What is on your mind?

Beck:

I have some good news for you

Me:

Really!

Beck:

Yeah

Me:

Okay I am listening for now

Beck:

Guess what the good news may be

Me:

Um, let me think! You have found yourself the flight fee

Beck:

Wow you guess right John

Me:

I thought so. So what are you going to say now? I know I didn't sound very excited, you're right. With you there is always a "But Something" I am waiting for that "But Something".

Beck:

How come you guess right?

Me:

Because it is the only thing you have been asking me for, that was easy. What are you going to do now you have the flight fee? I am going for dinner. Drop me a line sometime with your intentions / flight details (if ever) or you can catch me as usual tonight as usual after 11pm EST

Beck: 12/5/2011

How are you doing my love?

Me:

Hi freezing my tits off. It is snowing in the mountains

Beck:

Oh sorry babe, how I wish I am there to keep you warm. Babe I have the flight fee but not yet completed. Do you still want me to come over?

Me:

If you can afford to get here that would still be nice, then you could help keep me warm for winter. I always wait for the day you actually arrive.

Beck:

Babe, I have the flight fee with me but not yet complete

Me:

Okay, send me the flight details when it is all complete. I can meet you at KSA

Beck:

Babe, can you help me with the remaining fee?

Me: Nop

Beck:

Why babe?

Me:

I have already paid once, and you have a diamond to sell. Why don't you ask Kate?

Beck:

She will not give it me. She doesn't like me anymore. I told you John, Kate has totally changed to me

Me:

And you to me Beck

Beck:

How babe?

Me:

Josh told me to tell you to "drop dead" I am telling you that I put a lot of faith and belief in you and you let me down. That is why

Beck:

Hmmm. John I am very sorry about that. I promise I will not let you down this time.

Me:

So am I, that is why I said to you it is up to you to prove yourself to me now. I have accepted my financial loss to you and will not send more cash on the "Off Chance"

Beck:

Babe I am trying my best. The money remains 200 pounds to complete the flight fee

Me:

Try harder. I did last time for you

Beck:

Babe pls, I really want to be there with you. I will not disappoint you this time babe.

Me:

Same answer. Call me from the airport if you arrive. There is no need for us to talk anymore about this. If you do arrive then you can slap my face, because I will do the same to you.

Beck:

Sad

Me:

Sorry love but you need to know how I feel

Beck:

Yeah, I do but you need to know that I love you very much and I want to pay back everything you have done for me. That's why I am trying my best, I just need help with 200 pounds,

that's all I need to complete the money

Me:

Then I need you show it and prove it. I won't give it to you love

Beck:

Okay it's okay

Me:

Yes I know it is

Beck:

I love you

Me:

I want to love you. If the photographs of you that you emailed to me really are you, then as a pretty boy you will indeed be able to get 200 pounds easily

Beck:

I can't babe

Me:

Yes you can

Beck:

I can't. How can I?

Me:

It's easy, all you have to do is date an old guy for a couple of months, tell him you need 200 pounds for some convincing story he will believe, the buy you ticket and leave.

Beck:

No way, I can't do that

Me:

You have already done it to me when you think about it, in my case you never came. We could've been a great couple

Beck:

I still want that

Me:

You know honey, sometimes we have to work harder for something we really want. I know it works for me

Beck:

John, I really want to be with you

The question to ask yourself, is how badly do you want something and how far would you go to reach your goal. Then when you try it actually happens

Beck:

Am trying, that's why I am asking you to help me out.

Me:

Honey, I am pleased you are trying it's just that I can't help you

Beck:

Okay, it's fine if you can't

Me:

Sorry babe

Beck:

Okay

Me:

It would be nice if you do ever make it

Beck:

Okay John I will try my best

Me:

Bye love

Beck: 20/10/2011

Hello

Me:

Hello, I noticed you were online, are you still there?

Beck;

Yes I am, how have you been?

Me:

I see what are you doing with yourself?

Beck:

I'm now in South Africa

Me:

Well! At least you made it to the Southern Hemisphere finally! Why South Africa?

Beck:

Because my mum has a relative here

Okay, how is your mum?

Beck:

She is doing good over there. How is things with you?

Me:

I'm fine. All back to normal with me. I am happy to stay single, I am still living with Josh and he has a new lover that might be moving in.

Beck:

I am happy for him

Me:

How long are you staying in South Africa?

Beck:

I have been here two months

Me:

You'd better be careful with your diamond there they could think you stole it and shoot you. Haha!

Beck:

I didn't tell anyone that I had the diamond here babe

Me:

Good idea

Beck:

Are you still single?

Me:

Intending to stay that way now

Beck:

Why?

Me:

It's really what I should do. Who are you dating now?

Beck:

Why do you say so you need to find someone who can make you happy. John there's a man for you. Don't intend to stay single.

Me:

Maybe there is, but I am not looking, not after the "Bad Czech"

Bad Czech? What do you mean by "Bad Czech"?

Me:

Last year I met a HOT! Czech guy 29 y.o. We had a five month relationship

Beck:

So what happened between you guys?

Me:

He was only using me and I helped him out financially. I was going to try and keep in the country as my partner, but he was full of shit! He ended up dating a DRAG Queen and fucking behind my back so we split. I think he is now an illegal immigrant

Beck:

That's bad of him

Me:

I have changed all the accounts back into my name so they don't come here looking for him. He even had a quick relationship with Rupert who dumped him because he didn't want to hurt me.

Beck:

Really!

Me:

So I think I'll just stay single, that's what happened.

Beck:

That's bad of him I hate any man that cheats

Me:

I had the most amazing time with this guy. He is soooo HOT! great sex huge cock total bottom and 6'5" tall Amazing light blue eyes. Because my Great, Great Grandfather was Czech I thought it would be great. My father was thrilled about it (It was his Great Grandfather). Unfortunately, this guy was more Russian or Slovak than Czech.

Beck:

That's bad of him John but you shouldn't because of that step back there's a lot of good men out there, you can still find one. How I wish you still loved me and had trust in me. I can be your man and spend the rest of my life with you

Me:

I don't think you and I will work out Beck

Beck:

John we can. I can come over there from here

on your own finances.

Beck:

I wish I can, but you know I don't have a job

Me:

No! but you have a diamond.

Beck:

Yes I have but I can't sell it yet

Me:

Well you had finance to get to South Africa you must have some funds

Beck:

I didn't finance myself someone financed me here.

Me:

You are good at that

Beck:

You just have to understand that I don't have a job I will be there for you if you can really finance me

Me:

You just don't understand, I don't trust you anymore

Beck:

John I understand if you don't trust me because it's all my fault. I know I caused you lots of pain then but I'm ready to put a smile on your face. I want you to cut the past. Let's start a new life and I promise I will never be like the Czech Guy

Me:

Sorry babe I promised myself I will never spend any more money on anyone ever again. You are welcome if you get yourself here by your own financial means

Beck:

Okay I understand you John

Me:

Thanks I'm not interested unless you can pay your own way

Beck Alright John

Me:

Sorry but I realize I need to put my cash to good use for me and anyone I might meet

Me:

Thanks. You remember I took a loan out for you last year to cover the missing 1500 pounds, well I have one payment left on that next week then it's finished. I am not doing any more credit

Beck: 24/2/2012

Hello how are you doing?

Me:

Hi off to dinner with the Germans

Beck:

Okay

Beck:

how are you?

Me:

Hi babe

Beck:

hello John how are you?

Me:

Me staying home on a cold winter night even though it is a Long weekend to celebrate Queen Victoria's Birthday I mean really the old queen has been dead for 110 years

Beck:

oh ok am home as well with my mummy

Me:

and how is mummy ?

Beck:

She's doing good she's fine

Me:

did you watch the royal wedding?

Beck:

yeah I did it was great wedding

Me:

Yeah I sat alone at one of the favourite pubs I go close to a big screen with no one to get in the way and ordered my $10 steak and $10 jug and did not move

Beck:

Good

Me:

I have always wondered what it would be like to be a queen no pun intended

Beck:

a great thing ever yeah

Me:

but would I look good in a crown?

Beck:

yeah babe

Me:

my mother tells me I am 427000th in line for the throne of Scotland I have to kill my cousins first and their children

Beck:

really?

Me:

my uncle is older than my mother you see that's why, well the number might be a bit out but yes really

Beck:

oh ok then how is Josh?

Me:

sitting on the lounge watching Dr. Who on his Ipad

Beck: 23/4/2012

Hey John

Me:

I am fine have had a good night out with the Germans

Beck:

how are you doing?

Me:

Well I had a scare early March with blood pressure bit high now better than ever.

Another job as well as RHP love it the Maritime Museum. I love this always have, this is like it's a dream come true I get paid to sell tickets for people to board old ships

Beck:

really? John, pls buy me a ticket to come over there

Me:

Yep. Old navy ships and subs and 19th century colonial clippers lighthouse ships tugs and of course our Titanic Exhibition There was one nurse on board that was Australian she boarded lifeboat 16 and survived she moved to Sydney from Adelaide You know

Beck:

lovely to hear that I'm very happy for you John help my life

Me:

I thought you were happy in South Africa

Beck:

I am not happy hear John

Me:

Darling I. Would like to help you but you are a bad investment honey

Beck:

not again honey I promise you

Me:

If I bought you a ticket in your name HTR/SYD to be collected by you at HTR would you really get on the plane

Beck:

wow that would be very loveiy dear

Me:

Hmm

Beck:

yes that would be good if I won't have any-problem with the ticket

Me:

why are you unhappy is your mother ill?

Beck:

yes very ill it would be better if you can send me the money so I can buy the ticket here so I won't have any problem

Me:

Don't get excited I am only asking questions to which I might add, you are not answering

Beck:

what question is that John you really need to help me out here dear

Me:

Well you need to tell me why that is the question

Beck:

I am not happy here things are not good with me I need to come over there and get a good job

Me:

What has happened to you that is so bad?

Beck:

my mom is ill and I need to come over there and start working so I can help her

Beck:

are you there?

Me:

Yes

Me:

Love you are over the age bracket now for a work visa 30 is the cutoff point

Beck:

is that the new rules?

Me:

No same rules as before same rules I checked out when I was dating the bad Czech as when I was hoping to be dating you. Same conditions

Beck:

oh I see my love but we can make things work

Me:

Not if you don't have an income you will need to check this I don't think I'm wrong

Beck:

but I have my working visa from here already

Me:

Well fine if that is still valid you still need the PTA fee on arrival

Beck:

yes love I will still need the PTA

Me:

Good night Beck It's all such a shame

Beck:

but remember that the money won't be taking from me

Me:

That's what you said last time

Beck:

I promise you John every thing will be fine this time remember I need to be there so I want to be there so bad everything will work fine this time

Me:

That's what you also said last time

Beck:

John I am making a promise this time, remember my mom is ill so I really want to be there so I can help her I now this is help you want to do for me and I promise I won't make you regret this

Me:

Why all of a sudden have you come back to me

Beck:

I dream about you 4 days ago

Me:

that is nice I am also 2 years older now closer to old age

Beck:

I know you are good man who cares and ready to love I am ready to give you all of me

Me:

I wanted this to happen before so much but now after 2 years I am not that interested anymore we would now not make a good team

Beck:

John we can

Me:

I am sorry but you would need to prove it to me in advance. I am going to go to bed now and I will leave my phone on just in case you want to call Goodnight Beck

Beck:

are you there?

Me:

Yes

Beck:

I swear I really want to be there and start new life. You can put your trust on me this time

Me:

Uhm!

Beck:

I promise you John I won't make you regret this I want to be there for you till the eternity I want to make you proud to the world this time I am here now to make a change John, are you there John?

Me:

Yes

Beck:

good to talk to you

Me:

I will not go to jail for nonpayment of taxes it was nice to hear your voice

Beck:

I don't want you to go to jail as well

Me:

Thankyou

Beck:

Don't you think that we can borrow the money before you pay the tax then when I get there you can pay tax?

Me:

my phone is showing 2 missed calls I don't know why it didn't pick up the call

Beck:

oh I see that is ur cell phone

Me:

Yes but this bill I must get out of the way in a hurry

Beck:

oh okay

Me:

the phone I spoke to you on is the land phone I have been chatting with you all night tonight on my cell phone I am not logged in to my new fast PC

Beck:

really?

Me:

yes upgraded to a terabyte hard drive Only cost me $160

Beck: that's great

Me:

Yeah a second hand rebuilt PC I have 3 in the house I am building the other 2 to sell it is a hobby

Beck:

Alright, John so now you don't have any help you can render for me?

Me:

I have also applied for a place in a special cheap housing project

Beck:

rent or buying?

Me:

I have been accepted and am on their waiting list this is permanent rental but it is mine until I die or my financial situation changes. I will only ever have to PAY one third of whatever I earn in rent not like now where I am paying a lot of money for this house

Beck:

now that's reasonable that would be okay

Me:

Yes there are a lot of conditions to meet for this and I meet all of them. It is a project started by Sydney City Council

29/4/2012

Beck:

John

Me:

I am surprised to hear from you

Beck:

How are you doing?

Me:

I am staying in this evening

Beck:

Oh good to hear that, how is everything over there? And how is life with you?

Me:

How is your mother?

Beck:

She's not really happy about everything

Me:

Hmm. Well I like my new job, I like being single now and I am happy with myself.

Beck:

Oh. But remember you will still need a partner to be there for you

Me:

No! You don't have to answer to anyone. Although I still have to answer to the tax office

Beck:

Then you better go and answer to it

Me:

Yes indeed but after that don't have to answer to anybody. My mother thinks I will answer to her but I won't

Beck:

Why don't you want to answer to her?

Me:

Because it all creates stress and I don't have any and I won't allow it. I have a nice peaceful life. My mother is bossy and she thinks I am still a child

Beck:

John, but you have to appreciate your mother and be there for her when she needs you

Me:

She needs me now, she is losing her memory and her sight she is 80 this year/

Beck:

You just have to make her understand but you must be there for her whenever she needs you

Me:

My youngest brother still lives with them and does help a little. Anyway enough of my parents

Beck:

Alright cool

Me:

Is South Africa interesting? Have you shot a Rhino!

Beck:

It's interesting but I haven't

Me:

Have you been Tarzan! Running around in only a loincloth? lol

Beck:

I haven't John

Me:

That's a pity I had a vision of you swinging from the trees in a g- string

Beck:

Really?

Me:

Yes really. Quite sexy I think

Beck:

I really want to make things work between us

Me:

That would be nice then I can fuck your brains out. But I don't see how we can. But I do want to fuck your tight little arse.

Beck:

John I want to do everything with you. If you put your trust in me we can work things out

Me:

I have done with the trust my love you know where to find me

Beck:

If I have the money to come there I would have done that.

Me:

Then you can when you do my love

Beck:

I need your help so bad

Me:

Darling, as I said too many bills at the moment including TAX OFFICE! Maybe one day you will get the money and turn up unannounced on my doorstep. That's okay

Phone call from Beck followed this conversation 2:00 am with a South African country code prefix.

CHAPTER 20

THE STALEMATE

Beck: 3/06/2012
Hi

Me:
Hello sorry I was busy last message

Beck:
oh okay how are you doing?

Me:
working really hard have 3 jobs to pay tax bill and save
some money for Summer

Beck:
oh how is it going? Hope you enjoying it oh okay that's
good

Me:

I have a new job at the Maritime Museum Yeah there are old ships navy subs and plenty of exhibits I love it

Beck:

really good to hear. Pls help me to come there so I can be working for you

Me:

Yeah good pay rate

Beck:

Wow can you help so I can be working for you

Me:

I love ships I even get to work on board on some shifts

Beck:

That's good to hear John I really want to start a new life with you

Me:

That's fine I am not able to fund you now with added financial problems

Beck:

Crying

Me:

Can't help it sweetheart I thought you were making a new life in South Africa. Can't you find

A wealthy Jewish Man to give you the money just lie a little. **Yeah you should do that**

Beck:

Life is not easy here my love I am single here

Me:

I am single here too

Beck:

I want to come down there and build my relationship with **you**

Me:

They call me the merry widow

Beck:

why do they call you that?

Me:

they call me that because my boyfriend of 15 years died 5 years ago and I pulled myself back up and was happy (sort of). That's when I decided to try dating sites and thought I might have ended up with you so I only do cock bondage sites now No relationship sites

Beck:

You need to prove them wrong John you just have to prove them wrong I can be there for you if you really put your trust in me this time

Me:

I still. Can't afford you Beck

Beck:

Haaa what site is that?

Me:

that's called learning the ropes so to speak

Beck:

What's the site all about? What's the name of it? Are they gay? Why bondage sites?

Me:

Gay BDSM and BDSM chat

Beck:

I can't find it

Me:

they match you to guys in your area or as close as possible

Beck:

how am I going to type it on the web?

Me:

type in gaybdsm.com see what you get I also have gay military dating, have a meeting next week with one guy hope to do group bondage what a turn on.

Beck:

what's the military?

Me:

If you go into gay bdsm you can click on gay military at the top of the screen you have to create a profile first who knows we might see each other there

Beck:

I will try to see it later I have to go now

Me:

the guys are in uniform some are real soldiers. Me too bye

Beck: 28/06/2012

Beck: 28/06/2012

Hi

Me: Hello Beck:

how are you doing?

Me:

I am feeling like I am doing community service

Beck:

Wow

Me:

I am working 6 nights week and 4 days 83 hours a week it all finishes this Sunday I Get my life back

Beck:

oh sorry to hear that

Me:

I have decided to look for a new job yeah don't want to do nights any more I have an interview on Tuesday I Will keep the Museum but get rid of the RHP

Beck:

but you're getting paid a good salary

Me:

I haven't told anyone yet but the museum is better salary but not a permanent position

Beck:

really?

Me:

so looking for 3 days permanent

Beck:

oh okay

Me:

yeah I was motivated to do so by a friend and my housing allocation has progressed in the queue things are looking good I just have to get past this weekend

Beck:

I am very happy for you

Me:

I may then go with Friends to North Queensland for a week. What about you?

Beck:

my life is boring as you know I just need someone to help me and start a new life

Me:

have u tried out some of those bondage. Sites yet? 1 get weekly phone sex row hot athletic guy in Queensland he is 26 Only $80 to fly up and meet him

Beck:

I don't have money to pay for the site

Me:

you don't need money to pay for the site, you just have to send a message with your email address so you can read their messages

Beck:

I can't send message as I'm not a paying member

Me:

easy I don't pay either

Beck:

I will try it again

Me:

some sites let you read emails as a non member some don't. I might meet you on one of the sites

Beck:

Okay can you give me another good site?

Me:

█████████████████ but it is not only a gay site ████████████ ████████████ are a few

Beck:

oh okay

Me:

I have to get ready for work now start at 11pm

Beck:

Okay

Me:

bye. Dear

Beck:

Bye

Beck:

how are you John?   10/7/2012

Me:

Hello

Beck:

Hi how have you been?

Me:

I am ok at the moment looking for a new house to live in

Beck:

oh okay

Me:

This one is being sold at auction

Beck:

what happened to your own house?

Me:

I only rent the house

Beck:

oh okay how is work going with you?

Me:

If I want to buy I have to move out of the city to match my price range and I don't want to do that

Beck:

I understand I think you should try to buy

Me:

I rent instead the. Price is cheaper than a mortgage repayment but you don't end up owning

Beck:

Alright

Me:

and why should I struggle to pay for a house I don't have any responsibility to anyone

Beck:

I understand you now ok John

Me:

I have enough to move will start packing the house up today

Beck:

John pls I need your help

Me:

what help are you still in Africa?

Beck:

yes I am still here in South Africa. Do you want to call me? I will give you number to call

Me:

Yeah what is the number?

Beck:

+27735116614

Me:

great what time is it?

Beck:

11:50 pm

Me:

Okay

Beck:

are you going to call me now?

Me: Yes

Beck:

Okay

Me:

Number not working I will try again

Me: 22/07/2012

Good to chat

Beck:

good to hear your voice thank you very much your voice really warm my heart

Me:

It was nice to hear you too I hope things work out between us one day maybe I can kiss your lips

Beck:

Amen

Me:

Bye

Beck:

but I really need to pay some bills by the month and if I don't do that I will be thrown out of here

Me:

How come you are so bad with your finances end of month is next week

Beck:

yes end of month is next week but I don't have the

money yet things are very hard here and they don't like gay people here so I am not proud of who I am here because they hate gay people here

Me:

I will not be paying for new house until next week earliest.

Me:

Why did you go there if they are homophobic

Beck:

I don't know until I came here they don't want to give me work once they notice you are a gay person

Me:

there are lots of rallies in the world today to stop this hatred that is awful can't you get work

Me:

Yes that is why there are world rallies. Today to stop the discrimination

Beck:

I am fed up being here

Me:

No doubt

Beck:

I cried a lot life is tired to me

Beck: 12/02/2013

Hello

Me:

Hi I am sending this from my new free mini tablet

Beck:

I have 500 dollars with me now I want to come over there

Me:

You will need more than and I have a lot of expenditure

Beck:

pls help me with the remaining money it took me a long time to save up this money I am working at restaurant now

Me:

Where? Are you still in South Africa?

Beck: 14/02/2013

Hello John

Me:

I am in Melbourne I have to go to bed

Beck:

okay goodnight

Beck: 02/03/2013

hello john

Me:

I am at Mardi Gras picked up a Frenchman have to
go xxx

Beck:

Okay I miss you so much

Me:

Talk later, have Frenchman to deal with tonight

Beck:

Okay

Beck: 22/03/2013

how are you?

Me:

Things are going well

Beck:

good to hear that I miss you so much

Me:

Thanks how are things going with you?

Beck:

things are good on my side here I am happy now

Me:

That is good to hear

Beck:

are you still single?

Me:

Yes but I have a young guy staying with us a student from Ecuador Beck: is he gay?

Me:

Yes I am fucking him

Beck:

Hmmmmm you like this

Me:

Huge cock

Beck:

okay I want to come there

Me:

Well I don't have any room now he is here for 4 months and my house mate is not happy about it but he is fucking him too. I had to let my housemate fuck him to keep him happy.

Beck:

Hmmm

Me:

He's quite obliging

Beck:

Ok

Me:

Plus I am seeing guys on the ███ site

Beck:

which site is that?

Me:

████ it's like █████ but the guys on ███ are inked and have cropped facial hair. I met my boy from Ecuador on this site

Beck:

oh okay I will try that and what's any other site you know again?

Me:

You load it into your phone for free you can chat and meet each other it shows locals in your area or international and it tells you how close to you the guy is. Sometimes only a few steps away

Beck:

oh okay that's good to hear do you have any other sites again?

Me:

████████ the guys here are young twinks and Muscle Mary's. It is the same as ██████ you hook up with guys close by

Beck:

oh okay I need site for older people I don't want young guys

Me:

Then use ██████ young guys also use it. You can also try ████████████ this is for older guys

Beck:

okay I will try ████████████

Me:

There is also a site younger for older but these sites do not use GPS so there won't be any proximity notifications

Beck:

What's the site name?

Me:

Older for younger but these sites are not free like ██████

and ████ they put ads on the page so you don't have
to pay but ███ and ███ are the biggest and most popular

Beck: oh okay

Me: Bye

Beck: 20/09/2013
How are you doing John?

Me:
Life? Well I think

Beck: 21/09/2013
How's everything with you?

Me:
I am getting used to the complications of growing old
but life is still fine I need a holiday

Beck: 15/12/2013
John?

Me:
Good morning

Beck:
how have you been?

Me:
Still working too hard but sorting that out I am fine

Beck:

what have you been up to?

Me:

I have a new vocation gilding I gild important iconic buildings and get my photos in the paper we also work on cruise ships free accommodation and paid for the lessons we give

Beck:

oh good to hear that and how is it going?

Me:

Our first cruise is early next year

Beck:

Good can you pls borrow for me 200 dollars?

Me:

What for?

Beck:

I want to use it for something important I will return it back in 2 weeks' time I am serious about all this

Me:

Hum

Beck: 27/3/2014

Hope all is well with you? sorry I didn't inform you about my trip to Lagos Nigeria for a program, I'm presently in Lagos state Nigeria, and am having some difficulties here because I lost my wallet to some robbers on my way to the hotel where my money and other valuable things were kept, presently I have limited access to the internet. I will like you to assist me with a loan of $1,600 or any amount you can help me with to sort-out my

hotel bills, feeding and transportation.

I have spoken to the embassy here but they are not responding to the issue effectively, I will appreciate whatever you can afford to assist me, I'll refund the money back to you as soon as I return, let me know if you can be of any help. Please let me know immediately. Best regards,

Beck Hill

Me:

You should be happy now you are finally back home

Beck:

John

I need a financial assistance of 1,600 but anything you could assist with now will be helpful. I was extremely happy when I saw your mail, please bear in mind that I'll facilitate your reimbursement as soon as I get back, Beck

Me:

You should be happy now you are finally "back home".

THE END

CONCLUSION

This scam would no doubt be part of a pyramid scam, you move up one level when you have collected the total value of funds allocated to you. Beck keeps referring to the word funds rather than cost or price.

There is a set formula for profiles to be wary of, the profile will always contain the same message the person will always be an only child, the father will always be dead and they will fall in love easily. From these you can build compliments to your suitor and justify your "miserable life". Reading back through the original contact email I sent Beck this entire situation has gone a long way. I realize now that there are certain phrases to look out for in profiles. One such line is "someone who is ready to put his _miserable life_ behind him" I thought this strange at the time but my eagerness outshone any logic.

When you read all those emails in chapter 1 to each other it shows that your feelings are vulnerable on the internet if you let them be and how shattered you become when it turns sour financially and emotionally I was advised by both the

State and Federal Police to delete all emails and forget this person. This however was after I had already lost $6000 and was not going to lose any more so I had nothing to lose anyway. This whole adventure has cost money and time but now I am wiser and certainly have a story to tell.

Chapter 2 is full of hope and I am too trusting. He has already referred to himself as Beck Osborne and I am even at this stage his victim.

You find yourself falling when you receive so many compliments and you want to enjoy the best out of your experience, at this point you don't realize you will never see the person on the other end. Undoubtedly you are drawn into this web of deceit and at this early stage you are not aware of the scam. This is why Beck moved in so fast to secure the Visa fee and PTA fee. There is no doubt more than one accomplice in the scam the phone call from the Australian Embassy in London happening at the same time I was chatting via email with

Beck, they may well have been in the same room laughing Beck's comment when I told him was only (lol). The voice on the phone would later be identified as Scott Van Bowman and Beck himself had a similar voice possibly both Nigerian

Kate undoubtedly is involved and both her email address and the IDC email address have been deleted. Beck stopped using his address after I had complained to Google. He gave me his new email address (able.god) which later was cancelled and he is again using his previous email address

While Beck is hostage we are communicating via letters only.

Clearly other parties are writing them and I have a great deal of satisfaction being in control of the situation.

There is no professionalism within the group they badly executed the entire event of Becks' Kidnapping and possibly all of Beck's conversations in Chapter one he had assistance with writing, there is a notable difference in style afterwards.

I should have realized the scam at the point where the PTA fee was required, naturally his family should help i.e his mother to even contemplate a loan was stupid. He did make me feel good and obviously I was still vulnerable and very lonely. It would never be recommended to pursue internet dating in this state, otherwise you wouldn't.do it this is why the scammers are successful, they are aware of the human emotion and desperation fulfills a need so my journey has begun without seeing the picture.

I was very cynical about Beck refinancing himself after the robbery and horrified with myself that I did not terminate the relationship here.

It is amazing how "DUMB" Beck and Kate are when it comes to finances. Possibly deliberate with all the conversation in chapter 7 He goes to church but has no friends there.

Clearly I am the next target in this pyramid and someone was intended as soon as anyone answered his add on ▮▮▮. He deleted it straight away I don't thinks Kate's Father has any part in this scam and I doubt she even asked him for money In The Refinance. I speak of things in my life past I had created a lie about being a soldier when I wrote a letter to his captor. I was too young to be involved in the Vietnam

War but again needed some excuse to let them know I am not interested

When desperation is the only option a scammer would probably try for credit card details. I was not prepared for the credit card scam that was about to begin and it was not going to be my regret but his in chapter 17 this was the situation and I wanted him to feel regret

The final outcome of this entire event is not what I had planned for the conclusion. I had hoped to finish this book with me flying to Amsterdam to identify a headless handless body that had been pulled from a canal. But as I had never met Beck I would not know who I was identifying and this would involve the police, besides I have already written this in Chapter16

I was right all along. When I accepted this was a scam I thought a Nigerian Scam. The police told me Nigerian scam, when I heard his voice it sounded akin to someone Nigerian or from that region and it never matched the pictures he claimed were him. The voice of Scott Van Bowman could also be Nigerian and while I entertained some thought he was one and the some person. The voice of Scott Van Bowman was more educated, possibly he was the gang leader. Maybe he even assaulted Beck because he could not deliver the goods to Adam Winkleman "the final 1500 pounds"

The message is simple particularly for adolescent Girls there is no such thing as an international online relationship. If you are lonely and unhappy with your life and your looks stay away from the internet, it will cost you your self respect.